Unsmiling Faces

ONE WEEK LOAN

Unsmiling Faces

HOW PRESCHOOLS CAN HEAL

SECOND EDITION

EDITED BY **Lesley Koplow**

FOREWORD BY VIVIAN GUSSIN PALEY

Teachers College, Columbia University
New York and London

Published by Teachers College Press, 1234 Amsterdam Avenue, New York, NY 10027

Library of Congress Cataloging-in-Publication Data

Unsmiling faces : how preschools can heal / edited by Lesley Koplow ; foreword by Vivian Gussin Paley—2nd ed.
   p. cm.
   Includes bibliographical references and index.
   ISBN 978-0-8077-4803-9 (pbk : alk. paper)—ISBN 978-0-8077-4804-6 (cloth : alk. paper)
    1. Preschool children—United States—Psychology. 2. Education, Preschool—United States. 3. Behavior therapy for children—United States. 4. Child psychotherapy—United States. I. Koplow, Lesley.

  LB1117.U57 2007
  372.14'6—dc22

2007003918

ISBN 978-0-8077-4803-9 (paper)
ISBN 978-0-8077-4804-6 (cloth)

Printed on acid-free paper
Manufactured in the United States of America

14 13 12 11 10 09 08   8 7 6 5 4 3

Contents

Foreword by Vivian Gussin Paley   *vii*

Preface: The Changing Landscape of Early Childhood Education   *ix*

Preface to First Edition   *xi*

Introduction: Knowing What We Know Now   *xiii*

PART I: Making Room for Emotional Life in Preschool

1. Developmental Reality and the Reality of Experience   3

   Lesley Koplow

2. "If You're Sad and You Know It": The Value of Children's Affects   17

   Lesley Koplow

3. A Look in the Mirror: Self-Concept in Preschool Children   29

   Judith Ferber

Part II: Structure and Relationships in Preschool

4. Therapeutic Teacher, Therapeutic Classroom   47

   Judith Ferber

5. Play Therapy as Early Intervention   65

   Lesley Koplow

6. Therapeutic Technique: The Tools of Preschools That Heal   79

    Lesley Koplow

Part III: The Meaning of Curriculum

7. Playing for Keeps: The Value of Open-Ended Play   97

    Lesley Koplow

8. Affect Meets Cognition: Building a Curricular Bridge   114

    Lesley Koplow, Virginia Hut, and Judith Ferber

9. Lesson Plans for Emotional Life   132

    *Virginia Hut, Beverley Dennis, Lesley Koplow,
    and Judith Ferber*

Part IV: Understanding Special Populations

10. The Traumatized Child in Preschool   175

    Lesley Koplow and Judith Ferber

11. Helping Children with Autistic Spectrum Disorders   194

    *Lesley Koplow, Suzanne Abrams, Judith Ferber,
    and Beverley Dennis*

12. Why Homeless Children Can't Sit Still   215

    Lesley Koplow

Part V: Preschool as Home Base

13. Caring for Families and Staff   229

    Lesley Koplow

About the Editor and the Contributors   251

Index   253

Foreword

IS THERE A PRESCHOOL anywhere that does not include those who at times feel sad, angry, and helpless? Young as children are when they enter school, few can escape the sudden fear of abandonment and the inability to make their feelings known. There is the frightened or aggressive child we are unable to calm, the isolate who refuses to emerge from hiding, the child too worried to play: We see them in all our classrooms.

Even so, when I read the title of this moving and eloquent book, I was tempted to limit its use. Here is a message, I thought, meant solely for special schools in extraordinarily stressful communities. Indeed, those schools that draw heavily on the population of the most endangered families will be eager to find new ways to heal and give comfort to their often traumatized children. These institutions already see themselves as islands of safety in a tormented world. They are not afraid to appear "therapeutic."

The rest of us, teaching in relatively stable circumstances, tend to resist the idea that some form of therapy may be a part of our job, even as we encourage larger numbers of families and children to meet with therapists. We tell ourselves, in the face of worrisome and unpredictable behaviors, "The ordinary classroom is not meant to be a therapeutic community." Then we go about picking up the random pieces of confused, frustrated, and otherwise unfinished development that surround us as we try to create the facsimile of a caring family.

The problem, I suspect, is that we do not know what a therapeutic classroom looks like; we think it must be very different from the "norm," beyond our reach and understanding. Well, then, here at last, in *Unsmiling Faces*, we have a book that provides, in eminently readable prose, the background, stage setting, plot, and script to help us see ourselves as actors in the theater of affective communication. Remarkably, it has the sound and feel not of esoteric and unnatural posturing, but of recognizable good teaching.

Their vision of the classroom makes sense. It is doable. I plan to study and practice this approach in my own kindergarten. I want to know more about how to structure an environment in which frightened children can be calmed, the timid dare to emerge from hiding, and those too worried to speak and play can learn to tell their own stories and listen to mine. For, by now, we must all realize that when we acknowledge and learn to deal with children's emotional needs, in the classroom, we directly influence their social and cognitive development. The reader will find ample evidence of these connections as the lives of the children in the book unfold.

Most certainly, in preschools that offer, in many cases, a first chance for children to experience trust and dependable attachments, *Unsmiling Faces* should be required reading. It is important to emphasize, however, that the environment so clearly depicted here in anecdote, discourse, dialogue, and doll play also represents the highest standard for teaching every young child. In today's troubled society, the image of the healing classroom seems compelling and urgent, no matter where we live.

Be assured, the therapy room is not being replaced. Rather, teachers, administrators, and therapists are invited to take joint responsibility for integrating the children's experiences during the school day and beyond, with parents an important part of the process. As the staff studies and applies this roadmap to a school that prepares children to learn *by dealing with the issues that interfere with learning*, each adult becomes a learner as well. We learn, individually and in supportive collaboration, that when the classroom is a healing place, it becomes a home for us all.

—Vivian Gussin Paley

The Changing Landscape of Early Childhood Education

THIS SECOND EDITION of *Unsmiling Faces: How Preschools Can Heal* is being written 11 years after the first edition was published. Early childhood programs look different than they did 11 years ago, but the children look the same. There are still emotionally fragile, traumatized, and developmentally challenged children in preschools in 2007, but they are more likely than their predecessors to be included in mainstream classroom settings. These classrooms themselves exist within a variety of public and private systems. A growing number of states now offer prekindergarten programs within the public schools. While there are still large numbers of young children being served in small child-care centers, Head Start programs, and private preschool centers, in 2007 there are also thousands of such children being educated in public prekindergarten programs in the less intimate setting of a large school building full of older children.

The changing landscape of early childhood education in the United States brings new resources and new challenges to our children. Young children today may be more likely to have teachers with a master's degree in education than they were in 1995. They are more likely to attend preschool programs with peers who have strengths and weaknesses that are unlike their own. Fragile children in preschool today are more likely to be able to receive support services within the mainstream school environment as an alternative to self-contained special education classrooms and to have these services funded by the city or state where they live.

While there are more possibilities for meeting the needs of young children through a network of early childhood programming, today's preschool children are being educated at a time when politics have an unprecedented influence on the quality of educational practice itself. Although the most recent outcomes of child development and brain research strongly support interactive learning with strong teacher–child–parent relationships and ongoing opportunity for play and social interaction, conservative politics have dictated that early education become increasingly performance-oriented. Indeed, federal, state, and city funding formulas are now frequently based on strict performance requirements. The result is that preschool children in 2007 may have more options for attending early childhood programs, but they are also more frequently placed in classrooms with less time for open-ended play and more focus on early academic learning. While children in preschool in 1995 could count on their teachers to be involved in and present for important caregiving routines such as arrival and departure, snack, lunch, rest, and toileting, children in 2007 often find those essential routines in the hands of less familiar and less qualified adults assigned by administrators who consider "noninstructional" time unworthy of the teacher's attention.

The changing landscape of early childhood education presents both great opportunities and great risks for young emotionally fragile children today. Certainly, we want young children to reap benefits from the increasing numbers of early childhood programs available to them in 2007. Yet we know that if those programs are designed to meet the needs of politicians instead of those of young children, the early childhood setting loses its capacity to function as a psychological home base for the children and families it serves. Young emotionally fragile and traumatized children need the same kinds of environments that they have always needed. They need warm, nurturing teachers who have the capacity to develop deep relationships with the children in their care and who know how to address the developmental and life experience issues of the children they teach. Young children need their caregiving routines to be supportive, consistent, and comforting and to involve the adults in the classroom to whom they are attached so that they feel valued and worthy of care. Young children need to explore their learning environment through interactions with their peers. Young children need to have open-ended play time protected so that they can develop symbols for inner life and actual life experiences and play out conflicts and confusing issues in order to better integrate them. Young children need to have curriculums that reflect their own developmental agendas and offer opportunities to construct their own worlds with clay and paint and blocks and projects that hold meaning for them. Young children who have lived with trauma, loss, and disruptive life experience desperately need the early childhood classroom to offer a safe haven, full of invitations to connect to teachers who can listen and hold their complex stories. All children need us to listen to the outcomes of recent brain development research that find relationships to be the building blocks that create potential for cognitive learning. Are we listening?

The editor gratefully acknowledges the contributions of teachers, directors, and clinicians who have used these ideas in the classroom and given us feedback that has enriched this edition of the book. Special thanks to Rachel Hass, who assisted with the preparation of the manuscript.

Preface to First Edition

UNSMILING FACES is written for teachers and clinicians who are concerned about the emotional well-being of young children. It is a book for early childhood professionals who want to create programs that acknowledge the emotional lives of their students, thus facilitating the integration of emotional, social, and cognitive learning in preschool.

Unsmiling Faces may be of special interest to educators and therapists who are working with highly stressed, emotionally fragile, and developmentally arrested preschoolers who erase our images of the young child as joyful, receptive, curious learner. The book is intended for the professional reader who works in mainstream preschool programs, day-care centers, special education preschools, and clinical preschools, since emotionally fragile children can be found in every early childhood setting. Given the enormous variation in program structures and program resources, the reader will be best qualified to judge how to adapt and apply the material offered here to her particular school situation. Certainly, there will be paragraphs, chapters, and perhaps entire sections that can be readily implemented within the motivated reader's existing program structure. Just as certainly, there will be suggestions made that would require programs to reorganize their resources in order to support their program's growing emphasis on emotional life.

It is the contention of the authors that any preschool can become a healing environment if it is respectful of the young child's developmental process *and* acknowledges the impact of a child's life experience on this process. The psycho-educational approach advocated here assumes that a child's behavior is meaningful. As emotionally fragile children are often described as "hard to read," *Unsmiling Faces* helps the reader to organize her perceptions about children's behavior in a way that highlights the salient emotional issues and allows her to formulate effective intervention responses. A psychodynamic perspective is offered to early childhood professionals from diverse disciplines as well as to mental health clinicians who may be well versed in dynamic theory but unsure of its implications for very young children.

Unsmiling Faces extends an invitation to the early childhood community. It invites the professional early childhood community to make room for the emotional lives of children within the preschool classroom. The only walls that will need to be torn down to accommodate this project are psychological walls—the walls between the disciplines of early childhood education and mental health—which have stayed erect for decades in spite of our commitment to the "whole child." As young children delight in the destruction of block towers of their own creation, perhaps the reader will feel liberated by the opportunity to break through these divisions of our own design. *Unsmiling Faces: How Preschools Can Heal* can be used as a manual for this breakthrough.

INTRODUCTION

Knowing What We Know Now

OVER THE 11-YEAR PERIOD that has gone by since the initial publication of *Unsmiling Faces*, we have become more knowledgeable than ever before about the way that children's brains develop. This recent brain research has rendered the nature versus nurture argument obsolete, finding clear evidence that children come into the world with multiple capacities that are dependent on relationship experiences in order to unfold (Shonkoff & Phillips, 2000). We have always known that children can thrive when they have secure attachment relationships and opportunities to see, hear, and playfully explore their worlds within protective family and community structures. We now know that these psychosocial supports affect not only a child's clinical presentation but also the actual physiology of his or her developing brain (Meany, 2001; Thompson, 1999). We now know that early emotional experience creates essential pathways for learning in the developing brain, and sets in motion a blueprint for reactivity that can promote or arrest the development of cognition and socialization for years to come (Francis, Diorio, Plotsky, & Meaney, 2002). We also now know that while there are optimal periods for the development of language, social skills, and motor capacities, the brain remains receptive to stimulation in these areas for many more years than previously thought. The plasticity of the brain allows for physiological changes to support development throughout childhood and adolescence and into adulthood.

Understanding more about the discoveries made by brain researchers and learning about the implications of these discoveries may be empowering for early childhood professionals. The first part of this book focuses on the ways that life experience impacts development in the early years. It invites practicing professionals to view the process of a child's unfolding capacities through the lens of their own life experience and encourages teachers and clinicians to consider psychosocial history as a primary factor when assessing a child who evokes concern. It asks the reader to value both positive and negative affects in young children, and to invite the expression of both in the early childhood classroom so that children are not left alone to manage their distress. It describes the evolution of children's sense of self within the context of their primary relationships, and highlights the role of the classroom teacher in the young child's development of self-image and a sense of self-worth. Research on brain development in the early years supports these core concepts, which underlie the creation of early childhood programs that heal.

Some of the recent studies on the impact of psychosocial experience on the developing child are particularly compelling for understanding the physiology that parallels our clinical findings. Research shows that children who grow up in adverse circumstances with high levels of environmental stress are at biological as well as psychological risk. When infants, toddlers, and preschool children live in threatening environments, the threat can produce a toxic level of stress. Children who are constantly stressed by the threat of abuse, neglect, parental substance abuse or mental illness, or any other factors that result in young children feeling overwhelmed and unprotected are likely to have elevated levels of stress hormones in the brain (Gunnar & Donzella, 2002). While the release of stress hormones are helpful to people in the process of coping with short-term stressors and help the body mobilize a response, when high levels of these stress hormones become the developmental norm, they can be destructive to the developing brain and cause emotional, behavioral, and learning difficulties for the growing child. Specifically, children who experience toxic levels of stress develop high cortisol levels that remain elevated long after a particular stressor alleviates. The sustained level of the stress hormone cortisol can cause damage to the hippocampus region of the brain and can interfere with learning, memory, and the ability to regulate responses to stress (Lupien, King, Meaney, & McEwen, 2001).

Certainly, we have seen many children from highly stressed environments who are quick to react to perceived threats in the classroom. A 3-year-old boy stomps on a little girl's finger so hard that he breaks it because the little girl lightly brushed against him in the process of sitting down in the circle. A 4-year-old shoves 10 graham crackers into her mouth and begins to choke seconds after the teacher put the basket on the table in preparation for snacktime. She later explains that she was afraid she wouldn't get a cracker. The "fight or flight" response that challenges teachers has an experiential explanation as well as a physiological one. The little boy has often had to fend for himself in a family with a history of violence. He is hypersensitive to perceived threat and too quick to react when someone intrudes. Experience has taught him that someone intruding into his space may be dangerous, and his high adrenaline and cortisol levels leave his body ready for action at all times. The little girl lives in a homeless shelter where no cooking is allowed and has often been hungry. She has older siblings who grab toys and food from her. Experience has taught her that she is on her own and to make sure she has enough. Her high adeneline and cortisol levels leave her body in a state of high alert and ready for action and suppress the higher level brain functions that might have helped her remember not to put so much in her mouth at once, or might have allowed her to use language to gain reassurance that she would indeed be given crackers. If the stress is persistent and the ways of reacting become physiologically and psychologically habitual, the impulse to act precedes and precludes higher level thought processes from developing (Karr-Morse & Wiley, 1999).

Where are children like these likely to be on the continuum of development when it comes to the social emotional milestones that are precursors for healthy relationships and receptive learning? What messages about self-worth are they likely to internalize, and what tools will they have to develop self-concept? How does their social and emotional status effect brain development, and vice versa? We now know that cognition and emotional development are interdependent systems that engage several areas of the brain, including the prefrontal cortex, limbic cortex, basal forebrain, amygdala, hypothalamus, and brain stem (Davidson, et al., 2002). The pathways that develop when children exercise emotional regulation not only allow for emotional maturation but also are needed to engage with other circuits, such as those governing the brain's "executive function" and cognitive mastery. In order for children to solve problems, use good judgement, plan their actions, and engage in higher level symbolic thinking, they need to be able to express and regulate emotions (Bush, Luu, & Posner, 2000; Greenspan & Wieder, 2006; Shonkoff & Phillips, 2000). When children are flooded with feelings that they can't sort out or regulate, there is interference with attention, problem solving, and other cognitive functions. The actions of the children described earlier may be behavioral examples of the vicious circle involved: Emotional experiences of violence and deprivation affect brain physiology, the physiological damage inhibits cognition and produces dangerous responses, and those responses are likely to result in more negative emotional experience. Children who act out in impulsive ways may not be well liked by peers and teachers. When other children and adults react to the behaviors of such children in a rejecting or punitive manner, they reinforce a negative self-image that is in process of crystalizing.

While research confirms the real dangers to the brain development of underprotected and highly stressed children, it also confirms the power of strong attachment relationships to ameliorate the effects of stressful environments on young children. During World War II, Anna Freud advised against sending English children to the countryside to protect them from the bombing in London unless their mothers could accompany them. She found that children who stayed with their mothers and experienced the trauma of the war within the intimacy of parent–child relationships did better than the children who were sent to the countryside to live with families who were strangers to them. We now know the mechanism involved: Attachment relationships can ameliorate the effects of stress on a child's physiology so that the stress level stays tolerable and does not become toxic to the developing brain (National Scientific Council on the Developing Child, 2005). Young children who have nurturing, supportive relationships with their parents and caregivers have more controlled stress hormone reactions when they are alarmed or are exposed to something frightening (Gunnar & Donzella, 2002). The psychosocial support that securely attached, well cared-for children enjoy often translates into life experience within a more protected environment, which in turn translates into less emotional vulnerability when stress does occur. The intimacy of the attachment relationship is a protective factor that helps to filter stress and buffers the developing child. It is not surprising that well cared-for children whose parents are nurturing and responsive show both stronger social competence and stronger cognitive achievement in the school setting.

There are many reasons why parents may be unable to be active relationship partners in their young child's developmental process. The parents themselves may be experiencing a crisis during their child's infancy and toddlerhood that exhausts their inner resources and diminishes responsive parenting. There may be depression or other mental health issues that intrude on the parenting process. There may be intergenerational patterns of abuse and neglect that a parent is not consciously aware of, but which threaten to surface as the young child's oppositional or provocative behavior evokes the parent's childhood experience. The need to include family intervention in service plans for at-risk children has been well documented (Brooks-Gunn, Berlin, & Fuligni, 2000; Shonkoff & Phillips, 2000). This need exists not only for children under age 3, who may be eligible for early intervention services, but also for children in highly stressed families from pregnancy through the childhood years. Studies of offspring born to animals who were highly stressed during pregnancy found elevated cortisol levels in young animals who showed regulatory disorders and learning disorders into adulthood (Weinstock, 2001). This research suggests that leaving highly stressed parents unattended may be setting the stage for stress-related developmental problems, such as regulatory disorders, learning disabilities, and emotional difficulties in their children. The implications for the value of preventive mental health practice for at-risk pregnant teens, young adults, and children within the early childhood education and child care community are enormous.

Another exciting body of literature is developing that highlights the value of nurturing caregiver–child and teacher–child relationships for children who attend high-quality child care, preschool, and kindergarten programs. Not only are warm and supportive teacher–child relationships associated with higher levels of social and emotional competence, greater receptivity to the school setting, and better reasoning skills that result in higher achievement during the school years, but there are indications that these important relationships can also play a part in buffering the adverse effects of stress on the developing brain (Francis, Diorio, Plotsky, & Meaney, 2002; National Scientific Council on the Developing Child, 2005). It is interesting to note the research indicating that children in high-quality child care centers with nurturing teacher–child relationships have stable cortisol levels during the school day, but children in poor-quality centers without well-supported attachments have elevating levels of cortisol as the day progresses (Watamura, Donzella, Alwin, & Gunnar, 2005).

Paradoxically, all of this research has become available during a period when conservative politics has dominated educational policy in the United States.

While funding sources now require "evidence-based research" before considering a proposal to be valid, there is now a wealth of evidence to support a mandate for healing practices in early childhood education. Yet few programs have been funded sufficiently to do this important work. On the contrary, there has been increasing pressure on early childhood programs to withdraw social supports and focus on academic performance in order to "prepare" children to succeed on standardized tests in the early grades. When large numbers of highly stressed and emotionally fragile children fail to do well on these tests, there is a public outcry. Academic remediation is required for the children who are failing, and a heightened level of pressure is put on teachers and administrators to achieve the desired statistics, producing toxic stress within the school building itself. If we are going to create preschools, kindergartens, and elementary school programs that meet the needs of young children, our education and mental health policies need to be informed by this existing credible evidence. Anything less constitutes medical, educational, and emotional neglect of our most vulnerable children.

REFERENCES

Brooks-Gunn, J., Berlin, L. J., & Fuligni, A. S. (2000). Early childhood intervention programs: What about the family? In J. P. Shonkoff & S. J. Meisels (Eds.), *Handbook of Early Childhood Intervention* (2nd ed., pp. 549–577). New York: Cambridge University Press.

Bush, G., Luu, P., & Ponser, M. (2000). Cognitive and emotional influences in anterior cingulated cortex. *Trends in Cognitive Sciences, 4*(6), 215–222.

Davidson, R. J., et al. (2002). Neural and behavioral substrates of mood and mood regulation. *Biological Psychiatry, 52*(6), 478–502.

Francis, D., Diorio, J., Plotsky, P. M., & Meaney, M. J. (2002). Environmental enrichment reverses the effects of maternal separation on stress reactivity. *Journal of Neuroscience, 22*, 7840–7843.

Greenspan, S., & Wieder, S. (2006). *Engaging autism.* Cambridge, MA: Da Capo.

Gunnar, M. R., & Donzella, B. (2002). Social regulation of the cortisol levels in early human development. *Psychoneuroendocrinology, 27*, 199–220.

Karr-Morse, R., & Wiley, M. (1997). *Ghosts from the nursery: Tracing the roots of violence.* New York: Atlantic Monthly Press.

Lupien, S., King, S., Meaney, M. J., & McEwen, B. (2001). Can poverty get under your skin? Basal cortisol levels and cognitive function from low and high socioeconomic status. *Development and Psychopathology, 13*, 653–676.

Meaney, M. (2001). Maternal care, gene expression and the transmission of individual differences in stress reactivity across generations. *Annual Review of Neuroscience, 24*, 1161–1192.

National Scientific Council on the Developing Child. (2005). *Excessive stress disrupts the architecture of the brain* (Working Paper #3). Retrieved Sept. 15, 2006 from www.developingchild.net/reports.html

Shonkoff, J., & Phillips, D. (2000). *From neurons to neighborhoods: The science of early childhood development.* Washington, DC: National Academy Press.

Thompson, R. A. (1999). Early attachment and later development. In J. Cassidy & P. R. Shaver (Eds.), *Handbook of Attachment: Theory, research, and clinical applications* (pp. 265–286). New York: Guilford Press.

Watamura, S. E., Donzella, B., Alwin, J., & Gunnar, M. R. (2003). Morning to afternoon increases in cortisol concentrations for infants and toddlers at child care: Age differences and behavioral correlates. *Child Development, 74*(4), 1006–1020.

Weinstock, M. (2001). Alterations induced by gestational stress in brain morphology and behavior of the offspring. *Progress in Neurobiology, 62,* 427–451.

Unsmiling Faces

Making Room for Emotional Life in Preschool

Developmental Reality and the Reality of Experience

LESLEY KOPLOW

MUCH HAS BEEN WRITTEN about the process of child development in the early years. While theories of development may differ, no one can deny the transformation process that propels the cheerfully seated 5-month-old to crawl across the room 1 month later or that compels the compliant young toddler to take an increasingly oppositional stance as she nears her second birthday. Given a supportive and nurturing environment, the healthy child's developmental agenda will unfold, including the predictable milestones charted on the pediatrician's checklist. Each will be achieved with the unique style and expressive quality of the individual child. Yet, unlike the slow-budding blossom of a flower best captured in the silence of time-lapse photography, the baby's developmental process requires an eye for action and an orchestra of sound. There is nothing neat or quiet about a baby's struggle to grow up.

The early childhood education community has grown to respect the child's developmental process and has fought to structure early childhood education programs in accordance with the child's developmental agenda. The National Association for the Education of Young Children's (NAEYC) Developmentally Appropriate Curriculums guide the early childhood professional and help her refrain from imposing expectations that are at odds with the developmental tasks of each age group. Piaget's belief that a child's intelligence unfolds through her own interaction with the environment informs our values and gives open-ended experience a primary role in the education of our young children.

Then along comes a child who seems ill-equipped to follow his own developmental agenda. Many essential ego functions may seem out of sync or qualitatively different from those of other children. This child's internal disorganization spills over the classroom like a geyser, threatening to drown children and staff and compelling the teacher to act swiftly to stem the flow.

3

The social worker who referred the child to the program may have little to say about his puzzling developmental status but much to say about the reality of the child's experience. The child's psychosocial history may include disruptions, deprivations, and traumas that are painful for the staff to consider. The teacher may feel empathic toward her student, yet exasperated as she struggles to contain his difficult behaviors and to follow his idiosyncratic developmental path.

The frightening tales that fill the little boy's psychosocial history may give the teacher insight into her young pupil's environmental reality but may leave her at a loss as to how to proceed with the job of acting as a facilitator of his development. She may ask herself, "How does it happen that difficult experiences arrest or actually alter the developmental process of a young child?" Indeed, in order to build a bridge between developmental reality and the reality of experience, the early childhood professional must reconsider the genesis of healthy ego development in well-supported children. Only by revisiting the origins of typical developmental achievements can the atypical child's struggle become clear.

IMAGE AND DEVELOPMENTAL REALITY

Certainly, we must begin our journey toward understanding developmental reality before the baby is born, by visiting the mother who is giving birth to a psychological image of her child-to-be (Cohen & Slade, 2000; Galinsky, 1987; Huth-Bocks, Levendosky, Bogat, & von Eye, 2004; Lieberman, 1997). During pregnancy, both parents endow the unborn child with identities and attributes, creating fantasies that prepare them for the reality of making room for a new person in their lives. The baby who comes is seldom the baby of fantasy, and much depends on the parents' ability to let go of "would-be" images and replace them with images that can change and be modified by the real, live child. The woman who longs for a daughter and has imagined herself braiding long hair will need to develop new images if she gives birth to a son. When parents can evolve images that are ever-changing and modified by the actual child, the images serve an important purpose. They can become the psychological equivalent of setting up and decorating a nursery for the coming child, ensuring that there will be a space ready to receive him right from the start. Parents who have done this psychological work of imaging may be more available for the intimate experience of bonding and building an attachment relationship once the child arrives.

Partnership

When the baby is born, she and her caregivers must engage one another in a profound and mutual way, allowing the umbilical cord that has been cut and tossed away to be replaced by an invisible, durable, and more elastic connection. Bowlby (1973; Waters & Cummings, 2000) conceptualized the child's need for care and the parents' caregiving response as the nucleus of the attachment relationship. The well-nurtured child who has the experience that his dependency needs can be attended to and satisfied within the context of a loving relationship will develop a secure attachment. The baby works just as hard as the parent to contribute to this union, making winning facial expressions, flashing beautiful smiles, and emitting irresistible cooing sounds in order to ensure that parental response will be forthcoming.

If the baby is successful, she will have a partner in the early developmental work of regulating state and will develop comfortable body rhythms and maintain physical and emotional equilibrium. She will have protection from overwhelming or toxic environmental influences—shielded by the adult's body as she rides securely in her snuggly or lulled by the hum of the dehumidifier that drowns out the discordant sounds of the street. As the baby begins to hold up her head, pull away from a close hold, and strive to maintain a sitting position, her growing interest in the world becomes overt and perceptible to the well-attuned adult. The well-attached baby will not be bored or understimulated. The culture of the responsive adult may determine whether the infant is stimulated with toys or solely through parent–child or sibling–child play. But the essential elements of response to the child's need for exploration can be answered and accommodated without damage to the relationship.

First Steps

During the second half of the first year of the baby's life, she begins a journey of locomotion that takes her farther and farther away from parental arms and results in her standing, however precariously, on her own two feet. The crawling, standing, cruising, and then walking child is faced with many new dilemmas. If she is to explore the beckoning world beyond mommy's lap, she must be comfortable being physically separate from the mother. She must risk adversity that may befall her when out of her parents' sight, and she must know the road back to safety if feared events occur. Indeed, the mobile child will prefer to station the adult in one spot, and then to journey out into the world and back again to make contact with the parent. Mahler, Bergman, and Pine (1975/2000) referred to this as "refueling," that is, returning to the source of emotional sustenance and then resuming exploration (Honig, 2002). In this way, the parent acts as a psychological "home base," allowing the toddler to develop an orientation to the environment by exploring it within the organizing influence of the parent–child relationship. The caregiver's predictable location gives the securely attached child a destination when she meets adversity, allowing her to evade danger as she seeks proximity to the attachment figure (Ainsworth, 1973; Bowlby, 1973; Main, Kaplan, & Cassidy, 1985).

When these parameters of closeness are no longer satisfying to the child whose motor urge has intensified, she may solve her dilemma by using a transitional object. A blanket, stuffed animal, or other soft toy is endowed with meaning and symbolizes the attachment figure that the child must leave behind. Armed with this comforting symbol, the toddler is able to journey beyond the confines of the parental circle.

Essential Discoveries

Before we let this toddler walk away, there is another important event to record that occurs while the baby is still crawling. At 4 or 5 months, she may play with interest with a rattle toy but take no action to recover the toy if it falls out of sight. Indeed, although the crawling 6- or 7-month-old has the motor means to seek a lost object, she cannot pursue it. The rattle exists for her only if it is pressed into her hand, making shaking sounds within her hearing, turning before her eyes, or being explored in her mouth. The infant is dependent on her sensory perception of it in order to realize its existence. Piaget tells us that before 9 months of age, the infant perceives items only as part of herself. Once out of contact with the self, the item ceases to be. Yet, somewhere between the ages of 9 and 12 months, the baby begins to pursue the lost object (Piaget, 1974). This achievement of object permanence lets us know that the infant has acquired the ability to differentiate between self and other-than-self, and can maintain the image of an item as a separate entity.

The baby or toddler who has acquired object permanence makes a tremendous discovery. If each item in his world is an entity unto itself, separate from the baby and distinctive from all other items, then each must have a name of its own. Thus, the young toddler begins his mission of identifying and labeling the world around him. He points, and his pointing is rewarded with names. While object permanence is primarily considered to be a cognitive milestone, the parental role in developmental mastery is significant. The persistent baby engages the patient adult in hours of play around retrieving lost objects. Pacifiers, rattles, and squeaky toys are thrown from cribs and high chairs with a twinkling expression that challenges the caregiver to prove that what is out of sight can be recovered.

When the young toddler points to his stuffed bunny and looks at his caregiver with an inquiring expression, he is inviting her to share in and help define the new world (Greenspan & Wieder, 2006; Siegel, 1999; Stern, 1985/2000;). The special names that children and parents often invent for toys, people, and routines are charged with personal meaning, helping children make an intimate and creative connection between language and experience. These personal symbols are precursors for more abstract and elaborate uses of language.

Challenge to the Self

The walking, talking toddler has much to accomplish. While transitional objects may help to bridge the increasing physical distance between child and caregiver, the toddler can now also use words to connect with others who are out of sight. As toddlers are driven to explore the world around them, they experience a heightened ambivalence about their newly acquired independence and their very real dependency needs. Parents often have the feeling that they can never be completely satisfying to their children at this stage. The child seems to assume an oppositional stance in spite of the parents' best efforts to be accommodating.

In fact, the toddler's oppositionalism serves him well. He needs to counter the adult in order to feel his emerging autonomy. He needs to have the freedom to test the limits of the adult authority so that he can feel safe and contained as his own person within the secure boundaries provided by the adult. "No" helps him more clearly delineate himself from the other he is opposing. "Mine" states his claim on the world and announces his intention to relinquish the passive infantile position for a more active, initiating role.

By continually testing his parents and making sure they are there when needed, the 2-year-old is helping himself to internalize a constant parental presence. Over and over again, the toddler in his third year of life challenges himself to integrate the adult's shifting affects into one stable image. The mommy who looks angry and says "no" is the same mommy who smiles a comforting smile and gives a bottle of milk. Once able to integrate positive and negative experiences with the nurturing adult, the child will have achieved object constancy: an ability to access the image of the nurturer even when he or she is out of sight. This developmental milestone will help the child to feel confident in the face of separation.

There is a parallel task confronting the child: to internalize a constant image of himself. Indeed, the volatile, moody toddler must come to feel whole and complete as one individual person with many feeling states. This is a difficult task. The child at this age has many worries about his caregiver's safety and many worries about his own safety. He worries about the integrity of his body and frequently fears injury, medical procedures, bathtub drains, haircuts, toilets, and so forth. While haircuts may not be physically painful, children feel threatened by any experience that implies a loss of self at this age. The falling hair may symbolize part of them that is now dispensable to their parents.

During this period, toilet-training issues are paramount for both parents and children. Children may want to comply with their parents' wishes to gain approval but fear parting with something they have produced that may still feel like part of their bodies. Young children worry about being as dispensable as their body products that are being flushed away. Their feelings require much patience and reassurance during this period in order to resolve these fears and accomplish the challenge of toileting.

The Preschooler's Agenda

The well-functioning preschool child is generally able to show at least partial mastery over these developmental issues, but she remains vulnerable to frequent regressions. She enters preschool with a belief in the permanence of objects and in the constancy of people. She carries an image of caregiver with her and is able to use this image to comfort herself in times of stress. Strong and stable attachment relationships at home allow her to develop trust in her surrogate caregivers at school and to seek and accept help when needed. The child's symbolic capacities have expanded beyond the use of transitional objects and language labels and have grown to include rich and elaborate symbolic play, accompanied by descriptive, action-filled language.

While adults remain central to the child's feeling of well-being at this age, peers are also compelling, and relationships with other people are growing in significance. Children are motivated to negotiate with one another over toys and shared space in order to have the pleasure of each other's company. As the negotiations proceed and the socialization process unfolds, there is less struggle over issues of domain, and more energy can be devoted to the emergence of dramatic play skills. Children begin to pool their symbols and their play metaphors and to create collaborative play ventures that allow a more profound level of sharing to occur. Not only can children share materials, but they can share experiences with one another through play. This important avenue allows them to diminish feelings of isolation and to feel empowered in a miniature world of their own design.

The preschool child's receptivity to more structured input will depend partially on her ability to feel relieved of survival concerns and relaxed in her environment. The well-cared-for, well-attached preschool child is free to devote her attention to her own learning and will be receptive to story time and other teacher-directed activities.

The needy infant and toddler undoubtedly continues to surface at times in the preschool classroom. There are frequent battles, tearful goodbyes, wet pants, and periods where dependency needs seem to cry out more loudly than the child's call for independent mastery. Yet, in developmentally healthy children, these small regressions often herald a new cycle of growth as children revisit their younger selves before moving on. This dance between progress and regress is essential to the young child's process of internalization and integration. It allows them to test the reality of their own self-constancy, as well as the stability of the adult who can accommodate both dependency needs and the need for independent mastery.

As children realize their ability to have an impact on their environments, they explore the extent of their own personal effectiveness and discover their own limitations. In order to avoid feeling overwhelmed by relative helplessness, preschool children borrow strength through their identifications with parental figures and "superheroes" who become sources of pride and hopefulness. While it is difficult for children to fulfill their desire to "be big like Daddy" in the here and now, enacting superhero fantasies allows them a less conflicted route to a position of power and status. The well-functioning 4-year-old has no problem assuming the role of caped crusader on the playground and later relinquishing the cape in favor of a flannel blanket when the lights go out for rest time. For the preschool child, strength and fragility are dual realities. The child's pockets must be large enough to accommodate the Power Ranger as well as the blanket square.

EXPERIENTIAL REALITY AND THE DISTORTED IMAGE

The child whose experience does not support development may not be able to hold onto these two essential developmental realities simultaneously. Teachers are often overwhelmed by needy children who vacillate between phases of pseudomaturity, disconnectedness, independent functioning, and complete emotional disintegration in the face of the most basic challenges. The psychosocial histories of these children may indeed provide clues to the gaps in development that their teachers observe.

Consider the child whose history indicates that the prenatal period was highly stressed by survival issues, maternal or paternal depression or illness, or the experience of loss or trauma. The psychological work of imaging may be preempted under those circumstances, as parents attend to the crises or to the intrapsychic issues that preoccupy them. The birth of a baby then occurs within the context of crisis. For instance, the baby born to a family whose survival needs are unmet may come to symbolize burden or parental failure because the parents fear they will not be able to care for their child adequately. Women who ignore their need for prenatal care, or who engage in high-risk behaviors such as drinking or drug use, may be denying the existence of the growing child inside of them. There may be a poverty of images surrounding the child-to-be. The birth of the child may not pierce that denial. The child may be the recipient of the unrealistic expectations that she will meet the mother's needs, while her own dependency needs continue to be denied.

The child born to depressed or grieving parents may come to symbolize the only hope for the family's future, thus assuming a grave responsibility at birth.

In all of these situations, the experience of the parent casts a shadow over the relationship with the infant. The urgency of parental need may cloud the parents' abilities to hear actual messages coming from the new baby and affect the quality of the emerging parent–infant dialogue.

Children Without Partners

If a parent is emotionally or physically unavailable to the infant during the first 6 months of life, and there is no other consistent caregiver acting as surrogate, the baby may be deprived of the opportunity to attach. We have seen the dire results of the most extreme cases of maternal deprivation in Spitz's (1965) study of institutionalized infants who became depressed and lifeless. Indeed, some developed failure-to-thrive and lost their lives. More recently, researchers have studied the results of neglect on infants and toddlers by following the developmental course of Romanian orphans who were cared for in extremely depriving conditions before being adopted. These children showed a range of medical, developmental, and psychological problems as well as atypical attachment behaviors (O'Connor, Marvin, Rutter, Olrick, & Britner, 2003; Zeenah, Smyke, Koga, & Carlson, 2005; Zilberstein, 2006).

While it is rare for early childhood professionals to encounter children who have experienced such extreme deprivation, it is, unfortunately, increasingly common to see children whose opportunity to attach has been severely limited, disrupted, or arrested.

If the adult who cares for a baby cannot be attentive to his dependency needs, the infant may frequently be uncomfortable and in distress (Lieberman, 1997). His own attempts to maintain emotional and physical homeostasis without help from the adult may consume all of his energy and result in less awareness and responsiveness to environmental stimuli. If the infant's cries do not bring a response of compassionate care, there may be less investment in communication in general. The baby may shut down and become uncommunicative or unresponsive, or may be overwhelmed by high levels of stress that activate a physiologic "high-alert" response that leaves him hyperalert, impulsive, and difficult to comfort or calm (Essex, Klein, Cho, & Kalin, 2002; Lieberman, 1997).

The diagnosis of reactive attachment disorder is given to infants, toddlers, and young children who have been deprived of the opportunity for attachment and who have developed a pattern of undifferentiated relatedness, or who have become distant, disconnected, and unresponsive to others (American Psychiatric Association, 1987/2000; Zilberstein, 2006). These children face serious developmental dilemmas as they move through infancy to the toddler stage and on to early childhood. Their ability to develop social relationships may be severely restricted or may be indiscriminate and dangerous as the child attempts to compensate for the lack of internal connection to another.

When locomotion becomes an imperative, the toddler who has no secure attachment may be inhibited in his exploration of the environment. He may fear abandonment if he invests in his own activity. On the other hand, many such children do proceed to explore, but in a driven, impulsive, and disoriented manner. Lacking a psychological "home base" in the relationship with the adult, the toddler's forays into his world appear chaotic and unproductive. If the child meets adversity, he is at a loss to avoid danger by seeking comfort.

When actual separations occur from familiar adults or from the child's familiar environment, the child without consistent experience of nurture will not be able to solve his dilemma in the usual way—via the transitional object. Since the transitional object represents the child's attachment relationship, the attachment-disordered child lacks the experiential resources to accomplish this symbolic feat.

A Poverty of Symbols

Sadly, this is only one example of the ways that deprivation acts to depress symbolic functioning. When we review the developmental precursors for meaningful language acquisition, there are many essential roles reserved for the adult partner in the parent–child dyad. It is the adult who engages with the baby in preverbal dialogues of reciprocal cooing, eye gaze, and peek-a-boo games. It is the adult who retrieves the pacifiers that the 10-month-old gleefully tosses from his crib in a game of differentiating items from self and reexperiencing the viability of items that leave the sensory field. It is the adult who responds to the child's inquiring gesture of pointing at an object once object permanence has been achieved and who provides her with word labels and demonstrations of an item's function. It is the significant adult whom the toddler invites on his mission to co-define his expanding world, creating his own words and phrases to code his discoveries. It is the magic of the primary attachment relationship that endows the child's discoveries with symbolic value and, thus, brings the world to life. Therefore, it is likely that the attachment-disordered or neglected child will have difficulties with these early achievements and may demonstrate impoverished symbolic abilities. For example, delays in speech and language development are often present in children with histories of disrupted attachments, as well as delays in ability to generate symbolic play.

The Disrupted Self

Logically, the autonomy-seeking toddler cannot do the work of testing the limits of his attachment relationships if there is no attachment relationship to oppose. Without the secure base of attachment, the toddler's forays toward a deeper sense of self are hampered. Of course, not all children experiencing difficulty in toddlerhood have been attachment-deprived. In many instances, parents and children seemed to have the opportunity and capacity to form secure attachment relationships. Problems may have arisen later in the child's developmental course, when issues of autonomy, body integrity, separation, and constancy of self and other are primary.

Difficult situations that exist during the child's infancy may become more problematic in toddlerhood. For example, a family living in inadequate housing, with exposed wiring and rotten floor boards, may have used a snuggly or baby seat to provide a safe environment for their infant. However, this family might have been forced to inhibit the curious toddler's motor learning by confining her to a crib. The equation of confinement and safety may thwart the child's movement toward separation-individuation and delay the child's struggle for autonomy. On the other hand, the experience of confinement might generate frustration in the child, who then protests her situation by becoming increasingly oppositional and provocative. Certainly, experience impinges on the process of development in either case, although the meaning of the experience is unique to the individual child in question.

Because the toddler in his third year of life is in the process of internalizing stable representations of self and other, major disruptions during this period may be particularly harmful to the developmental process. Psychosocial histories that include multiple or persistent separations from primary attachment figures, instances of abuse or neglect, foster-care placement, mental illness in parental figures, exposure to violence, death of family members, illness, hospitalization or intrusive medical procedures, or loss of home due to fire or eviction will alert professionals to the need for developmental monitoring.

It is easy to see why the highly stressed toddler would be at risk for developmental difficulty. Recall that children at this age have many fears about injury and physical integrity. They require much parental support and reassurance to favorably resolve toileting fears and to maintain self-esteem in spite of the failures inherent in the learning process. They need patient parental intervention to allow themselves to sleep in a darkened room without experiencing an invasion by monsters born of their own aggressive impulses that come back to haunt them at night.

When children are neglected during this period, they not only sustain more physical injuries but are also vulnerable to becoming overwhelmed by their own fears and feelings of fragility. Without appropriate adult attention, children are unlikely to develop adequate mastery of toileting and other self-care routines. The experience of failure may be accompanied by feelings of shame and may discourage involvement in more age-appropriate challenges for fear of defeat. Often children who are not well supported develop a pseudomastery of these tasks, learning to comply without achieving psychological mastery and thus without pride of ownership. Children may assume an aggressive stance to defend themselves from their feelings of deprivation and vulnerability. Because aggression is not adequately contained within the parent–child relationship, it cannot be contained by the child and is likely to come out in social situations away from his parents.

An Image Divided

Physically painful experiences are often problematic for toddlers who are in the process of trying to master body integrity issues. Intrusive medical procedures are especially risky during the toddler stage. The already vulnerable toddler must suffer intrusions that seem to be sanctioned by his parents. Psychological recovery may require more time than physical recovery, since the toddler must regain feelings of sure-footedness and being physically intact.

Abusive behavior is also extremely damaging to children during this period. Children who are physically abused by their parents within the developmental context of establishing stable and positive concepts of self and other are unable to successfully complete their developmental task. The abuse shatters both constructs simultaneously. The child who is alternately injured and nurtured by his parents is in the untenable position of being dependent on someone who is hurtful. Many children survive this dilemma by identifying with the aggressive parent and detaching from their own pain. Their image of themselves as someone who needs or deserves punishment may become the strongest self-representation. If abuse is the parental response to the normal 2-year-old's oppositional stance that heralds the toddler's emergence of self, the self that emerges may be fused with negative feeling. The toddler may be withdrawn and compliant in order to remain as pleasing to the adult as possible at the cost of her own sense of autonomy and mastery. Conversely, the toddler may be driven to engage the adult's wrath because he does not recognize himself as separate from the punishing incidents.

Clearly, the achievement of object constancy is complex and difficult for abused and neglected children. Children cannot internalize a stable, comforting image of an adult if adults are intentionally harming them. Frequently, abused children cope with the impossible task of integrating the good and bad experience with their parents by splitting the image in two. They develop an idealized image of their parents to replace the conflicted one and attribute the danger that belongs to the parent–child relationship to the environment itself. Therefore, the world may be experienced as menacing, and the child may cry out in panic for the idealized mommy's and daddy's comfort. Sadly, the child cannot evoke the comforting image internally, since the idealized image does not represent the child's actual experiences. Children with poor object constancy feel as though they are alone when adversity strikes in preschool and rarely can use the teacher as a source of help or comfort. Rather, they are likely to use preemptive aggression or physical retaliation when they feel threatened in socializing with other children.

Similar to children with abusive histories, children who have mentally ill parents or substance-abusing parents may find it very difficult to achieve object constancy. Since parents with these issues often have extremely discordant moods and unpredictable affects, children struggle to integrate their disparate experiences with their parents. Parents with mental illness or substance-abuse issues may find it hard to take in and mirror their children's affects. Therefore, their children may have difficulty expressing affects that reflect their true feeling states. Their emotions may be difficult for their teachers and caregivers to read.

A Whole Child

Let us return to the troubled child mentioned earlier in the chapter. This child is out of sync with classmates, and it requires heroic measures to maintain him in his early childhood classroom.

There are several manifestations of dysfunction in this little boy. He is marginally verbal, inattentive to the language of others, and uninterested in age-level tasks. He has a high activity level, appears random and disoriented as he moves about the room, and shows a low frustration tolerance when challenged. He is alternately fearful and aggressive, has difficulty with separation, and seems at a loss to comfort himself or accept comfort from others. Routines such as eating, napping, and toileting are fraught with conflict. He is unable to play productively, ignores the play of his peers, and uses toys only for hoarding.

When faced with such a child, there is a temptation to push the troubling history aside and instead to evaluate his performance and then provide remediation for each deficit area noted. While the little boy may not be functioning on a typical 4-year-old level, this child's behaviors are understandable within the context of his life experience. The psychosocial history tells us that the child's mother became involved with drugs when he was 6 months old and that he was placed in his grandmother's care at age 2½, after his mother was charged with neglect. His grandmother reports that her grandson still has difficulty sleeping and frequently awakens with nightmares. She notes that during the day he is "all over the place" and doesn't seem to be deterred by being told "no." He cries and becomes fearful when he has to use the bathroom.

Clearly, this 4-year-old's developmental processes were disrupted at critical stages. How can a neglected 6-month-old discover the permanence of objects in an unattended, chaotic world? How can he internalize a safe and stable adult presence if he experiences extreme inconsistencies and unmet dependency needs? How can he learn to symbolize his relationship with toys and words if he has no true relationship partner? How can he sleep through the night or be calm and attentive at school if he is preoccupied with his own survival?

There is much unfinished business in this child's early developmental process. Intervention for him cannot be effective unless it acknowledges history and addresses those developmental issues that could not be resolved initially, given the nature of the child's experiences. In order for the preschool child to build a solid developmental basis for learning, he must have new experiences that support the acquisition of essential developmental precursors. In order to heal this child, his preschool will have to acknowledge the primacy of relationships as the organizer of development for young children and the foundation for symbolic learning. This preschool will have to infuse its caregiving routines, teacher–child interactions, and curriculums with its knowledge about attachment and symbolic development. Preschools that heal will have to provide children with an opportunity to attend to their unfinished business before insisting that they devote their energies to the mastery of abstract preacademic tasks. These preschools will consider the child's unresolved developmental issues to be his or her primary agenda during the schoolday. Staff will work to foster the child's ego capacities, but recitation or writing of the ABC's will not be the goal. Rather, staff members will look forward to the day when the child's development supports language, play, and drawing that symbolizes his emotional experience and allow him to tell his own story.

REFERENCES

Ainsworth, M. D. S. (1973). The development of infant–mother attachment. In B. M. Caldwell & H. N. Ricciuti (Eds.), *Review of Child Development Research* (Vol. 3, pp. 1–194). Chicago: University of Chicago Press

American Psychiatric Association. (2000). *Diagnostic and statistical manual: DSM-IV-TR.* Washington, DC: Author. (Original work published 1987)

Bowlby, J. (1973). *Attachment and loss, separation anxiety and anger.* New York: Basic Books.

Cohen, L. J., & Slade, A. (2000). Psychology and psychopathology of pregnancy. In C. H. Zeanah (Ed.), *Handbook of infant mental health* (2nd ed., Chap. 2). New York: Guilford.

Essex, M. J., Klein, M. H., Cho, E., & Kalin, N. H. (2002). Maternal stress beginning in infancy may sensitize children to later stress exposure; Effects on cortisol and behavior. *Biological Psychiatry, 52*(8), 776–784.

Galinsky, E. (1987). *The six stages of parenthood.* Boston: Addison-Wesley.

Greenspan, S., & Wieder, S. (2006). *Engaging Autism.* Cambridge, MA: Da Capo.

Honig, A. S. (2002). *Secure relationships, nurturing infant/toddler attachment in early care settings.* Washington, DC: National Association for the Education of Young Children.

Huth-Bocks, A. C., Levendosky, A. A., Bogat, G. A., & von Eye, A. (2004). The impact of maternal characteristics and contextual variables in infant–mother attachment. *Child Development, 75*(2), 480–496.

Lieberman, A. F. (1997). Toddler's internalization of maternal attributions as a factor in quality of attachment. In L. Atkinson & K. J. Zucker (Eds.), *Attachment & psychotherapy* (pp. 277–291. New York: Guilford.

Mahler, M., Bergman, A., & Pine, F. (2000). *The psychological birth of the human infant.* New York: Basic Books. (Original work published 1975)

Main, M., Kaplan, N., & Cassidy, J. (1985). Security in infancy, childhood, and adulthood: A move to the level of representation. In I. Bretherton & E. Waters (Eds.), *Growing points of attachment theory and research* (pp. 66–104). [Monograph of the Society for Research in Child Development, 50 (1–2).] Chicago: University of Chicago.

O'Conner, T., Marvin, R., Rutter, M., Olrick, J., Britner, P., & the English and Romanian Adoptees Study Team. (2000). Child–parent attachment following early institutional deprivation. *Development & Psychopathology, 15*, 19–38.

Piaget, J. (1974). *The origins of intelligence in children.* New York: International Universities Press.

Siegel, D. J. (1999). *The developing mind: How relationships and the brain interact to shape who we are.* New York: Guilford.

Spitz, R. (1965). *The first year of life: A psychoanalytic study of normal and deviant development of object relations.* New York: International Universities Press.

Stern, D. (2000). *The interpersonal world of the infant.* New York: Basic Books. (Original work published 1985)

Waters, E., & Cummings, E. M. (2000). A secure base from which to explore close relationships. *Child Development, 71*(1), 164–172.

Zeenah, C. H., Smyke, A. T., Koga, S. F., & Carlson, E. (2005). Attachment in institu-
    tionalized and community children in Romania. *Child Development, 76*(5), 1015–
    1028.
Zilberstein, K. (2006). Clarifying core characteristics of reactive attachment disorders: A
    review of current research and theory. *American Journal of Orthopsychiatry, 76*(1),
    55–64.

CHAPTER 2

"If You're Sad and You Know It": The Value of Children's Affects

LESLEY KOPLOW

> If you're happy and you know it, clap your hands
> If you're happy and you know it, clap your hands
> If you're happy and you know it, and you
> Really want to show it
> If you're happy and you know it, clap your hands
> —Children's song

EVERY EARLY CHILDHOOD TEACHER will recognize the song above. It is a song familiar from our own childhoods, apparently received as eagerly by the current generation of children as it was years ago. Yet if we end the song here, we risk neglecting many of the children sitting before us whose predominant affects are not happiness but sadness, anger, fear, worry, and the like. If we conceive of childhood only as a carefree, joyful time, we may be denying the experiential and emotional realities of many at-risk children who enter our classroom each morning. Paradoxically, by letting these negative affects go unattended, we may be barring the children from an avenue of connection and learning that can increase their capacity for joyful sharing.

Clearly, denial of children's negative emotions is an occupational hazard. We use clowns to comfort hospitalized children; the hallways of children's homes and shelters are decorated with cheery-faced Disney characters. These attempts to "cheer" children may convey our own difficulty acknowledging, affirming, and tolerating a range of affects in young children, including those that communicate emotional pain and distress. Unfortunately, adult denial of children's negative affects puts some children in the untenable position of having to join the adult in denial mode or risk emotional alienation, because they find no mirror for their affective states in the classroom.

The importance of an educational environment that reflects a child's experiences has been well documented by educators concerned with multicultural education (e.g., Derman-Sparks, 1989). We no longer populate our housekeeping corners with only blond-haired, blue-eyed baby dolls. We stock our bookshelves with stories that include children of all races and cultural backgrounds and depict urban as well as rural and suburban imagery. The support of diversity in the early childhood curriculum empowers children on many levels. On a cognitive level, these curriculums introduce children to symbols that are personal and that represent what is relevant and familiar to them. Hence, representational capacities are enhanced as children are better able to embrace the symbols as "old friends." On a social/emotional level, a curriculum that reflects diversity helps children feel culturally affirmed and prideful about what is their own. Each factor contributes positively to a young child's ability to learn.

It is this author's contention that affirming the value of children's diverse affects is similarly empowering. At-risk children need to experience their own affective expressions as understood, mirrored, and valued before they will be able to take in affective information from others. Research shows us that without experiencing this fundamental form of communication, which stimulates the development of multiple synaptic connections in the young child's brain, children may have difficulty moving toward more sophisticated forms of communication and learning (Greenspan & Wieder, 2006; National Scientific Council on the Developing Child, 2004; Shankoff & Phillips, 2000; Shore, 1997/2003; Siegel, 1999).

This chapter will focus on the process of affect development in the early years and suggest ways for early childhood professionals to strengthen the foundations for healthy affect development in at-risk preschool children.

THE BIRTH OF AFFECT

There is much evidence to suggest that infants are born biologically prepared to enter into an affective discourse with their caregivers. Indeed, affect may be considered to be the primary vehicle for communication between infant and parent. The baby's cries communicate his distress, invite the mother to share the distress, and motivate her to address its source. The mother's delight at presenting the baby with a new rattle is transmitted to the baby, who shares in the affective mood and is motivated to bat playfully at the toy. The infant's attunement to affects becomes increasingly evident at 2 months of age, when she appears enchanted with a responsive, social smile. The infant's ability to differentiate among maternal affects and inform her behavior accordingly has been demonstrated in studies involving

6-month-olds who checked their mother's faces before proceeding to crawl toward a situation that appeared dangerous (Beebe & Lachmann, 2002; Sorce, Emde, Campos, & Klinnert, 1985).

The infant's capacity to regulate affects evolves as she experiences herself as a social partner in a relationship where each makes adjustments in response to the affects of the other. This relationship must be strong enough to "hold" the baby's affective core, supporting her through the extremes of her emotional ups and downs but helping her avoid sustained distress by balancing these affects with pleasurable affective experience (Beebe & Lachmann, 2002; Emde, 1989). Nathanson (1986) postulates that the infant learns to evaluate experiences of intense affect by checking the affects of important adults around her, thereby determining whether an affect is originating within the self or is being elicited by the other. This process then allows the infant to take defensive measures to protect herself from affects that are overwhelming (Beebe & Lachmann, 2002).

Emde (1989) refers to the infant as endowed with an affective core that "becomes exercised within the infant–caregiver relationship" (p. 48). Certainly, the quality of that primary relationship and the nature of affective communication within it will impact on the growing child's differentiation and affect regulation. Because affect can be conceptualized as a primary organizer of a young child's experience, as a vehicle for communicating emotions, and as a marker of developmental integration, the child's overall developmental integrity is partially dependent on his affective core getting the right "kind" of "exercise." Children are biologically equipped for this affective activity, but they are reliant on the stimulation of a responsive adult in order to begin the affective dialogue (Shore, 1997/2003; Siegel, 1999).

One can imagine that a well-attuned baby will attend to the affective cues of her mother, but if the mother is ill attuned and misses the baby's cues, the communication is disrupted. The baby may continue her affective monitoring of the mother, but as a survival mechanism and without the sense of shared meaning that motivates joyful interaction. Difficulty with affect regulation may be anticipated in an infant such as this because the caregiver's lack of attunement will not convey a sense that affects can be contained or accommodated. One can also imagine that a constitutionally compromised infant who does not send distinct affective messages, or appear interested in receiving them, will affect the caregiver's responsiveness negatively (Beebe & Lachmann, 2002). Clinicians have found that mothers of such infants provide care in a way described as mechanical, since there is little feedback to sustain a more related interaction (Greenspan & Wieder, 2006; Solnit & Stark, 1961).

Beebe and Sloate's (1982) studies of psychotic mothers and their infants found that infants turn away from affects delivered in intrusive, overwhelming ways. Infants in relationships with disturbed caregivers learn to avoid affective information, thus impoverishing their own abilities for attunement (Beebe & Lachmann, 2002). Infants whose caregivers are active substance abusers, and who are therefore exposed to intense, inconsistent, and abruptly shifting affects in adults, may have difficulty with affect differentiation and regulation, since these abilities are impaired in the caregivers whom they are monitoring for affective information.

The role of affect as an organizer of development and developmental integrator has been described in the literature. Sroufe's (1979, 1996) work suggests that stranger anxiety may be the 8-month-old's reaction to the difference in affective climate when in the presence of someone other than the primary caregivers. Emde (1989) notes the heightened affects and affective shifts that typically accompany developmental milestones and interprets this phenomenon as an emotional declaration that "adaptation is providing for integration at a new level" (p. 41). Thus the suddenly separation–anxious baby expresses distress that heralds the child's developmental reality, which is that separation has new emotional meaning for her. The ecstatic shrieks of the 12-month-old who has just begun to walk announce the presence of a toddler who will never again function like the baby he was only a week before.

Both positive affects (joy, interest, excitement, surprise) and negative affects (distress, fear, anger, disgust) are thought to be innate and can be identified in every culture (Eisenberg & Qing, 2000; Izard, Huebner, Risser, Mcginnes, & Dougherty, 1980; Siegel, 1999). We suppose that these affects are available to the infant for expression as well as for reception of affective messages in others. While the function of the baby's affects within the infant–parent relationship can be considered essential for communicating the baby's needs for engagement and care, the function of the adult's affects within the infant–parent relationship merits discussion. We have referred to the function of the adult's negative affects as a danger signal to the baby to alert him if a feature of the environment is not safe. Adults often exaggerate their affects when communicating in this way (e.g., "Yuk! That's dirty!" or "Uh-Oh! Hot!"). On the other hand, when adults use negative affects to mirror a child's distress or anger in order to provide affirmation or empathy, the affective tone is often slightly toned down. This kind of affective mirroring may serve to communicate a sense that negative affects can be shared with and understood by adults, but they are not so powerful or adversive as to destroy either parent or child.

Negative affects expressed by an adult who is not part of the parent–child relationship but are demonstrated within the baby's perception are likely to interest him and, perhaps on some level, be retained.

Negative affects that are directed at the baby may constitute an assaultive or dangerous element to the primary relationship and cause the baby to withdraw for self-protection. Infants and toddlers who are overwhelmed with painful affects that cannot be ameliorated by primary adults are at risk for not being able to develop age-appropriate tolerance for painful affects as they grow older. Emde (1989; Emde, Oppenheim, Nir, & Warren, 1997) and others emphasize the role of positive affect sharing and affect exchanges within the parent–child relationship as necessary motivation for social interaction, as well as "food" for the inner sense of emotional well-being. Without these social and emotional foundations, the play and learning capacities of toddlerhood and early childhood are compromised (National Scientific Council on the Developing Child, 2004).

THE FUNCTION OF AFFECTS: PRESCHOOL YEARS

Affect will be defined here as the outward facial and postural expression of one's feeling state. In essence, affects communicate feeling states to others and provide them with a nonverbal means of assessing our emotional needs and responding accordingly. Thus, we can recognize a not-yet-verbal toddler's fearful expression when the noisy vacuum cleaner is turned on, and we can then offer comfort and reassurance.

The work of infant researchers gives us insight into the birth and evolution of affect as a language of feeling that develops within the intimacy of the infant–parent relationship. Affect initially serves a social function within the first relationship and later serves a similar function in the growing child's wider social milieu. Healthy affect development requires a young child to maintain a connection to her feeling state and at the same time reflect that state outwardly in pursuit of connection to others who might provide comfort, emotional affirmation, or emotional confrontation. In effect, the child's ability to express true affect prevents emotional isolation.

Consider the many ways that the healthy preschool child uses affect to engage other children. He may skip toward a playmate with an eager, smiling face and an inviting posture, holding out a canister of Legos on a nonverbal but effectively engaging play mission. The same child may later read an expression of dismay on a classmate's face as she discovers the lack of dessert in her lunch box and offer to share his own. He may begin to cry when another child inadvertently bumps a sore spot on his arm, ensuring that his peers treat him gently for the rest of the afternoon. Another child's face may redden in anger when she is pushed into the snow, alerting the teacher to the need for intervention before the angry little girl retaliates. In each of these examples, affect is the primary communicator, but verbal language will most likely be used to elaborate the affective messages and facilitate social interaction and conflict resolution.

The child who has a narrow range of affect, who projects false affect, or who is ill attuned to the affects of others is likely to experience constant failures in social functioning. Without the ability to project and read emotional messages, a preschool child is lacking the necessary tools for successful peer interaction, whether or not he is adequately verbal. Such a child may be equally ill attuned to his own emotional status, resulting in his inability to predict his own affective shifts. Therefore, this child may seem to have intense emotional outbursts that come "out of the blue," as no corresponding affects serve to inform self or others of the internal emotional distress that is brewing. Teachers and peers may both feel frustrated with these children, whose emotional needs are difficult to anticipate and whose distress is difficult to manage.

Healthy preschool children display a range of affects during the course of a schoolday and receive a range of affective messages from others. Observant early childhood professionals can describe the interplay of affects, language symbols, and play symbols weaving intricate connections through the peer group. In addition to this kind of clinical evidence, there have been several studies inquiring into affect development in young children. The results of these studies may help to inform our thinking about what is normative for young, emotionally healthy children (National Scientific Council on the Developing Child, 2004; Shankoff & Phillips, 2000).

Researchers have found preschool children to be capable of accurately identifying the affects of happiness, sadness, anger, and fear both in video characters and among peers in naturally occurring situations (Fabes, Eisenberg, McCormick, & Wilson, 1988; Strayer, 1989). The way that children's knowledge about affects informs their behavior has also been a subject of inquiry. Terwogt and Olthof (1989) show that children can regulate their emotional behavior before they are aware of what they are doing or before they are able to talk about it (Beebe & Lachmann, 2002). Experts on infant development see emotional regulation as a capacity that emerges within the parent–child relationships of shared affective states (Beebe, 2004; Beebe & Lachmann, 2002; Greenspan & Wieder, 2006; Lieberman, 2000). The adult's ability to mirror, identify with, elaborate, and contain the baby's range of emotional expression helps the baby to develop her own emotional ability to regulate emotions little by little.

Strayer (1989) posits that children's feelings and knowledge about emotions in themselves and in other people evolve as they mature cognitively and socially (National Scientific Council on the Developing Child, 2004). She points out that newborn babies share affect in the nursery, responding to another baby's cry by also becoming upset. This level of empathy, born of the infant's inability to differentiate self from other, evolves as the child individuates and becomes capable of differentiation, language, and other mediational functions. While preschool children are able to recognize and identify a range of positive and negative affects, they seem to distance themselves from dysphoric emotions in others for fear of regression to more undifferentiated forms of empathy. The present author's work with emotionally disturbed school-age children who had not yet mastered self–other differentiation at age-typical levels found "epidemics of empathy" to be a regressive force in the group (Koplow, 1986).

The work of Fabes and his associates (1988, 1999) shows that preschool children understand emotional reactions in peers to be the result of social interaction within the classroom environment (Eisenberg & Qing, 2000). Children were more accurate in attributing situational cause and effect to anger and distress reactions in peers than to happy or sad reactions in peers (Cicchetti, Macfie, Toth, Rogosch, Robinson, & Emde, 1999). This discrepancy seemed related to the children's perception of anger and distress as reactive to external provocation or frustration, whereas antecedents for happiness and sadness were more difficult to observe and more likely to be related to inner states (Favez, de Roten, & Bonvin, 2003; Roseman, 1984).

Fabes and his associates (1988, 1999) also found preschool children able to devise effective strategies for remediation of stimuli that produce negative emotions. He found that when children were able to recognize the source of a negative emotion, they could generate strategies to address that source (Cicchetti et al., 1999). Emde's more recent studies emphasize the role of co-constructed parent–child narratives in the development of the child's ability to regulate emotion and address complex emotional themes (Ontai & Thompson, 2002; Oppenheim, Nir, Warren, & Emde, 1997).

DILEMMAS FOR THE CHILD AT RISK

Research tells us that well-functioning preschool children are able to distinguish one affect from the other, perceive a cause-and-effect relationship between affect changes and social interaction, and generate remediational strategies to address negative affects in young peers (Cole, Michael, & O'Donnell-Teti, 1994; Fabes et al., 1988). However, we also know that young children have difficulty tolerating negative affects in themselves and others and become defensive when they feel threatened by overidentifying with another child's potentially contagious emotional state. These findings imply certain dilemmas for at-risk children and for the early childhood professionals who work with them. Clearly, children achieve social as well as emotional gains when they are able to show a range of genuine affect and to recognize and respond to these affects in others (National Scientific Council on the Developing Child, 2004). Programs that invest in helping children to develop prosocial behaviors rely on the child's ability to process affective information and on the developing capacity for empathy. Yet these goals may seem out of reach when we consider emotionally fragile children whose experiences have not supported age-appropriate levels of self–other differentiation and are therefore vulnerable to regressed empathy states. Many such children have not had the crucial affective mirroring that allows the child to feel comfortable and contained when expressing negative affects. Neither have they had the ongoing dialogue of responsive parent–child interaction that allows for the birth of language and other symbolic capacities, thus limiting their ability to put feelings into words and play symbols (Ontai & Thompson, 2002). For good reasons, emotionally fragile and traumatized children often express a predominance of negative affects. These negative affect states are often healthy manifestations of the internal distress felt by children whose needs for nurture or protection have been frustrated. Nonetheless, the weight of these negative affects may feel threatening to children and their teachers. The threat that negative affects will somehow "take over" may cause programs that include at-risk children to minimize opportunity for peer interaction and to give selective attention to children's happy affects. While this strategy of structuring and preventing affective events is understandable, it may deprive young children of opportunities to accomplish some essential precursors for the development of empathy and prosocial behavior; it may also diminish the child's potential to use his relationships with his teachers to improve object constancy. Preschools concerned about promoting affect development in their students must provide them with the following:

1. *Opportunity for connection with primary adults within a safe and stable environment.* While all preschool environments afford children with this opportunity to some degree, many are not conscious of the import of this program function. It is important to take into account the at-risk child's enormous need for teacher–child interaction when planning staffing patterns and classroom activities. Heightened opportunity for connection is necessary in order to promote strong attachments to classroom adults. Attachment may be "unfinished business" for at-risk preschoolers and is an important precursor for attaining the level of self–other differentiation needed to support receptivity to one's own affect states, as well as to the affect states of others. When children enter preschool with psychosocial histories that indicate that their attachment processes were disrupted by multiple separations, maternal illness or unavailability, or traumatic family events occurring during infancy, the preschool must create an intimate environment where children can safely "exercise" their affect development. Therefore, contact with classroom teachers and assistants cannot be limited to task-oriented interactions where adult responses are contingent on a child's performance. Teacher–child interactions must be open-ended, spontaneous, and genuine in order to facilitate emotional growth.

2. *Opportunity to receive empathic responses from adults.* This ensures that young children experience their affects as effective agents of communication and have even negative feelings affirmed in the context of social relatedness. If children feel less isolated with their emotional distress, there will be less need to surrender to emotional loneliness by either distancing from emotions or losing control.

3. *Opportunity for dialogue concerning affects and emotionally salient experiences.* Prior to attending preschool, many children may lack a consistent partner for preverbal and then verbal dialogues that identify, refer to, and explore affect states. Engaging children in dialogues about their affects and the affects of others may be done on varying levels. An adult may approach a toddler who has just fallen with an empathic expression and the words, "Aww, boo-boo hurt?" whereas a 4-year-old waiting for her mother to come is helped by the teacher's attentive words, "You look worried about not being picked up on

time!" and comforting gestures. These kinds of dialogues communicate adults' willingness to share in and contain negative as well as positive affects, producing a kind of "holding environment"—described by Winnicott (1965) as an essential feature of the healing relationship. By initiating dialogue about affect and affect-related events, the adult implies her ability for tolerating and surviving the child's emotional pain. This helps him develop his own capacities for dealing with difficult emotional experience. In addition, using language to describe affect states allows the young child to mediate emotional experiences by employing ego strengths. Instead of drowning in emotion or evading emotionally charged situations, children who have developed a reciprocal dialogue with significant adults concerning affects will be more likely to use words, representational drawing, and symbolic play materials to elaborate affective themes and thus to go beyond the diffuse expression of sadness, anger, fear, and happiness.

4. *Opportunity for peer interaction.* During open-ended play periods, children are encouraged to focus on and interpret naturally occurring affective events. These opportunities give children experience in reading affect messages from peers in the classroom milieu, where teachers can help them interpret messages and provide protection from emotional content that may be overwhelming. If opportunity for open-ended interaction is limited to outdoor play periods, or to the beginning of the day, when teachers are occupied by facilitating entry, there will be a lack of the kind of teacher–child contact needed to make affect-laden interactions meaningful. This generally results in children acting out emotional distress and contributes to a chaotic environment.

PRESCHOOL TEACHER: MIRROR AND MODEL

This discussion of the value of children's affects has several implications for the early childhood professional. Teachers, assistants, and clinicians who care for and interact with children on a daily basis can play a significant role in helping young children comfortably show a range of affect and respond appropriately to affects expressed by others. To do this, adults must give children permission to feel and express sadness, fear, anger, worry, and loneliness as well as joy, delight, excitement, enthusiasm, and other positive emotions. This permission will be readily conveyed by the teacher's mirroring of children's affects, by identifying those affects, affirming them, and representing them in drawing, stories, and so forth (see Chapter 9). Emotional mirroring is important because it feels affirming to the children and heightens teacher–child connection, but its effects go beyond what is observable to teacher and clinician. There is evidence that emotional mirroring underlies the development of memory and higher-level symbolic thinking (Beebee, 2004; Greenspan & Wieder, 2006; Siegel, 1999).

In addition, permission will be conveyed by the teacher's use of modeling to express her own genuine affects when interacting with the children.

It is impossible for classroom adults to serve as healthy models if they are falsely cheerful, speak to children in an unnatural or forced tone of voice, offer empty compliments, or interact with children in an effusive and undifferentiated manner. Teachers who allow themselves to discretely express and verbalize the cause and effect of their own affects will give their students a valuable lesson in emotional life. The teacher who gasps in fear when a mouse dashes across the classroom can later say, "Do you remember how scared I looked before when I saw that little mouse run out of the closet? Did you feel worried when you saw my face? I was really scared for a minute. Do you know anyone else who gets scared when they see mice?" The teacher who becomes exasperated by a child's difficult behavior can later acknowledge her feelings. She might say, "I bet I looked pretty angry before when you were stomping on those crackers! I'm glad we're both feeling better now."

In general, preschool classrooms must be relaxed, interesting places where children and adults share the joy of discovery and creativity. The sharing of pleasurable experiences will infuse the environment with the social strength necessary to accommodate the expression of negative as well as positive affects. Instead of trying to minimize the expression of negative affects in the classroom, teachers might use naturally occurring expressions of affect to help children become better attuned to affects, to differentiate among them, and to develop strategies for affect regulation when necessary. A teacher who habitually advises children in her class to ignore a classmate who is having a tantrum might try instead to engage the other children in a dialogue about what the angry child might be feeling or about their own experiences of being so out of control. Children can create strategies for helping their classmates feel calmer.

THE AFFECTIVE CONNECTION

Teachers who allow the true affects of at-risk children to have a voice in the classroom may fear that negative affects will become pervasive and overpowering. While at-risk children may be "overflowing" with negative affects as the result of depriving and traumatizing experiences or of developmental disabilities, teachers will find that giving these affects a voice need not result in a depressing environment. On the contrary, children who are allowed to sing "If you're sad and you know it, you can cry" and "If you're angry and you know it, stomp your feet!" will sing with interest, energy, and genuine shared feeling. The preschool experience then becomes a true "holding environment," where children feel safe with all of their feelings and learn to communicate about themselves. The teacher then becomes an important link in the child's affective connections, enabling her to be herself while reaching out to others.

REFERENCES

Beebe, B. (2004). Faces in relation, a case study. *Psychoanalytic Dialogues*, *14*(1), 1–51.

Beebe, B., & Lachmann, F. M. (2002). *Infant research and adult treatment, co-constructing interactions*. Hillsdale, NJ: Analytic Press.

Beebe, B., & Sloate, P. (1982). Assessment and treatment of difficulties in mother–infant attunement in the first three years of life. *Psychoanalytic Inquiry*, *2*, 601–623.

Cicchetti, D., Macfie, J., Toth, S. L., Rogosch, F. A., Robinson, J., & Emde, R. N. (1999). Effect of maltreatment on preschoolers' narrative representations of responses to relieve distress and of role reversal. *Developmental Psychology*, *35*(2), 460–465.

Cole, P., Michael, M., & O'Donnell-Teti, L. (1994). The development of emotion regulation and dysregulation: A clinical perspective. *Monographs of the Society for Research in Child Development*, *59*(2–3, Serial No 240).

Darwin, C. (1965). *The expression of emotion in man and animals*. Chicago: University of Chicago Press. (Original work published 1872)

Derman-Sparks, L. (1989). *Anti-bias curriculum: Tools for empowering young children*. Washington, DC: National Association for the Education of Young Children.

Eisenberg, N., & Qing, Z. (2000). Regulation from a developmental perspective. *Psychological Inquiry*, *11*(3), 166–171.

Emde, R. (1989). The infant's relationship experience: Developmental and affective aspects. In A. Sameroff & R. Emde (Eds.), *Relationship disturbance in early childhood* (pp. 33–51). New York: Basic Books.

Fabes, R. A., Eisenberg, N., Jones, S., Smith, M., Guthrie, I., Poulin, R., Shepard, S., & Friedman, J. (1999). Regulation, emotionality, and preschoolers' socially competent peer interactions. *Child Development*, *70*, 432–442.

Fabes, R., Eisenberg, N., McCormick, S., & Wilson, M. (1988). Preschoolers' attributions of the situational determinants of other's naturally occurring emotions. *Developmental Psychology*, *24*(3), 376–385.

Favez, N., de Roten, Y., & Bonvin, P. (2003). The effect of experienced emotions on preschoolers'narration. *Swiss Journal of Psychology*, *62*(1), 19–26.

Greenspan, S., & Wieder, S. (2006). *Engaging autism*. Cambridge, MA: Da Capo.

Izard, C., Huebner, R., Risser, D., Mcginnes, G. C., & Dougherty, L. (1980). The young infant's ability to produce discrete emotional expression. *Developmental Psychology*, *16*, 132–140.

Koplow, L. (1986). Contagious sneezing and other epidemics of empathy in young children. *Exceptional Child*, *33*(2), 146–150.

Lieberman, A. F. (2000). *The emotional life of the toddler*. New York: Free Press.

Nathanson, D. (1986). The empathic wall and the ecology of affect. *Psychoanalytic Study of the Child*, *41*, 171–187.

National Scientific Council on the Developing Child. (2004). *Children's emotional development is built into the architecture of their brains*. Working paper # 2. Retrieved July 15, 2006 from http://www.developingchild.net/reports.shtml

Ontai, L. L., & Thompson R. A. (2002). Patterns of attachment and maternal discourse effects on children's emotion understanding from 3 to 5 years old. *Social Development*, *11*(4), 433–450.

Oppenheim, D., Nir, A., Warren, S., & Emde, R. (1997) Emotion regulation in mother–

child narrative co-construction: Associations with children's narratives and adaptations. *Developmental Psychology, 33*(2), 284–294.

Roseman, L. (1984). Cognitive determinants of emotion: A cognitive theory. In P. Shaver (Ed.), *Review of personality and social psychology* (Vol. 5, pp. 11–36). Beverly Hills, CA: Sage.

Shankoff, J., & Phillips, D. A. (2000). From neurons to neighborhoods. Washington, DC: National Academy of Sciences.

Shore, R. (2003). *Rethinking the brain; New insights into early development.* New York: Families and Work Institute. (Original work published 1997)

Siegel, D. (1999). *The developing mind: How relationships and the brain interact to shape who we are.* New York: Guilford.

Solnit, A., & Stark, M. (1961). Mourning and the birth of a defective child. *Psychoanalytic Study of the Child, 16*, 523–537.

Sorce, J. F., Emde, R. N., Campos, J. J., & Klinnert, M. D. (1985). Maternal emotional signaling: Its effect on the visual cliff behavior of 1-year-olds. *Developmental Psychology, 21*(1), 195–200.

Sroufe, L. A. (1979). Socio-emotional development. In J. D. Osofsky (Ed.), *Handbook of infant development* (pp. 462–516). New York: Wiley.

Sroufe, L. A. (1996). Emotional development: The organization of emotional life in the early years. New York: Cambridge University Press.

Strayer, J. (1989). What children know and feel in response to witnessing affective events. In C. Saarni & P. L. Harris (Eds.), *Children's understanding of emotion* (pp. 239–289). Cambridge, UK: Cambridge University Press.

Terwogt, M., & Olthof, T. (1989). Awareness and self-regulation of emotion in young children. In C. Saarni & P. L. Harris (Eds.), *Children's understanding of emotion* (pp. 209–237). Cambridge, UK: Cambridge University Press.

Winnicott, D. W. (1965). *The maturational process and the facilitating environment: Studies in the theory of emotional development.* New York: International Universities Press.

CHAPTER 3

A Look in the Mirror: Self-Concept in Preschool Children

JUDITH FERBER

A QUESTION THAT CHALLENGES and compels us from our earliest years through-out our lifetime is "Who am I?" We are universally drawn by surfaces that reflect us back to ourselves: We search mirrors and the faces of others and catch our images in storefront windows and still waters, hoping these reflections will offer critical clues into the nature of our individual experience and identity. While the forma-tion of self-concept is a process that spans a lifetime, the years encompassing in-fancy, toddlerhood, and early childhood are a critical time during which the foundations of self are put into place. Developmentally sensitive early childhood programs recognize this fact and strive to foster greater self-awareness, self-expression, and self-esteem on the part of the child. Such programs offer the child ample opportunities to represent and see himself represented in play, art, litera-ture, and songs. They also provide developmentally appropriate challenges that allow children to actively explore the boundaries of their newfound autonomy and build upon their competencies. Understanding and addressing the nature of self-development is especially important in working with emotionally fragile and at-risk preschoolers, for whom the process can be complicated.

This chapter will analyze the growth of healthy self-concepts in young chil-dren and explore ways that early childhood professionals can support the devel-opment of self in the preschool classroom.

DEFINITIONS AND THEMES

What do we speak of when we use the term *self-concept*? The "self" as a psychological and developmental construct has been described in a variety of ways. Kohut (1977) has defined the self simply as "the center of one's psychological universe." For Stern (1985/2000), the self is a "unique subjective organization." Many have wondered about the viability of "the self" as a unified entity and have focused instead on the various facets of the self, such as self-concept (e.g., Harter, 1983, 1999).

Among the various theories of the development of the self, there are several points of convergence. One theme that runs like a thread throughout the literature is the distinction between two fundamental aspects of the self: the self as subject ("I"), which is the active, knowing, experiential self; and the self as the object ("Me") of one's awareness and evaluation, which is what we often refer to when we use the term *self-concept* (Lewis & Brooks-Gunn, 1979). Another major theme is that the self develops in the context of relationships with others (Beebe, Rustin, Sorter, & Knoblauch, 2003). There is wide agreement that the quality and characteristics of the child's early relationship with his caregiver shape the child's emerging self in fundamental ways and that social feedback continually influences the child's developing image of himself.

THE BEGINNINGS: PERSPECTIVES ON THE DEVELOPING SELF

How and when does the infant begin to develop a sense of self? There has been much agreement on the point that it is not until toward the end of the second year, with the onset of language and symbol development, that the child develops an objective awareness of self, what is known as "self-concept" (Kagan, 1981; Lewis & Brooks-Gunn, 1979; Mahler, Pine, & Bergman, 1975/2000; Roth-Hanania, Busch-Rossnagel, & Higgens-D'Alessandro, 2000; Stern, 1985/2000). However, the questions of how this happens and what leads up to this development have been approached in a variety of ways.

Visual Self-Recognition

Much of the empirical work on the development of self-concept has focused on visual self-recognition (Beebe & Lachmann, 1998). Lewis and Brooks-Gunn (1979) studied infants' responses to their images in mirrors, on videotapes, and in photographs. They observed that during the first year, infants demonstrate a growing awareness of the fact that they exist as subjects distinct from others and are capable of exerting an effect on their environment. Drawing on the work of Piaget, these authors maintain that contingency cues presented by kinesthetic feedback, interaction with objects and mirrors, and especially social responsiveness provide information about the relationship between one's actions and outcomes in the external world. These cues create the store of knowledge out of which grows an awareness of the "existential" self, or the self as an active subject.

It is not until toward the end of the second year, note Lewis and Brooks-Gunn, that infants demonstrate what is frequently known as "self-concept": a consolidated awareness of self as the object of one's knowledge, or the "categorical" self. Beginning around 15–18 months and consistently by 21–24 months, children differentiate between self and others and display self-recognition in noncontingent situations (Roth-Hanania et al., 2000). For example, when confronting mirror images of their rouge-marked faces, they tend to direct behavior toward the mark, which indicates that they have developed a schema of themselves as objects with invariant, identifiable features and recognize that the mark violates this schema. Around this same time, children begin to recognize and label themselves in pictures as well as systematically use verbal self-referrants, including names and personal pronouns. A child might point to herself in a picture and say, "Dat Katie. Katie blue dress." Kagan (1981) also found that toward the end of the second year, children show increasing signs of self-awareness, including self-descriptive utterances.

According to Lewis and Brooks-Gunn (1979), self-knowledge depends on knowledge of others; the child must have a schema of the other in order to develop a schema for himself. "What can be demonstrated to be known about the self can be said to be known about the other and what is known about the other can be said to be known about the self" (p. 231). Knowledge about others informs the child's definition of himself vis-à-vis the external world. Children from this age forward increasingly use social categories such as age, gender, and familiarity, according to which they define themselves vis-à-vis the external world. At first, these criteria are fairly concrete (Harter, 1983, 1999), but they become more abstract as the child gets older.

Not only is visual self-recognition a reflection of the acquisition of self-concept, but vision is also an important source of feedback contributing to the development of self-image (Beebe, 2004). Fraiberg (1987) studied blind children's self-representations in language and play and found that they were consistently delayed in the acquisition of "I" as a stable pronoun. The role of parent-to-child visual and auditory affective mirroring as a foundation for integrating information about self and other has been recently acknowledged (Beebe, 2004; Friedman, 2005). Daniel Siegel (1999) highlights the role of parent–child co-construction of narratives as an organizer of self and an integrator of self–other experience.

Psychoanalytic Accounts

Psychoanalytic accounts of the self have had a more socioemotional thrust. They tend to emphasize the dynamic and affective aspects of the infant–caregiver relationship and the separation and individuation process that was previously outlined in Chapter 1.

Freud (1915/1950) first described the processes by which the rudimentary ego develops out of the realization that the mother does not automatically fulfill the infant's every need. However, Mahler and her colleagues (1975/2000) have been the most influential in terms of delineating the process by which the child separates and individuates during the early years.

According to Mahler, in the first few months of life there is no differentiation between self and other. The infant–parent bonding process takes them into a "symbiotic" state, during which the intimacy of the parent–child relationship is all-encompassing for the baby and for the parent. This period is followed by several phases characterized by increasing differentiation, separation, and individuation. Locomotion is seen to spur on the child's movement away from his caregiver, while increasingly stable mental representations of the caregiver support his ability to tolerate periods of separateness. A turning point for Mahler comes in the latter half of the second year and the crisis of "rapprochement." At this point the child is able to differentiate between self and object, internal and external, and becomes acutely and painfully aware of his separateness.

Mahler's turning point coincides with the finding by Lewis and Brooks-Gunn that children exhibit a consolidated awareness of themselves as distinct entities in the latter half of the second year. However, Mahler's emphasis is different and has more to do with the importance of the mother as an emotional object in the infant's life, the affective components of the child's struggles to separate and individuate, and the formation of intrapsychic representations of self and other (Harter, 1983, 1999). In Mahler's view, the end of the second year is a stormy time, marked by the child's distress and anger about his separateness and the helplessness it entails, his conflicting wishes to be both connected and autonomous at the same time, and his conflicting image of mother as good (need-gratifying) and bad (frustrating). If the mother continues to be available and responsive to her child's needs, however, by the third year this conflict is largely resolved and the child is able to integrate the good and bad (gratifying and frustrating) aspects of his caregiver into one unified image. Aided by his increased cognitive capacities for symbol formation and object permanence, the child establishes a more secure and integrated intrapsychic representation of his caregiver, or "emotional object constancy." This enables the child to consolidate a stable image of self as a separate entity with an enduring individuality ("self-constancy"), one important aspect of which is a rudimentary consolidation of gender identity.

Around the same time, says Mahler, there is a far-reaching structuralization of the ego and establishment of many basic ego functions. Greenspan (1981, 1997; Greenspan &Wieder, 2006) has pointed out that many basic ego functions, such as reality testing, regulation of impulses, and regulation of thought and affect rest on the stable differentiation of self and nonself, inner and outer reality, and establishment of sense of self as a separate causal agent.

Object relations theorists such as Winnicott also emphasize the role the parent plays in laying the intrapsychic foundation of self. Winnicott (1965) theorized that when a "good enough" mother is able to provide empathic response to the infant's needs,

> each infant is able to have a personal existence and so begins to build up what might be called a continuity of being. On the basis of this continuity of being, the inherited potential gradually develops into an individual infant. If maternal care is not good enough then the infant does not really come into existence, since there is no continuity of being; instead the personality becomes built on the basis of reactions to environmental impingement. (p. 54)

Empathic response entails meeting the baby's needs, not only physical but also psychological, through holding, so that the baby is allowed a brief experience of omnipotence and is protected from such "unthinkable anxieties" as the feeling of "going to pieces" and "falling forever" (Winnicott, 1965, p. 58). The mother must then remain emotionally responsive as she *gradually* presents the infant with masterable levels of frustration, or external reality, whereby the infant comes to successfully separate out the self from other. The infant slowly internalizes the ego-supportive environment (the object), which becomes the basis for the child's self and the child's capacity to be alone.

More recently, Stern (1985/2000) brought observations from the field of developmental psychology to bear on psychoanalytic theories of self-development. Stern challenges earlier psychoanalytic notions of a symbiotic phase of development, maintaining that there is evidence that some senses of self as distinct from other exist from birth and long prior to self-awareness and language. These preverbal, experiential senses of self serve as the subjective organizers of experience, particularly social experience. They are "the preverbal existential counterpart of the objectifiable, self-reflective, verbalizable self" (Stern, 1985/2000, p. 7) and continue to grow and coexist with later senses of self. Each newly acquired sense of self creates new and greater capacities for interpersonal relatedness. Separation and union experiences, like other clinical issues, are not phase-specific; rather, they proceed simultaneously and are issues for the life span. Stern's later work introduced the concept of "the motherhood constellation" as a way of understanding maternal experience and its impact on the mother's sense of self. In this way of conceptualizing maternal experience, the new mother's sense of self includes not only the baby, as Mahler had implied in her definition of symbiosis, but also the mother's own mother (Stern, 1995).

Stern (1985/2000) postulates four different senses of self in the developing infant, each describing different domains of self-experience and interpersonal relatedness. With the sense of an "emergent" self (birth–2 months), there is rudimentary organization of experience and orientation toward interaction with the external world. With the development of the sense of a "core" self (2–6 months), infants become aware of themselves as distinct physical entities with their own agency, affectivity, and continuity in time and a sense of others as distinct and separate interactants. With the development of the sense of a "subjective" self

(7–15 months) comes infants' discovery that both they and others have distinct mental states and that these inner subjective experiences, which include attention, intention, and affective state, can be shared. The sharing of affects paves the way, in Stern's view, for symbol formation and language development during the second year and the development of a "verbal" self (15–18 months and on). With language and symbols come the toddler's awareness of himself as an objective entity rather than just as a subjective experiencer. Language and symbols also provide the vehicle through which the child can create and share meanings with another.

Emde (1983) has also proposed a process view of the self:

> We must avoid getting caught up in the idea of a sharply focused age period in which the self emerges. Such a way of thinking tends to reify the self as a developmental acquisition and implies that it is something like walking, learning to ride a bicycle, or beginning speech. Nothing could be further from the truth. I believe we must remind ourselves that the self is a process, and refers to a vital set of synthetic functions which increase in complexity and depth as development proceeds throughout the lifespan. (p. 168)

While self-recognition per se begins in the latter half of the second year and successively evolves to higher levels of organization, prior to the second year and the development of representational capacity, an "affective core" of the self exists (Beebe & Lachmann, 1998). This affective core monitors experience according to what is pleasurable and unpleasurable and helps to guide both self-regulation and social interaction. It gives continuity to our experience even as we change the course of development and ensures that we can understand others. We all possess in common an innate, universally shared set of affects. Long before language develops, the affective core of self makes possible both communication and the sharing of affective states. For example, through what is termed "social referencing," infants can communicate about affects with adults and use adults' affects to help guide behavior in ambiguous situations.

THE SHARING OF INNER STATE: VALIDATING THE SELF

Parents play a crucial role in fostering their child's sense of self through their willingness and ability to share in their child's inner state. This not only offers the child knowledge about himself but also gives validity to what the child is feeling and thus helps bring the child's true self into existence. Winnicott (1965) introduced the notion of the "true self," which he said can only arise if the mother is able to meet and make sense of the infant's gesture rather than imposing one of her own. Moreover, the mother's reflecting back to the child what she sees there, or "giving back to the baby the baby's own self," allows the baby to exist psychologically and to feel real (Winnicott, 1971/2005). When caregivers excessively impose their own external agenda on the child instead of responding to the infant's needs, the child constructs a "false self" that is characterized by an attitude of compliance and hides the child's true inner reality. Stern (1985/2000) refers to a similar phenomenon when he discusses "affect attunement," which involves the parent's matching of her child's inner, affective state. "Affect attunements" allow for intersubjective relatedness and strengthen the child's subjective sense of self (Beebe, 2004). Failures in affect attunement on the part of the parent exclude certain portions of the child's subjective experience from the realm of intersubjective sharing (Beebe et al., 2003). In order to maintain a connection with his parent, the child creates a false self that utilizes only those portions of inner experience that can be shared. This effort to meet the needs and wishes of another comes at the expense of remaining, very real portions of inner experience and can result in the disavowal or splitting off of portions of self-experience.

Internal Working Models of Self and Other

Bowlby (1969, 1973) first introduced the idea that the child develops internal working models of self and other based on early attachment experiences. If a caregiver is emotionally responsive and available, a secure attachment relationship develops. In turn, this fosters positive internal working models of both self and others. As Bowlby (1973) stated:

> The model of the attachment figure and the model of the self are likely to develop so as to be complementary and mutually confirming. Thus an unwanted child is likely not only to feel unwanted by his parents but to believe that he is essentially unwantable. (p. 204)

Followers of attachment theory have elaborated on this notion. Sroufe (1990, 1996) defines the self as an "inner organization of attitudes, feelings, expectations, and meanings which arises itself from an organized caregiving matrix" (Sroufe, 1990, p. 281). The core of self has to do with expectations regarding the maintenance of basic regulation and positive affect. A responsive caregiving relationship, which promotes smooth regulation of affect and maintenance of behavioral organization in the face of stress, will foster the development of a well-defined and functional self-core (Sroufe, 1990, p. 293). This will influence later adaptation of the child, particularly with regard to social interaction and relationships (Oppenheim, Nir, Warren, & Emde, 1997).

The interrelationship between self-organization and history of care has been explored in a number of empirical studies (Kochanska, 2001). Sroufe (1989, 1990, 1996) reviews these findings. In summary, children who have histories of sensitive care and are securely attached have been observed to have complementary models of themselves as potent and worthy. They are more ego resilient, independent, resourceful, and confident in their approach to the environment. They are able to utilize adult resources effectively and tend to interact positively with peers, displaying empathy and the capacity for emotional closeness. Children with histories of insensitive care who have anxious-avoidant attachments, on the other hand, seem to have complementary models of themselves as unworthy and impotent. They are less self-confident and resourceful in their approach to the environment and, despite a seeming precocious independence, are generally less self-reliant. While they are deemed to be highly dependent, they are not able to utilize adult resources effectively. Avoidant children exhibit feelings of low self-worth and tend to interact negatively with peers, displaying hostility, aggression, and lack of empathy. Expecting rejection, these children tend to elicit rejection from others.

Who Am I? The Struggle for Self-Concept in the Preschool Child

While the different theories thus far presented have different points of emphasis and even contradict each other at times, they all contribute to a picture of the developing self during the toddler years. In working with emotionally fragile preschoolers, theory can be used selectively, according to what is relevant, to guide our understanding of individual children's experiences. The overall picture of self-development describes an infant who, in the context of a supportive caregiving relationship, is beginning to organize and monitor experience. Affect is an important organizer of experience and lies at the core of self. Patterns of experience become the basis for the child's developing sense of self. In the first year and a half, the child has a growing experiential sense of himself as an active subject ("I") who exists as both apart from and related to others, who is capable of having thoughts and feelings and exerting an effect on his environment. Toward the end of the second year, there is a major developmental turning point when the child crystallizes a reflexive awareness of self; this is referred to by many as a "self-concept." This awareness continues to grow and undergo modification throughout one's lifetime. There is wide agreement about the importance of the early caregiving relationship as initially helping the infant regulate and organize experience, laying the emotional foundation for self-development, and providing the infant with ongoing feedback about self and others.

Given nurturing and supportive provision of his needs, by the time a child enters preschool, he should have established a strong and secure relationship with his caregiver and upon this foundation begun to construct a sense of himself as a separate and autonomous person. He is able to internally maintain his connection with his caregiver even when he is not in her presence and, bolstered by this connection, confidently set off to explore independently in his nursery classroom, knowing that he will later return to the comfort and security of his caregiver. Knowledge he has gained through his interactions with others enables him to define himself as an individual with his own unique set of attributes, such as gender, age, competencies, and familiarity. He knows he is a boy, that he is 3 years old, that he has curly hair, that he lives with his mommy and his sister, and that he can ride a tricycle. The well-functioning child deems himself to be a potent agent who is capable of exerting an effect on his environment. He feels that he is valuable in the eyes of others, worthy of both care and friendship, and able to maintain his self-esteem even in the face of stress.

Unfortunately, however, this is not every child's reality. For example, what of the child whose caregiver has not been a reliable and available attachment figure? Or the child who has been separated from parents and placed in foster care? Or the child whose parents are so preoccupied with their own pressing intrapsychic needs or the realities of survival that, instead of attending to their children's needs, they demand that their children adapt to theirs? Or the child of parents who themselves are depressed, have low self-worth, and send messages of failure to their children? Or the child whose parents are prone to extreme mood swings and outbursts of violent behavior? These situations will have important consequences for the young child's self-concept.

Self-Esteem

An often discussed aspect of self-development, which can be problematic for young children, is self-esteem. Harter (1983, 1999) says that self-esteem has to do with one's cognitive evaluations of oneself as well as the affective reactions to these judgments. She distinguishes between self-esteem, the evaluation of one's worthiness and acceptability in the eyes of others, and self-confidence, one's sense of oneself as a competent, effective agent. While many factors affect self-esteem, early relationship experiences as well as reflective feedback from significant others are fundamental influences in its development. Attachment studies have demonstrated that children who have histories of insensitive care develop complementary models of themselves as unworthy and ineffectual in eliciting care (Osofsky & Roberson-Jackson, 1994). Children carry these feelings into the nursery classroom. Thus, teachers might observe a little girl who frequently engages her peers in negative ways: She teases her classmates until they respond aggressively, at which point she seems oddly smug, somehow satisfied that the outcome confirms her expectations of rejection. The teacher might have to struggle herself to overcome her frustration and find positive ways to engage with the child who constantly seeks her attention in negative, confrontational ways. We might observe children who scribble over photos or pictures of themselves, spit at or hit their mirror images, and display a lack of attention to body care—allowing, for example, their noses to go unwiped and their shoes untied. Self-representations in artwork can offer clues to the teacher and clinician about the child's self-concept. A child's confusion or ambivalence about who he is might be manifested in representing himself in distorted ways. He might appear to be extremely small and fragile in his drawings of himself; lack arms, legs, or other significant features; or have features belonging to the opposite gender, perhaps even an animal. Teachers have in some cases reported having seen children climb into the garbage can, expressing through a very poignant metaphor the feeling that they are disposable. One little girl, who had by the age of 4 lived in three separate foster homes, put it pointedly: "I should be in the garbage can. That's where I belong."

Diminished Sense of Agency

Another aspect of self that can suffer is the young child's sense of agency. We have seen that the child's sense of self as an effective agent or actor in the world grows out of experiences of being able to have an impact on others and on his environment. The infant's opening and closing of his fist, his cries to bring his caregiver to his side, the toddler's incessant turning on and off of the light switch and demands to do things "myself" have all been ways of developing and practicing this sense of agency, of learning that there is an "I" that can "do" many things. From this perspective, it follows that children would have a sense of themselves as being ineffectual if they are growing up in an environment that is unresponsive to their needs and actions, where they have little opportunity to exert autonomy in developmentally appropriate ways, and that emphasizes their inadequacies. Children who have been excessively challenged by experiences that are beyond the scope of their comprehension and mastery, such as trauma, or who are presented with unrealistic demands, such as babysitting their younger siblings, might have a diminished sense of their own agency and instead feel powerless and overwhelmed.

Pseudo-Autonomy

With some children, we observe a developmental paradox. The child is precociously independent, disconnected, and competent. At the same time, he has a diminished sense of agency and is emotionally immature. Often, these children come from deprived or multistressed families. Parents who are themselves needy often are unable to meet their children's needs; at the same time, they place unrealistic demands on their children, such as cleaning and other household chores or comforting the parent when he or she is upset. Children who experience this are often unable to strike the important developmental balance between dependence and independence. These children give the distinct and unsettling impression of being at once very old and very young. On the one hand, they are precociously competent and independent and can accomplish tasks beyond their years. A preschool teacher might marvel at how competently her 4-year-old pupil goes about readying the table for lunch and diapering her baby sister. However, this same child backs away from age-appropriate challenges such as making a block building with disclaimers such as "I can't do it." In many ways she is highly dependent on her teacher; she is terrified, for example, when the teacher goes out of the room for a few brief moments. The shallowness of the child's independent stance becomes quite clear in ordinary situations of stress. For example, when her friend refuses to share the toy stove with her, she becomes extremely upset and regresses to rather infantile behaviors, screaming, crying, and pounding the floor with her fists.

Unstable Self-Concept

Mahler has shown us that the emotional constancy of the mother is the cornerstone of the child's development of self-constancy. A child whose mother is inconsistently available will not develop trust in her constancy and will continually fear her loss. In a parallel fashion, this child might fear losing himself. We observe children in the classroom who do not have a sense of body integrity and fear getting paint on their hands, lest it entail a change or loss of self. We observe children who insist on using the potty, fearful that when the toilet is flushed they will be sucked down into the hole along with everything else.

A child whose parent has extreme fluctuations in behavior—for instance, violent mood swings, maltreatment alternating with caretaking—will have difficulty integrating the good and bad aspects of the parent into one unified image (Osofsky, 2005). This child will consequently have trouble establishing a unified self-image and might vacillate between having an inflated, idealized self-image and one that is utterly diminished. He might identify exclusively with one aspect of his caregiver and have little tolerance for the suggestion that he or his caregiver is anything other than all good. Cicchetti, Beeghly, Carlson, and Toth (1990) observe that maltreated children may be prone to idealize qualities of themselves and their attachment relationship, perhaps as a defense against the rejecting behavior on the part of their primary attachment figure.

False Self

Although affect is at the core of our self-experience, many emotionally fragile young children are confused about or disconnected from their inner experience and manifest what has been described above as a false self. We might notice the child who falls down and lets out a strange laugh, one that resounds with a false and hollow ring. We might notice the child who giggles when his friend cries because he is too cut off from his own feelings to be able to empathize. Too often, children are required to meet the emotional demands of adults while their own inner affective experiences remain unvalidated. Consumed by their own pressing needs, some parents are unable to respond empathically to their children and have little tolerance for displays of negative emotion (Osofsky & Roberson-Jackson, 1994). When a parent tells a child to "stop crying or I'll give you something to cry about," he encourages the child to suppress his true, feeling self and present instead a "false self."

IMPLICATIONS FOR TEACHERS AND CLINICIANS

Early childhood educators and clinicians can exert a powerful influence on a child's self-concept. Unfortunately, many attempt to promote a positive self-concept through blanket statements of praise, such as "good boys and girls," which have little connection to the child's real attributes, affects, and competencies. Praise is often doled out in the form of smiley-face stickers, which encourage children to put up a sunny front in spite of what they might really be feeling inside. When a child is exhibiting an undesirable behavior and negative affects, he might be warned not to be a "bad" boy. Statements such as these attach global estimations of self-worth to particular behaviors and affects and reflect more the adult's agenda than who the child is. Such statements might effectively modify behavior and encourage an attitude of compliance. However, in conveying the message that worth is contingent upon a certain adherence to adult standards of behavior and affects, they also have the potential to undermine a child's self-esteem and encourage her to put on a false front and push the true self underground.

Self-worth rests on the experience of being loved, accepted, and cared for unconditionally. Adults can help improve children's self-esteem by giving them the message that they are fundamentally valuable in the eyes of others and worthy of care regardless of their behaviors or affects. In order to be meaningful and not rote, positive feedback must be offered in the context of a caring relationship and should be connected to the child's real successes, affects, and attributes rather than the adult's agenda. In this way, the adult can help the child make positive, successful experiences her own. A therapeutic reflection might be, "Alexis, you have gotten really good at riding that tricycle. I remember when you used to say, 'I can't do it.' You worked really hard at it, and now you ride so well!"

It is more helpful to respond to a child's acting out by conveying the message that the behavior, not the child or his affects, is unacceptable. A therapeutic teacher might tell a child, "Natasha, it is not okay for you to hit Theo. You can feel angry, but hitting is not okay. Hitting hurts, and we need to keep everyone safe." By offering meaningful explanations of limits, we can actually help build children's sense of self-worth, the message being that we set limits because we value children and want to protect them.

In addition to providing meaningful feedback, the therapeutic teacher can help improve a child's self-concept and self-confidence by creating opportunities for the child to have successful experiences in the school setting, in the context of both interpersonal interactions and interactions with materials. Adults can help the child whose poor self-concept impels him to seek attention in negative ways by creating opportunities for the child to have positive interactions with both adults and peers, interactions that have the potential to improve the child's working models of self and other. At first, the adult might need to initiate these interactions, for example, by joining the child on the floor to engage in a mutually pleasurable game of ball play. She might also encourage the child to develop positive strategies with peers. Observing a child who would like to join in another child's play but goes about it in a maladaptive way, a teacher might say, for instance, "Tanya, Paul didn't like it when you knocked down his building. Maybe you could ask him if you can build with him instead. You have a lot of good ideas about building, too." Similarly, for a child who has a diminished sense of agency, the therapeutic teacher might present the child with learning challenges that he is able to master and help him to overcome his fears by encouraging him, reminding him of past successes, and assisting him in a way that adds to rather than takes away from his experience of mastery in the activity. A teacher might position the puzzle pieces to make it easier for a child and then gently encourage the child to place them himself: "I'll bet you can figure out where that one goes. I remember yesterday, you did the whole butterfly puzzle all by yourself. (*Child hesitates.*) I'll give you a hint. It's part of the ice cream cone. (*Child places piece successfully and smiles.*) See? You did it!"

Teachers and clinicians can help children who have simultaneously too much and too little agency establish a balance. The preschool years are an important time for children to consolidate their concept of age and belonging to the social category of little girl or boy, not baby or grown-up, a time to strike a balance between big and little. The well-functioning preschooler can approach new challenges confidently and at the same time draw upon adults for help and support when needed. The therapeutic teacher can help children establish this important balance by providing children with many appropriate opportunities for mastery and at the same time reassuring them that they are children and that grown-ups are there to take care of them. Children should be able to feel "big" as they run around the playground pretending to be superheroes, or as they practice a new trick on the monkey bars, and then curl up into a little ball with a teddy bear at naptime as their teacher reads them a soothing story. Teachers might also heighten children's awareness of age categories through a curriculum such as "big and little," which compares babies, children, and adults and connects these observations to the children's own experiences: "When you were a baby, you drank from a bottle. Mommy and Daddy gave you your bottle. Now you are a 3-year-old girl. You know how to eat with a fork. But you still need grown-ups to help cook your food."

Teachers and clinicians can help children develop a more stable and integrated self-concept. The adult's consistent availability and responsiveness to the child is a powerful intervention in and of itself, enabling the child to build trust in the constancy of the adult and correspondingly stable and integrated images of self and other. Teachers can also help children develop a unified image of self and other by offering realistic feedback about a child's ambivalence: "Yesterday you were really mad at me when I said it was cleanup time. Now you are happy with me again and we are playing together. You are still you and I am still me."

Ironically, many preschool programs perpetuate the problem of the false self by failing to validate a child's full range of emotion, reflecting images of a bright and happy but unreal world. Instead, adults can help children develop greater connection to their true selves by reflecting and accepting their full range of inner experiences. At times, the adult might need to reassure the child that she can survive the child's negative emotions and still remain available: "I see that you are angry. Even if you are angry at me, I will still be your teacher." Adults can help children develop their inner sense of who they are, how they feel, and what makes them feel that way. This can only be done in the context of a real relationship. It is the teacher or therapist's ability to recognize and share in the child's feelings—even difficult feelings—that can help the child to accept those feelings as his own and integrate them into a sense of self that reflects his own true inner experience.

REFERENCES

Beebe, B. (1994). Representation and internalization in infancy: Three principles of salience. *Psychoanalytic Psychology*, *11*, 127–165.

Beebe, B. (2004). *Faces in relation, a case study. Psychoanalytic Dialogues*, *14*(1), 1–51.

Beebe, B., & Lachmann, F. M. (1998). Co-constructing inner and relational processes: Self- and mutual regulation in infant research and adult treatment. *Psychoanalytic Psychology*, *15*(4), 480–516.

Beebe, B., Rustin, J., Sorter, D., & Knoblauch, S. (2003). An expanded view of intersubjectivity in infancy and its application to psychoanalysis. *Psychoanalytic Dialogues*, *13*(6), 777–804.

Bowlby, J. (1969). *Attachment and loss: Vol. 1. Attachment*. New York: Basic Books.

Bowlby, J. (1973). *Attachment and loss: Vol. 2. Separation*. New York: Basic Books.

Cicchetti, D., Beeghly, M., Carlson, V., & Toth, S. (1990). The emergence of the self in atypical populations. In D. Cicchetti & M. Beeghly (Eds.), *The self in transition* (pp. 309–344). Chicago: University of Chicago Press.

Emde, R. (1983). The pre-representational self and its affective core. *Psychoanalytic Study of the Child*, *38*, 165–192.

Fraiberg, S. (1987). Self-representation in language and play: observations of blind children. In L. Fraiberg (Ed.), *Selected writings of Selma Fraiberg* (pp. 525–545). Columbus: Ohio University Press.

Friedman, D. (2005). *Interaction and the architecture of the brain*. Washington, DC: National Scientific Council on the Developing Child. Retrieved July 7, 2006 from http://www.developingchild.net/papers/020705_interactions_article.pdf

Freud, S. (1950). *Instincts and their vicissitudes*. London: Hogarth. (Original work published 1915).

Greenspan, S. (1981). *Psychopathology and adaptation in infancy and early childhood*. Madison, WI: International Universities Press.

Greenspan, S. (1997). *The growth of the mind and the endangered origins of intelligence*. Cambridge, MA: Perseus.

Greenspan, S., & Wieder, S. (2006). *Engaging autism*. Cambridge, MA: Da Capo.

Harter, S. (1983). Developmental perspectives on the self-system. In P. Mussen (Ed.), *Handbook of child psychology* (4th ed., Vol. 4, pp. 275–385). New York: Wiley.

Harter, S. (1999). *The construction of the self, a developmental perspective*. New York: Guilford.

Kagan, J. (1981). *The second year*. Cambridge, MA: Harvard University Press.

Kochanska, G. (2001). Emotional development in children with different attachment histories: The first three years. *Child Development, 72*(2), 474–490.

Kohut, H. (1977). *The restoration of the self*. New York: International Universities Press.

Lewis, M., & Brooks-Gunn, J. (1979). *Social cognition and the acquisition of self*. New York: Plenum.

Mahler, M., Pine, F., & Bergman, A. (2000). *The psychological birth of the human infant*. New York: Basic Books. (Original work published 1975)

Oppenheim, D., Nir, A., Warren, S., & Emde, R. (1997). Emotion regulation in mother–child narrative co-construction: Associations with children's narratives and adaptations. *Developmental Psychology, 33*(2), 284–294.

Osofsky, J. D. (2005). Ghosts and angels: How can we find them in the nursery and beyond? *Infant Mental Health Journal, 26*(6), 525–528.

Osofsky, J. D., & Robertson-Jackson, B. (1994). Parenting in violent environments. In J. D. Osofsky & E. Fenichel (Eds.), *Hurt, healing, hope: Caring for infants and toddlers in violent environments* (pp. 13–19). Arlington, VA: Zero to Three.

Roth-Hanania, R., Busch-Rossnagel, N., & Higgins-D'Alessandro. (2000). Development of self and empathy in early infancy: Implications for atypical development. *Infants and Young Children, 13*(1), 1–14.

Siegel, D. (1999). *The developing mind: How relationships and the brain interact to shape who we are*. New York: Guilford.

Sroufe, L. A. (1989). Relationships, self, and individual adaptation. In A. Sameroff & R. Emde (Eds.), *Relationship disturbances in early childhood* (pp. 70–96). New York: Basic Books.

Sroufe, L. A. (1990). An organizational perspective on the self. In D. Cicchetti & M. Beeghly (Eds.), *The self in transition* (pp. 281–307). Chicago: University of Chicago Press.

Sroufe, L. A. (1996). Emotional development: The organization of emotional life in the early years. New York: Cambridge University Press.

Stern, D. (1995). *The motherhood constellation*. New York: Basic Books.

Stern, D. (2000). *The interpersonal world of the infant*. New York: Basic Books. (Original work published 1985)

Winnicott, D. W. (1965). *The maturational processes and the facilitating environment*. New York: International Universities Press.

Winnicott, D. W. (2005). *Playing and reality*. New York: Routledge. (Original work published 1971)

Structure and Relationships in Preschool

CHAPTER 4

Therapeutic Teacher, Therapeutic Classroom

JUDITH FERBER

THE THERAPEUTIC CLASSROOM is a place where troubled children are helped to sort out their complicated experiences so that development can proceed. Here, children have opportunities to go back to earlier levels and accomplish developmental tasks they could never before accomplish. Here children are encouraged to explore their inner lives as well as their external environments to achieve learning.

The children who need therapeutic classrooms are not unique. There are many like them—in Head Start programs, day-care centers, and private nursery schools. Teachers and other early childhood professionals struggle to meet their needs, searching for ways to maintain a responsive but structured preschool environment. This chapter will describe essential components of a therapeutic classroom and will invite the reader to adapt suggested techniques to a variety of preschool situations.

EXTERNAL ORDER, INTERNAL FREEDOM: THE MEANING
OF STRUCTURE IN THE THERAPEUTIC CLASSROOM

The therapeutic classroom maintains an external structure that helps children feel safe, contained, and organized in the context of a productive learning environment. Within this structure, the therapeutic classroom provides freedom for children to explore and develop their inner lives.

Historically, special education programs for emotionally fragile children went to great lengths to contain what they saw as the potentially disruptive emotional lives of their students. They created highly structured programs in which stimulation and emotionally charged situations were kept to a minimum. Shelves were often turned around, and materials were kept out of sight and out of reach. Children's

behavior was controlled through behavioral reinforcement and curriculum con-
fined to the more neutral arenas of cognition and skill acquisition.

Undoubtedly, structure has great value in the therapeutic classroom. It is vital
in maintaining an orderly and constructive learning environment. A classroom is
not a therapy room where a child's agenda can be the sole determinant of process.
If the whims of the children dictated the agenda of the therapeutic classroom, the
result would be chaos. However, the developmental and emotional *needs* of children can and should be attended to in the therapeutic classroom. This is especially
important in the preschool years, when children's intrinsic motivation for learning will help determine future success. A young child's cognitive and emotional
development progress hand in hand. In order for a young child to find meaning in
learning experiences, her whole being—including her emotional self—must be
involved in the process.

The key to creating a therapeutic milieu lies in creating a balance. The therapeutic classroom is guided by a structure that gives permission for children to think
and feel while providing them with the means to safely contain and organize powerful thoughts and feelings. Because it is consistent and meaningful, the structure
of the therapeutic classroom is one that can be mastered and internalized by children. This mastery helps the children build the growing set of competencies required for the successful navigation of the world around them.

Several structural frameworks guide the process in the therapeutic classroom:
the daily schedule and routines, the organization of the classroom environment, a
consistent set of rules and limits, the cognitive framework of the curriculum, and
the teacher–child relationship itself.

Physical Environment

One structure that allows for the exploration of emotional life in the therapeutic
classroom is the organization of the physical environment. The classroom offers
a rich array of materials, thoughtfully arranged according to use and theme. There
are shelves full of brightly colored manipulative materials, such as duplo and bristle
blocks, puzzles and stacking cups, as well as some developmentally younger toys,
including a mirror, a soft ball, and a pop-up toy. There is a dress-up area and a
play kitchen for dramatic play. There is a shelf full of wooden building blocks
and nearby a variety of toys that lend themselves to representational play: a doll
house; toy cars, animals, and people; and puppets. The bookshelf displays a variety of picture storybooks with developmentally salient themes. There is a cozy
corner with a bed for baby dolls and, next to it, a menagerie of soft animals. There
is playdough, sand, and a table for water play. Paper, markers, crayons, scissors,
and collage materials are available on the art shelf; nearby is an easel for painting.

Many of these materials invite children to represent their experiences—to
reach within themselves, explore, and express what they have internalized about
these experiences. They are not designed to keep experiences outside the class-

room walls and feelings locked within each child. Rather, they are selected precisely for their ability to bring thoughts and feelings together. To this end, all the materials in the classroom are carefully chosen to reflect the real world in which the children live, including their urban environment and the racial and cultural diversity that surrounds them.

For children who have difficulty focusing, organizing their behavior, and controlling impulses, a classroom where such a collection of toys and materials is easily accessible might seem like an invitation for chaos. To be sure, children do sometimes become distracted and grab toys when it is not time to play. Rather than prevent these situations from occurring by removing the source of distraction or stimulation, the therapeutic teacher organizes the use and accessibility of materials within this environment. Children are encouraged to put away what they have used before using something else. Limits are placed on dumping. Children are not allowed to destroy materials or use them to hurt other children, and everything gets put away in its place at the end of free play.

The fact that everything has a place in the classroom reinforces the development of object permanence. A toy might leave its place, but it is always returned. During free play, the floor might be littered with blocks, legos, dolls, and the pieces of the doctor's kit, but at cleanup time, everything is neatly returned to the shelves before snack can begin. A toy will be in its place when a child looks for it: This is as important for a child who comes from a chaotic home and has had little stability in her life as it is for a child whose organic impediments to development have prevented her from acquiring a solid concept of object permanence.

The physical environment is one that is endowed, consistent, and cared for. Materials are kept clean and organized. If something is lost or broken, the loss or breakage is acknowledged and mourned. This is a new experience for children who have had extreme loss in their lives but never had the chance to experience their feelings about it. Children learn that adults will take care of their toys just as they will care for and protect children. This investment is transferred to the children, who become, in turn, more able to invest emotional energy in their learning environment.

Daily Schedule and Routine

The structure of the daily schedule is facilitating for children with emotional difficulties in many ways. By taking responsibility for determining the schedule and routines, adults convey to children that there is someone—larger and stronger than themselves—who will make sure their school world is a safe and predictable place where basic needs will be consistently met. Many of the children come from homes where life is chaotic and unpredictable, where they are sometimes left to fend for themselves. The consistency of the schoolday helps these children develop—in Erikson's terms—a certain level of "basic trust" in their environment (Erikson, 1950/1985). Knowing that they can always rely on certain things, such as the presence of their teachers, the availability of food, and the repeated occurrence of certain activities each day, helps the children relax their emphasis on survival needs, diminish hypervigilance, and invest attention and energy in learning activities.

Although adults take responsibility for deciding the sequence of events during the day, children are still allowed room for feelings and choice. For example, the teachers determine that lunch will happen at the same time every day and that each child must wash hands before eating, sit at the table to eat, and eat at least some lunch before dessert. However, within this basic format, the children eat how and what they want to. One little boy expresses his dependency needs by sipping his juice with a spoon, like a baby. One girl, who is overfed by her mother in a rather intrusive way, never wants anyone to touch her lunch and chooses to eat only small portions of it.

By including long periods of open-ended playtime, the daily schedule offers children ample opportunity to explore their inner lives. While most regular, developmentally based preschool programs include playtime as an important part of the schoolday, many special education programs take pains to avoid such open-ended activity in the fear that bringing children's emotional concerns into the classroom will balloon the anxiety level and unleash unwanted behaviors. However, therapeutic classrooms that provide children with opportunities during the day to work through feelings actually reduce anxiety and the need to act out.

Although free play is open-ended and children can pick and choose materials and activities, teachers impose an invisible structure. By organizing and helping children to elaborate on play, teachers weave together the threads of activity into a constructive process. The therapeutic teacher helps children create a beginning, middle, and end to their activities.

For example, a child pulls the bin of duplo blocks off the shelf and dumps them on the floor. She begins to make something but quickly becomes frustrated, then distracted by another child's activity. She begins to walk away.

> TEACHER: Krystal, it looks as if you were building something. What were you going to make?
> KRYSTAL (*turning back to the duplos*): A train.
> TEACHER: Come on, let's finish it. Do you want some help?
> KRYSTAL: Yeah.

Child and teacher spend several minutes working on the train. Krystal becomes absorbed in making a compartment with a person inside on each of the train cars, designating the people as the members of her family. She drives the train around the room. After a few minutes, she leaves this and goes to the dress-up corner to play.

> TEACHER: Krystal, are you finished with your train?
> KRYSTAL: Yes.

TEACHER: Okay, before you play dress-up, lets put your train on the shelf and put away the rest of the duplos. (*Krystal hesitates.*) I'll help you. Would you like to put your train away or clean up the duplos?

KRYSTAL: The duplos.

The activity is completed, and Krystal goes off happily to the dress-up corner.

A more emotionally charged topic can be handled in a similar way. Two children begin playing that there is a fire in the "house." In chorus, they yell "Fire! Fire!" and begin to run around the classroom, without direction.

TEACHER: Hold on. You need to stop running around, but we can think of something you can do. What happens next in your game? (*The children hesitate.*) Can you put the fire out? Is somebody going to be the firefighter? Should we build a firetruck?

TONY: Yeah! A firetruck—that's a good idea! (*He puts on a fire hat and begins lining up the chairs to make a firetruck.*)

JENNIFER: The babies! What about the babies? [Jennifer's apartment was burned down when she was 2 years old.]

TEACHER: Maybe you are remembering when there was a fire in your house. That must have been very scary. Should we find a safe place to put the babies?

JENNIFER: Yes. Let's get the babies. (*She begins rescuing the babies, pulling the doll bed to the other side of the room and carefully placing the babies in it, out of reach of the "fire." She joins Tony in his firetruck. They arrive at their destination, get out, and begin running around again, wildly spraying invisible water all over the classroom.*)

TEACHER: Slow down. If you want to put out the fire, you need to spray water on the fire. . . . Good work. . . . Is the fire almost out? It's almost cleanup time. Maybe you can finish putting out the fire and drive back to the fire station before we clean up.

TONY: Okay. Fire's out.

JENNIFER: Wait—the babies!

TEACHER: Let's all help put the babies back and then drive back.

Tony and Jennifer carry the doll bed back to its proper place, and the teacher replaces the babies. The children get back in the firetruck and pretend to drive back to the station. The activity is completed and the cleanup song is sung.

Rules and Limits

A consistent set of rules and limits helps to preserve a safe and orderly classroom environment. Limits are set for children in such a way as to safely contain disruptive or dangerous behaviors while at the same time allowing for emotional response. Rather than rigidly controlling isolated behaviors through the use of behavior modification, the interventions employed in the therapeutic classroom help children understand the feelings that underlie their behavior and find alternate ways of coping with them.

Many of our children are impulsive and tend to act out feelings in the moment. They grab toys, break materials, hit, run out of the room, jump on furniture, and so forth. Secondary process is compromised, and primary process takes over during moments of emotional crisis. While the teacher will help stop a child from engaging in maladaptive behaviors, she will also help a child mediate between feeling and behavior by offering the child alternative strategies, such as using his words or redirecting the feeling into symbolic forms of expression.

This is done in many different ways. The teacher might use verbal reflection or interpretation. If a child continually jumps up and asks "Can I go with you?" when a teacher leaves the room, the teacher might interpret this to mean that perhaps the child is worried that the teacher will not come back—and will then reassure her. For other children, the teacher might draw a picture, or even make a book about an issue that is particularly pervasive and persistent for a child. The use of visual forms of reflection are used frequently with children who are less receptive to verbal input.

For example, during the transition from snack to meeting one day, a child jumps up on the table and dances around.

> CHILD: Look at me!
> TEACHER (*lifting the child down*): That's too dangerous. Maybe you were
> worried and wanted to make sure a grown-up would keep you safe.
> I'm not going to let you jump on the table, but you can sit on my lap.
> CHILD: I want to sit on your lap.

Another child, after being told it is time to stop playing, dumps a bin of toy cars and is about to knock over a shelf when a teacher catches her arm.

> TEACHER: Pamela, I'm not going to let you knock the shelf over. That's
> dangerous. (*Child tries to hit teacher.*) I'm going to help you stop
> hitting, too. Hitting hurts. Did you get angry because we said it was
> time to clean up? (*Child nods.*) You can use your words and say,
> "That makes me angry. I don't want to clean up!"
> PAMELA: I'm angry. I don't want to clean up.
> TEACHER: Okay, I hear that you are angry, but we still need to clean up so
> we can have snack. Maybe you can take the baby doll you were
> playing with to the playroom later. We can put it right near the door
> so we remember.

For the child who is more receptive to visual input, the teacher might draw a picture afterwards of the child angry, with a simply worded caption: "Judy said, 'It's cleanup time.' That made Gail angry. She said, 'No cleanup.'"

Once a feeling has been expressed, the teacher can offer alternative ways of coping with it. Often, empathic response and reassurance is enough. Sometimes, a child needs more concrete help. A child who is angry, for example, might need to punch a punching bag, stamp his feet, or tear up paper. A child worried about being away from Mommy might need to carry around a transitional object, such as a soft toy from home, in order to feel reassured. A needy child who is grabbing food from other children's lunches might need a few extra crackers from the refrigerator in order to feel she has enough.

Because children are allowed to have their feelings even when the adult imposes a limit, a child can accede to a limit without compromising her integrity or losing self-esteem. By offering children some choice while remaining firm about setting a limit, the teacher affords children appropriate levels of autonomy. She might tell a child, for instance, "You can wash your hands in the bathroom or the classroom, but you need to wash your hands before lunch. Where would you like to wash them?" This is powerful for emotionally fragile children, many of whom come from chaotic homes where limits are set in rather arbitrary ways, where they are either excessively frustrated or excessively indulged. Insofar as the limits in the therapeutic classroom are meaningful and can be clearly explained to the children, they can be internalized and mastered, thus facilitating the development of greater frustration tolerance and impulse control.

Curriculum

Often it is helpful for children to deal with their feelings out of the moment, when needs are not so primary, the observing ego is stronger, and they can use cognition to make sense of experience. The curriculum in therapeutic classrooms provides for this by presenting a conceptual framework within which experiences and feelings can be symbolically represented and mastered. Because the curriculum is based on salient developmental issues, it is inherently compelling to the children. The curriculum consists of individually tailored play interventions as well as a thematically structured group curriculum.

Spontaneous play lends itself perfectly to the integration of cognition and affect. In their spontaneous play, children act out an endlessly imaginative collection of themes, including going away and coming back, caretaking experiences (both positive and negative), danger and protection, breaking and fixing, being big and being little, and countless others. Working within the child's metaphors, the teacher helps her to elaborate and make both cognitive and affective connections to the themes of the play. Sometimes the teacher will make a direct connection between what a child is representing in play or artwork and real-life experiences.

The following anecdote illustrates how a child's cognitive and emotional concerns are addressed simultaneously in the context of play. Nina is playing with water, emptying and filling bottles of various sizes.

> TEACHER: You have some little bottles and some big bottles.
> NINA: This one's little . . . it's a baby. (*She fills a bottle, then pours it into a bigger bottle.*) This one's big. It's a mommy. My mommy say I'm bigger.
> TEACHER: Hmm . . . You are bigger than you were when you were a baby.
> NINA: When I was a baby, I had a bottle. But now I'm big. Here, you stir this. My mommy stirs food.
> TEACHER: Do you think I'm like a mommy?
> NINA: Yeah, you like a mommy.
> TEACHER: How about you? Are you like a baby, a little girl, or a mommy?
> NINA (*Her face clouds.*): Mommy says I'm bigger!
> TEACHER: Mm-hmm, you are bigger than you were when you were a baby, but you're not as big as a mommy yet. Sometimes I think you worry that you have to be like a grown-up. Sometimes your mommy wants you to do things like a grown-up, like clean the dishes. But it's okay to do things like a 4-year-old girl, too.
> NINA: I'm 4. I had a birthday. See? (*She holds up three fingers.*)
> TEACHER: Yes, you are 4 years old. Here, let's count four fingers together. One, two, three, four. (*She helps Nina hold up four fingers.*)
> NINA (*smiling*): I'm four!

The group curriculum offers various conceptual structures that the children can use to symbolize and make meaning out of their experiences. The content is drawn directly from the themes children express in their play, language, drawing, and behavior, and it is shaped by our knowledge of child development. Themes are both conceptual and emotional in nature. Examples include going away and coming back, house and home, hiding and finding, hatching and growing, big and little, empty and full, messy and clean, and breaking and fixing.

After the teacher models different ways of representing the themes symbolically, the children then are helped to represent the themes themselves. Some activities are primarily conceptual in nature while some are more personally oriented. For example, when we implemented a "big and little" curriculum, the children used big and little bottles during water play, and they made collages out of big and little paper circles. Later in the week, they played dress-up—one day dressing up to be big, another day pretending to be little. There is always overlap, however: One little boy made his collage with one big circle and lots of little ones, thus turning it into a representation of his family constellation. Naturally, each child will bring something different to the curriculum. However, since the themes are drawn from the children's real-life experiences and developmental issues, they are universal enough so that they are meaningful to all the children (see Part III).

The Missing Link: The Teacher–Child Relationship

It is the dialogue implicit in the child's relationship with her teacher that provides the mediating link between structure and freedom. Initially, the teacher acts as the child's auxiliary or observing ego. By engaging in a dialogue with the child, the teacher helps the child integrate and build her own mediational capacities. The teacher helps the child organize her cognition and behavior around the structure in the classroom and eventually internalize it herself. By providing direction and limits as well as offering empathic response, the teacher permits but helps contain feelings. She makes a child feel safe with her experiences and helps channel them in a productive fashion, that is, to express them symbolically. Therefore, the child's relationship with her teacher becomes a pivotal force in the therapeutic classroom. The following section elaborates on significant aspects of the teacher–child relationship in the therapeutic classroom.

THE IMPORTANCE OF RELATIONSHIP: THE ROLE OF THE THERAPEUTIC TEACHER

Relationship is pivotal in the development of a young child. Cognitive and emotional development are intricately interwoven and bound up with a strong primary adult–child relationship. Often the relationships that emotionally fragile children have had have been problematic. Many children in a therapeutic nursery have not had the opportunity or the capacity to engage in a healthy primary relationship. As a result, no groundwork has been laid for healthy emotional and cognitive development. It is crucial that therapeutic teachers address the developmental requirements of these children in an integrated fashion and acknowledge the importance of their relationships in this process. Relationships must be the starting point and the context within which the work in the therapeutic classroom occurs.

To function successfully in a regular classroom setting, the young child must have achieved a certain level of emotional integration or ego strength. Some of the ego functions required for a successful preschool experience include a solidified sense of self and object constancy and the ability to organize and mediate experience through symbolic means (e.g., play and language). These ego functions must develop in the context of relationship. Behaviors rooted in basic ego functions cannot simply be taught in an isolated, external fashion, outside of a developmental context. When skills and behaviors are acquired by children in this manner, they are not integrated and quickly break down under stress. Often the children in the therapeutic nursery are missing the developmental precursors that underlie basic ego functions. These developmental precursors are rooted in the child's relationship with the caregiver and therefore must be fostered within the context of relationship.

In order to be free to invest attention and emotional energy in learning activities, a child must have a sense of object constancy and know that if she separates from her caregiver, her caregiver will be there when she returns. In order to use symbols in a meaningful fashion (an important developmental task for the preschooler), a child must have a strong relationship on which to draw. Winnicott (1971/1999) has shown that a child's very first symbol—a transitional object such as a soft toy or blanket—is a symbol of the primary relationship. Moreover, symbol formation presupposes a shared reality, or a state of "intersubjectivity," as Stern (1985/2000) has called it, which only relationship can provide. Without relationship, symbols remain inaccessible, idiosyncratic, or devoid of meaning for the young child. Clearly, the importance of the teacher–child relationship for a needy child is paramount in effecting the development of cognition as well as emotional well-being.

The therapeutic teacher thus finds herself in the complex position of having to wear several hats at the same time. She is many things to the child, including teacher, surrogate caregiver, therapist, and limit setter. The many roles the teacher plays come together in the totality of her relationship with the child.

Teacher as Instructor

By accommodating the child's learning needs, the teacher satisfies the preschooler's natural drive toward autonomy and progress. Typically, 3- and 4-year-old children are still dependent on the adult but are increasingly able to move away in order to explore and master the world around them. They learn best when they learn actively, through a variety of hands-on experiences. They integrate what they learn by symbolically re-creating experiences in play, art, and language. Piaget (1952) calls this the "preoperational" phase of development. Greenspan (1981; Greenspan & Wieder, 2006) refers to the development of "representational capacities" during the preschool years.

The teacher therefore provides young children with developmentally appropriate learning tools, through which they can discover concepts, acquire new skills, and organize experiences symbolically. The teacher encourages questioning and problem solving, highlights basic concepts, makes connections, and guides the mastery of basic skills. Helping a child to complete a puzzle, cut paper with scissors, remember the name of an animal, count the right number of cups to pass out at snack, pour her own juice, mix a new color, build a bridge, or ride a tricycle affords a child opportunities to gain mastery and assert autonomy in developmentally appropriate ways. The teacher takes each child's level of cognitive development as her starting point and helps the child move forward from there. She facilitates the integration of cognition and emotion by relating a child's learning activities to the child's personal experiences.

In the following example, Paul sits on the floor attempting to build with the duplo blocks. He tries to put two pieces together, becomes frustrated, and gives up.

PAUL: I can't do it!

TEACHER: You seem frustrated, but I'll bet you can do it. Let me show you, and then let's see if you can do it by yourself. (*Paul watches, then successfully joins two pieces.*)

PAUL: I did it!

TEACHER: That made you happy. What are you going to make?

PAUL: A house. (*He works intently for several minutes and makes a house, muttering "red, red, red" as he selects only red pieces to use.*)

TEACHER: You made a red house.

PAUL: I'm gonna make another house.

TEACHER: What color are you going to make this one?

PAUL (*picking up a blue piece*): Green.

TEACHER: Is that green? Let's see . . . it's the same color as your sneakers. Do you remember what that color is called? (*cuing*) That's bl . . .

PAUL: Blue! (*He smiles proudly. Paul completes the second house and puts a little boy in one of them, along with a mommy, a little girl, and a baby. In the other house he puts a daddy figure.*)

TEACHER: That's like your family. You live with Mommy, Veronica, and Shawna, and Daddy lives in a different house now.

Teacher as Surrogate Caregiver

In her role as teacher, by promoting the child's mastery of certain concepts and skills, the teacher fulfills the child's growing need for mastery and autonomy. However, sometimes a child must also regress in order to progress. She must return to earlier developmental levels in order to establish the missing developmental precursors that underpin the formation of later developmental gains. The therapeutic teacher helps the young child build a sound developmental foundation through the formation of a strong relationship. The therapeutic teacher not only attempts to strengthen the child's relationship with his caregiver, but she also makes herself available as a surrogate attachment figure.

Some children, due to an organic fragility, have had difficulty entering fully into relationship. The teacher actively attempts to bring such children into relationship by engaging them in activities such as reciprocal play, mirroring, peek-a-boo, and hide-and-seek. These are activities that children typically use at earlier developmental stages to develop a sense of self in the context of relationship with the other. Other children have the capacity but have not had available to them a stable or appropriate attachment figure. The teacher will offer such children permission to express their dependency needs and make herself available as a stable and nurturing attachment figure.

Within the context of the relationship with the therapeutic teacher, the child can do developmental work she was unable to do earlier. Often emotionally needy children must experience ways of relating to the adult that are more appropriate for a younger child because they have not had the opportunity to do so earlier. Many need help establishing trust in the consistent availability of an adult. The therapeutic teacher helps the child bridge the connection with her own caregiver through toddler-like "checking-in" behaviors, such as visits to the parents' room or telephone calls to Mommy. The teacher will also encourage the use of transitional objects, such as a soft toy from home or a photograph of Mommy. Within her own relationship with the child, the therapeutic teacher might indulge the child's dependency needs by carrying or holding the child on her lap, giving the child extra crackers if she needs them, allowing Band-Aids for imaginary boo-boos, or permitting the child to play baby. She will help the child solidify a sense of object constancy by playing peek-a-boo or hide-and-seek and remaining consistently available as the child moves away and comes back to her.

The therapeutic teacher provides a corrective experience to children who have been either overly frustrated or indulged by offering them appropriate levels of need gratification. She nurtures and accommodates need but at the same time sets limits and structures the experience for the child. She might, for example, address a child's preoccupation with hoarding crackers from the refrigerator first thing in the morning by allowing him to take two at a time, and two more if he is still hungry.

The following is an example of how a child was able to use her relationship with her teacher to work through important developmental processes. By age 4, Juanita had been in and out of three separate foster homes before she was finally placed in the care of her great-aunt. When Juanita first arrived in the nursery, she remained aloof but hypervigilant. Juanita's symbolic play was limited, but she found some comfort in water play. Often she would have her hands immersed in a bin of water while her gaze steadily followed the teachers as they moved around the classroom, as if she was trying to ward off the ever-present danger of abandonment. When a teacher went out of the room without her, Juanita would panic and cry inconsolably. During transitions, Juanita would become very anxious, run around the classroom, and climb on furniture as if testing to see if an adult would come protect her.

Interventions were employed that were designed to strengthen Juanita's relationship with her great-aunt and allow her to use her relationship with her teacher to foster a sense of basic security and reduce anxiety. Juanita's aunt was asked to send a photograph of herself, which the teachers hung on a string for Juanita to wear around her neck, as well as Juanita's favorite teddy bear for Juanita to carry back and forth to school each day. Juanita periodically called her aunt at home to "check in" and was allowed to visit her in the parents' room whenever she was at school.

In the classroom, the teachers helped Juanita learn that she could ask to sit on a lap when she was feeling worried. They played hide-and-seek and other activities that involved "going away and coming back" in order to reinforce Juanita's sense of object constancy. Juanita began to use transitional objects to symbolize the relationship with her teacher and would sometimes ask to wear a teacher's watch or hold her keys when she was going out of the room.

Sometimes, Juanita would opt to play baby and regress to a developmental stage where she was more receptive to nurturing input. One day, she got into the doll bed and asked for a bottle.

> JUANITA: Waaa! Waaa!
> TEACHER: Baby needs something . . . what do you need, baby?
> JUANITA: Ba-ba.
> TEACHER: A bottle? Hang on . . . here you go.
> JUANITA: Waaa! Waaa! The monsters!
> TEACHER: The baby is scared. (*picking her up*) Don't worry, baby, I'm
>   not going to let the monsters hurt you.
> JUANITA: Don' leave me!
> TEACHER: You're afraid I'm going to leave you. But I'm staying right
>   here.

By acting as a nurturing and protective "mommy" to the frightened "baby," the therapeutic teacher helps Juanita relive old fears in a new and corrective way, thereby helping her to build the sense of basic security she was unable to build at the developmentally appropriate time.

Teachers are frequently worried that if they allow for such regression, they will soon have a classroom full of screaming infants to contend with. The therapeutic teacher, however, allows for regression but is also able to contain it. By allowing children to feel alternately "big and little," the therapeutic teacher facilitates movement back and forth and maintains the delicate balance between progress and regress. Within the schoolday, the children are allowed to play baby during open-ended play periods but are asked to be their 3- and 4-year-old selves during structured group activities. When free play is over, the teacher helps Juanita "grow up" again:

> Okay, Juanita, it's time to clean up. You can play baby again later in the playroom. Now let's see if you can be 1 year old . . . now be 2 . . . now 3 . . . now be your 4-year-old self . . . are you ready to pass out the cups for snack?

By remaining consistently available to Juanita as she worked through these developmental processes, the teachers helped Juanita become more comfortable with her dependency needs and establish a sense of security and trust in the relationship. Eventually, Juanita became much less anxious, more autonomous, and able to invest more of her attention and energy in learning activities.

Teacher as Therapist

Helping the child to develop a significant relationship with an adult is one therapeutic function the teacher performs. Another is to act as an "interpreter of experience," to help children who have had traumatic or emotionally overwhelming experiences in their lives sort out what has happened to them. As children represent their experiences through play and art symbols, the therapeutic teacher will help a child elaborate and connect the experiences represented to real emotions and sometimes to real-life events. She thus enables the child to sort out confusing and powerful experiences. The therapeutic relationship safely contains these experiences and the child's powerful feelings around them.

Peter, a 4-year-old boy diagnosed with separation anxiety disorder, has been separated from his mother at 1 year and brought from Jamaica by his father to live in New York. In January, Peter learns that his father will be leaving shortly on a 2-month trip to Jamaica, without Peter. Peter begins to experience behavioral regressions. At the end of each day, he becomes highly anxious, screaming and crying in distress. Interventions are employed to address Peter's anxiety. During free play, Peter plays with the toy plane and people. Placing several people on the plane, including a daddy figure, Peter flies the plane away, leaving the little boy behind.

> PETER (*sternly*): I'm leaving . . . I'm going away.
> TEACHER (*playing the part of the boy*): Don't go, Daddy! Don't leave me! I want to go with you.
> PETER: You shut up, you're not coming with me. Now don't be a baby.
> TEACHER: But I'm afraid you won't come back.
> PETER: Oh, all right . . . Wait, wait . . . I come back. (*Taking his time, Peter eventually flies the plane back to the little boy.*) See? I come back. Now don't you worry.
> TEACHER: Maybe you are worrying about how your daddy is going to go away on a plane. But your daddy will come back, too.

Peter plays out similar scenarios for several days. His anxiety is reduced and behavioral regression diminishes.

The therapeutic teacher also "saves" experiences for children and helps them work through them out of the moment, when observing ego is stronger. By referring back to an upset that occurred previously, the therapeutic teacher reinforces the child's sense of object constancy, helps him bridge and integrate what might otherwise be isolated experiences, and establishes an emotional middle ground. A teacher might reflect to a child as follows:

> TEACHER: Do you remember yesterday when you got really sad at goodbye time?

CHILD: I was crying.

TEACHER: Yes, you said that you didn't want to go home. But you came back to school today. Are you feeling a little better?

CHILD (*smiling*): Yes. I'm gonna come back tomorrow and tomorrow and tomorrow.

By talking over with a teacher an incident that occurred earlier, children learn that they can have and express their feelings without becoming panicked or overwhelmed by them.

Teacher as Limit Setter

While there are many times when it is appropriate for the teacher to follow the child's agenda, the therapeutic teacher must also retain the role of limit setter and reality tester for the young child. Unlike the therapist, who sees the child in a uniquely removed situation, the therapeutic teacher is involved with the child for many hours per day and within the context of a group. Insofar as she must manage the needs of a group of children and maintain a certain degree of order in the classroom, the therapeutic teacher must make demands on the individual child to conform to certain routines and limits. In this way, she is responsible for enforcing a reality outside of that of the individual child. For children whose sense of self is fragile, this can be quite facilitating. Developmentally, children need to repeatedly come up against a parental "no" in order to establish themselves as separate, autonomous beings. By setting limits in a way that is firm and neutral but at the same time acknowledges the child's place within the situation, the therapeutic teacher helps the child delineate a sense of himself in relation to the other. When the teacher has access to her own feelings and is able to communicate them clearly, she offers children a nonthreatening model for self-expression. Her display of genuine affect and her ability to articulate the source of her feeling gives children permission to connect with their own feelings and to expand their awareness of emotional cause and effect.

Limit setting, which is done within the context of a supportive relationship, can also be a corrective experience for children who come from homes where adults exert authority in ways that might be hurtful and frightening. Because they have been presented with overwhelming levels of frustration, these children often become enraged and are unable to stop themselves from acting out. Frequently, when an adult in the nursery attempts to set a limit with the child, the child becomes terrified, as if she is actually seeing a monster, and runs to the "good" teacher to save her.

One day in the playroom, Keith is hitting another child who is refusing to get off the tricycle he perceives as his. The teacher intervenes.

TEACHER (*holding Keith's arms*): I'm going to help you stop hitting. Hitting hurts. Let's see if you can stop yourself and use your words instead of hitting. (*Keith becomes distressed.*)

KEITH: Get offa me! Get offa me! (*Breaking loose, he runs to the other side of the room and picks up a block to throw at the teacher. The teacher stops him and carries him to a chair at the side of the room.*)

TEACHER: Let's take some time out and talk about what's happening.

KEITH (*struggling to hit teacher*): Get offa me! Get offa me! (*calling to another teacher*) Chrissy, help!

TEACHER: You seem really scared. Are you afraid I'm going to hurt you?

KEITH (*yelling*): Yes! You're hurting me!

TEACHER: Maybe it feels as if I'm hurting you. I'm not going to hurt you, though. But I am going to help you stop hitting because hitting does hurt, and we need to make sure that everyone stays safe. (*Keith begins to relax in teacher's arms.*)

TEACHER: Okay, it seems as if you are ready to stop. Let's talk about what just happened.

When limits are set by the adult in a neutral, supportive, and meaningful manner, the child will come to trust that the adult can be authoritative without being hurtful. The teacher says "no" but continues to care for and be available to the child. In the service of the positive relationship with the therapeutic teacher, the child eventually comes to internalize the ability to adhere to limits and to tolerate frustration.

A COMMON WORLD, A COMMON LANGUAGE: THE CHILD WITHIN THE GROUP

A distinguishing feature of the therapeutic classroom setting is that it addresses the needs of individual children within the collective of the group. As the facilitator of this group, the teacher is faced with the challenge of balancing the needs of the individual with the needs of the group. Although the management of a group of young special-needs children is at times a difficult task, in the end the process of fostering group activity and interaction can be therapeutic and promote growth for the children.

One function the group serves is to diminish a child's sense of isolation. By participating in a curriculum that draws on universally relevant developmental themes, the children are enabled to share and compare their individual experiences with those of other children. Making an isolated trouble into a shared experience is powerful and healing for the young child.

In their spontaneous play, the children engage in a similar process. Very often, a group of children will join together in choreographing complex play scenarios where the collective imagination weaves together themes that are at once profoundly individual and universal. The teacher can facilitate this process by helping to mediate conflict situations, delegating roles, and organizing themes. As facilitator, it is crucial that the teacher be able to assess when to get involved and when to step back and let group process proceed on its own.

By participating in the dialogue that is created in group dramatic play, children are intrinsically motivated to establish a shared reality—and with it a shared set of play symbols. They must agree implicitly that a plate full of playdough is a pizza or that a cylindrical block is a firehose. These play symbols become the basis for meaningful communication among the children. This is especially important for children who have language difficulties and for whom the development of other symbolic capacities is an important precursor to effective language use.

For children whose sense of self is underdeveloped, group interaction helps them differentiate between self and other. Children who are still locked within a symbiotic relationship with their caregivers and who are relatively undifferentiated are suddenly confronted with the fact that there are other children, different from them.

Working through conflict situations helps diminish each child's sense of egocentrism. Children are helped by the teacher to check destructive impulses and to communicate with each other instead. As children are led to examine how their behavior impacts on others, they gain a greater awareness of emotional cause and effect. The teacher guides children in recognizing and empathizing with each other's feelings, so that cooperation, rather than competition, will become attractive to them.

CONCLUDING REMARKS

Creating a space for emotional life in the classroom is essential if troubled children are to realize their full developmental potential. Although it might be possible to manage a difficult child's behaviors without speaking to her emotional needs, in the long run this could be to the child's detriment. If this is not dealt with at this formative age, a child's emotional troubles may go underground but continue to interfere with optimal growth and psychological integration throughout the child's life.

Helping children cope with powerful emotions requires hard work, emotional strength, and ingenuity on the part of the teacher. Her multiple roles require the flexibility to move from instructional mode to caregiver mode to therapeutic mode in her relationships with children. A teacher who reaches out to embrace students on all of these levels gains access to children's energies for learning that may have previously been inaccessible. While the children's activity level may increase and the noise level may be higher at times, so will the level of spontaneous, constructive learning. That achievement is the therapeutic teacher's greatest reward.

REFERENCES

Erikson, E. (1985). *Childhood and society.* New York: Norton. (Original work published 1950)

Greenspan, S. (1981). *Psychopathology and adaptation in infancy and early childhood.* New York: International Universities Press.

Greenspan, S., & Wieder, S. (2006). *Engaging autism.* Cambridge, MA: Da Capo.

Piaget, J. (1952). *The origins of intelligence in children.* New York: International Universities Press.

Stern, D. (2000). *The interpersonal world of the infant.* New York: Basic Books. (Original work published 1985)

Winnicott, D. W. (1999). *Playing and reality.* New York: Routledge. (Original work published 1971)

CHAPTER 5

Play Therapy
as Early Intervention

Lesley Koplow

PRESCHOOL AND DAY-CARE centers frequently augment their programs by providing on-site therapies for children who need additional help. It is not uncommon for a Head Start program or day-care center to have a speech therapist on site to treat those children in the school community who have difficulty with communication. However, it is much less common for preschools to provide play therapy as a form of early intervention for children with emotional difficulties. This is true even in the face of increasing numbers of children with high levels of emotional distress. While early childhood professionals are generally quite knowledgeable about the importance of play skills in normally developing children, there is a general lack of sophistication about use of play as a therapeutic tool (Bratton, Ray, Rhine, & Jones, 2005).

Preschools that heal use play as a therapeutic modality serving as an integral part of the early intervention program for emotionally fragile children. This chapter will help readers become familiar with the play therapy process and create a context for including play therapy programs in the early childhood setting.

PLAY THERAPY: DEFINITION AND HISTORICAL CONTEXT

Play therapy may be defined as a process of using play symbols to establish a connecting dialogue between child and therapist as well as between the child's conscious and unconscious experience. Play is the child's tool for making sense of his world, and children's spontaneous play is in part motivated by their need to interpret and master salient experiences. When developmental delays or traumatic events inhibit a child's ability to master personal challenges, a play therapist may intervene.

An antiquated system of social stratification may cloud our vision about the potential use of play therapy for today's urban children. Well-known case studies elaborating on successful treatments of very young patients have often featured upper-class children, such as Axline's (1964) *Dibs* and Winnicott's (1977) *The Piggle*. Indeed, the analytic community's early attempts to integrate the principles of child analysis with the practice of early childhood education resulted in therapeutic models that depended heavily on treatment via the parent. These early models primarily served well-educated, upper- and middle-class families through a highly verbal psychoeducational process. Parents were educated to be auxiliary therapists for their own children. The children themselves received a cognitively oriented early childhood experience designed to strengthen their verbal and perceptual skills, which would eventually allow them to participate in more conventional forms of treatment (Weil, 1972).

The evolution of psychologically oriented treatment programs designed to meet the needs of delayed, deprived, neglected, and traumatized children can be seen in the work of the corrective object relations therapists of the 1960s. The corrective object relations approach stressed the need for young children to experience their dependency needs in the presence of a responsive adult before age-level independent mastery could occur. Although programs informed by this approach were designed to meet the emotional needs of children, they were also found to positively influence a child's learning capacity. A project in Florida gave academically precarious first-graders weekly sessions where nurturing play was the primary intervention. The children's academic status subsequently improved (Brody, 1978). Likewise, Zelman, Samuels, and Abrams (1985) found that young psychotherapy patients often showed increases in IQ when tested following treatment. Arietta Slade's work on using play in therapy with young children who have not yet developed language and other representational capacities makes a compelling argument for the value of interactive, presymbolic, and early-level symbolic play as a therapeutic catalyst for a child's ability to create more complex and meaningful symbols that can help them integrate their experiences (Slade & Wolf, 1994).

While progressive early childhood education values young children's play and provides rich play opportunities in the classroom, children in classrooms designed to meet the needs of children with developmental and social-emotional issues are often treated as though their play behavior is not meaningful. Paradoxically, play is often less likely to be a welcome part of the schoolday for these children. Intervention objectives tend to be defined in behavioral terms, and the child's struggle to develop symbols that can hold and communicate his experiences is unattended. Given research findings indicating that play increases brain activity (Mann, 1996; Meade, 1999), the exclusion of play as a form of therapy and early childhood education for children at risk is puzzling.

Where does this leave us as we attempt to meet the special needs of traumatized and emotionally arrested urban preschool children today? Clearly, many of the children we see lack the verbal skills of "The Piggle" (Winnicott, 1977) and fail to announce their intellectual potential via the IQ score, as Axline's (1964) patient *Dibs* was able to do. Many do not have parents who are physically or emotionally available to assume the role of therapist, as did the father of Freud's patient, Little Hans. Moreover, the children we see often show glaring developmental deficits or extremely disruptive behaviors that overwhelm the early childhood educator and the clinician alike. Trauma and deprivation act to create a kind of developmental paralysis in the child, sometimes preventing growth in several areas simultaneously. Unfortunately, this fragmentation in children results in programs that divide students into several pieces, each piece then becoming the province of the appropriate specialist.

Consider, for example, a little girl who was drug-exposed in utero, treated with intrusive medical procedures as an infant, and then removed from her mother and subsequently placed in two foster homes. At age 3, she displays high activity levels, delayed language development, fearfulness, and a detached quality of relatedness. She takes little initiative in manipulating her environment and does not follow through on the few activities she initiates. She can, however, dress independently, get her snack from the classroom refrigerator, and attend to her own toileting needs. Her early childhood program may refer her to a psychiatrist, who prescribes Ritalin for her activity level; to a speech therapist, who works on her delayed language; and to an occupational therapist, who improves her manipulative abilities. Yet no one is given the job of helping this fragmented 3-year-old integrate all of these disparate approaches, let alone helping her make sense of the real-life experiences that have impacted on her so tragically. Neither is there an assumption that this child's life experiences might have diminished her developmental processes, and that attention to the emotional injuries sustained might improve her developmental outcome.

When we ask this little girl's teacher whether she might benefit from play therapy, the teacher reacts with surprise. "But she doesn't know how to play!" the teacher replies.

CHILDREN WHO CAN'T PLAY

There are children who do not know the language of play. They come to preschool but cannot participate in the bubbling of creative activity surrounding them. Sometimes they remain silent, sullen, and preoccupied, maintaining a hypervigilant stance and refusing to allow themselves to become involved in the preschool world except to assume an almost precocious responsibility for their own self-care. Indeed, studies of deprived children in preschool identify a pattern of precocious self-care activity coexisting with impoverished cognitive and language development (Koplow, 1985; Pavenstedt, 1967).

Some children appear active within the confines of a world they seem to fill with rituals and idiosyncratic manipulations of the environment. Their "play" seems to lack the rich quality of personal interpretations and variations that characterize the drama in most housekeeping corners populated by 4-year-olds. Peers do not understand the meaning of their rituals and, therefore, do not seek to join in. Adults are confused by the unusual quality of the child's activity and may conclude that they do better with structured, task-oriented work.

Play, Language, and Trust

Many children who cannot play are also unable to use language effectively (Greenspan & Wieder, 2006; Westby, 1980). Some of these children are extremely volatile emotionally, expressing distress through frequent bouts of crying or violent outbursts. Children who cannot play may seem highly disorganized in the classroom environment. It is as if they are unable to orient themselves to the routine or to differentiate between one classroom area and another. Others may appear to organize themselves quite effectively by staying involved exclusively with structured materials, such as puzzles or pegboards, because these toys have a single purpose and do not require peer contact, communication, or personal elaboration.

If children come to preschool and are unable to speak at age level, they are referred for language therapy. If children come to preschool and are unable to play at age level, there is a tendency to lessen their opportunity for play instead of implementing therapies that will enhance this essential ego function.

"If we have toys, the children will hurt each other! They will become overstimulated! They will play about scary experiences and become upset." These comments illustrate the fears of urban teachers who are given the task of containing many emotionally fragile children without the benefit of play as an expressive outlet or form of emotional release.

How can nonplayers learn the language of play so that their own self-generated activity can become meaningful and promote growth? And how can traumatized children, whose play may consist of a grim repetition of traumatic events, come to use play as a healing process? Play therapy may be indicated for children in both categories.

Winnicott (1971/2005) tells us that the ability to play implies trust in the maternal environment. In order for play to develop, children must be able to rely on their primary caregivers to ensure their safety and meet their basic needs. The well-protected and well-nurtured child is then free to devote her emotional energy to her own developmental processes. She can interact with her environment playfully and explore her impact without the burden of having to guarantee her own survival. She can depart from the present qualities that her play materials may possess and fantasize about new and interesting possibilities. She does not fear losing touch with her primary caregiver as she plays because the caregiver has helped her give names and definition to her playthings, and therefore these playthings have become endowed with meaning and meaningful connections to the nurturer (Siegel, 1999; Stern, 1985/2000).

Many children who cannot play are children who have had to attend to their own survival needs. They cannot afford to take their attention from the here-and-now mission of staying alert to danger, obtaining food, tracking the adult, preventing abandonment, and competing with other children to collect mountains of materials that, sadly, fail to satisfy them because the toys are empty of maternal connection. It is often next to impossible for these children to involve themselves in abstract conceptual tasks, or play themes, because survival is felt to be dependent on maintaining a vigilant state. This tends to result in a diminished use of fantasy play or in fantasy invested as the only escape from the survival burden, thus compromising reality testing and making it difficult for the child to return easily to the present. Recent studies have highlighted the role of opportunity for stable adult–child interaction in the development of reality testing (Greenspan & Wieder, 2006). Therefore, in order to learn the language of play, children's needs for protection, nurture, and interaction must be met. Emotionally fragile children may require an individual relationship with a therapeutic adult in order to experience their dependency needs without overwhelming the group. The child's relationship with the therapist may become a pivotal catalyst in the development of play symbols, as he searches for ways to represent his experiences with the therapist.

A Space for Play

A play therapy space needs to be a safe, clean, and predictably accessible. It should be neutral, meaning it should not have other uses for those children being treated. Toys should be intact and well cared for and should either be items that convey the nurturing and containing features of the therapeutic relationship or items that lend themselves to becoming symbolic of children's actual and inner experiences. For example, available materials for preschool playrooms may include the following:

dolls	Russian dolls	fire hat
doll houses	bubbles	miniature firetrucks
little people	children's books	police figures
play food	sand, cornmeal	ambulance
playdough	hospital figures and paper	animal puppets
crayons	people puppets	baby bottles
chalkboard	mirror	a potty
marker board	play telephones	disposable diapers
pillows	dress-up items	a space for children to hide
blankets	a doctor kit	

Play therapists should keep in mind that material need not be limited to those typically suited for preschool age levels; many children using the space will be trying to resolve earlier developmental issues that were disrupted by difficult experiences. Materials such as lotto games, peg boards, and electronic toys are not recommended because they discourage interpersonal relatedness and do not facilitate representational play.

Traditional psychoanalysts have considered the child's imposition of order in the room to be part of the therapeutic process and, therefore, have not always attended to arrangement and position of materials. However, when treating children who have experienced chaotic living situations, including disruptions and multiple separations from caretaking environments, it is important for the play therapist to maintain a more organized space (Donovan & McIntyre, 1990). For example, instead of having one large toy box containing a variety of toys, the therapist should separate items thematically and locate similar items in distinctive places in the room. For example, all dolls may be kept in the doll bed, crayons and paper on the shelves, play food and play dishes in the cabinet, and so forth. This enables the children to consistently find materials when they seek them out and shows them that the therapist respects their investment in the therapy space. This is particularly important for children whose achievements of object permanence and object constancy may be tentative.

PLAY THERAPY: PERSON AND PROCESS

Who is the child that is an appropriate referral for play therapy?

Preschools should be aware of children who show extreme separation anxiety, maintain a preoccupied hypervigilant state, elect to be mute in the school setting in contrast to demonstrated verbal ability elsewhere, show extreme fearfulness or social withdrawal, do not show age-level ego development in spite of adequate cognitive ability, have language that is atypical and noncommunicative, do not develop fantasy play, or remain absorbed in constant fantasy and appear to lose their orientation to the present reality. Complete developmental histories should be taken during the preschool intake process, and children who have suffered the death of a parent or sibling, been a victim of abuse or neglect or other traumatic experiences, been affected by family or community violence, been hospitalized for illness and treated with intrusive medical procedures, or sustained long-term or multiple separations from caregivers should be considered for play therapy programs whether or not they are symptomatic. Children who have had these experiences are at great risk for emotional, developmental, and learning difficulties, and play therapy may prevent the evolution of more serious problems as they grow older.

Teachers are usually quick to point out those children in the classroom with the most disruptive behavior as likely candidates. Indeed, these children may be acting out psychological needs that they are unable to express verbally. However, there are also children who may not manifest distress through aggression. Preschools should be aware of traumatized children who may be driven to reenact traumatic experience through grim and repetitive play. Their behavior may seem unremarkable except for high levels of distraction and a preoccupied state. These children may show delays in overall development, indicators that the trauma caused developmental arrest.

Young children initially use toys as "transitional objects" that represent the caregiver and allow the child to move out of her sight. This can be considered a precursor to more complex symbolic play. It follows that children who have relatedness difficulties or attachment disorders typically lack transitional objects and show delayed ability to elaborate in play. Toys may have idiosyncratic uses, and dynamic features tend not to be perceived. While these children may not act out in an aggressive manner, play therapy may be indicated as a preferred intervention method.

Play therapy may be accomplished by professionals from a variety of disciplines. Interviews undertaken for this book found play therapy programs implemented by clinical social workers, school psychologists, clinical psychologists, and counselors, as well as by special educators and early childhood educators trained in play therapy technique and supervised by mental health clinicians.

Play therapists treating young children must have a deep understanding of child development in order to recognize unresolved developmental issues and address them using therapeutic technique. Play therapists must have the capacity to be with children who have sustained developmental and psychological injuries without becoming overidentified with the child's fragility. Attempts to deal with this problem sometimes result in the therapist usurping the maternal role or, at other times, assuming a defensive distancing in working with the child.

Clinical Premises and Methods

Clinical philosophies and methods vary considerably and range from nondirective approaches in which the therapist maintains a neutral stance and supports the child's unfolding themes (Axline, 1964), to approaches where the therapist directly nurtures the child using food, holding, and so forth (Alpert, 1963; Brody, 1993), to approaches where the therapist considers interpretation her primary task (Freud, 1926/1965; Klein, 1932). More recent work has focused on the value of the interactive play partnership as a springboard for the development of symbolic and social capacities (Greenspan & Wieder, 2006; Slade & Wolf, 1994). Certainly, the avenues of treatment will vary according to the background of the therapist and the need of the child (see Chapter 6). Yet there are some developmental premises that inform therapeutic work with young children and can be discussed apart from the particular method employed.

One such premise is that an individual relationship with a therapist will provide an organizing experience for a young child, whether or not the therapist is active in the play and assumes a role of alter ego or is neutral and reflective in her

manner. The special relationship and the special room that contains it may constitute a psychological home base for children who have been unable to internalize
a primary relationship.

Another important premise is that materials in the therapy room will become
endowed with meaning born of the therapist–child relationship. This will eventually allow the child access to underlying issues and enable the child to share these
issues with the therapist through the use of play metaphor. Once the troublesome
material can be shared or worked on, the child will experience less anxiety and
will be more available for social interaction and learning.

A third premise is that children who are preoccupied with survival issues or
with traumatic experiences will not be able to attend to structured teacher input.
Their energy will be spoken for in the cause of their own survival. In the case of
trauma, children may be tense with the effort of holding overwhelming experiences at bay or may be flooded with intrusive sensory remnants of the traumatic
experience. Therefore, in order to address these children's difficulties, the play
therapy process allows children to attend to their internal preoccupations and dra-
mas before requiring them to take in new information.

Finally, while play therapy technique was traditionally thought to be appropriate only for children whose symbolic processes are well developed, this
author also advocates its use for children who need to build a developmental
bridge from sensorimotor, ritualistic, or idiosyncratic play to a representational
play level.

A Case in Point: Dionne

Dionne was 2 years old when her mother was killed by a stray bullet when they
were entering their project building.

At 2½, when Dionne's pediatrician sent her for intervention, the trauma and
loss were part of her record, but the developmental delays that occasioned the
referral were presumed to be related to Dionne's mother's drug history. Indeed,
Dionne's grandmother spoke sadly of Dionne's unusual and arrested development
during the nursery intake, describing a nonverbal, withdrawn child who rocked
to soothe herself and who had violent outbursts with no obvious provocation.
Dionne did not play with toys and showed little interest in her environment.
Dionne's grandmother initially presented a positive picture of her granddaughter's
life prior to the murder but later acknowledged that she had been worried about
the quality of Dionne's care from the beginning. She told of coming to visit and
finding Dionne dirty and neglected. She feared the neglect might have been a sign
that her daughter had become increasingly involved with drugs.

In the classroom, Dionne was either withdrawn and glued to a tiny rocking
chair or highly anxious and in constant motion. She often panicked if anyone came
to the classroom and stood in the doorway conversing with the teachers, scream-

ing for her grandmother and becoming inconsolable if her screams did not immediately bring Grandma from the parent room.

After some months, Dionne internalized the classroom routine and became slightly less hyperactive, although the panic attacks continued. Her language became more elaborate, and she began to use short sentences as well as single words and phrases. Her play consisted of driven doll-nurturing, which was done in a serious, painstaking, and almost desperate way. The worried, empathic care shown to her baby doll was in sharp contrast to Dionne's demeaning treatment of her own mirror image. She frequently accosted herself in the mirror with angry language. "You're disgustin'," she would yell at her own mirror image. "You're sickenin'."

Dionne's teacher noted that while she became toilet-trained after her first few months at school, Dionne became anxious and hyperverbal while sitting on the toilet, often making odd associations that were difficult to follow.

Dionne's play therapy sessions allowed her to clarify her complex feelings about caretaking, toileting, and mirror play and gave the staff insight into the issues that preoccupied Dionne and took her away from the work of developing her own ego capacities. In addition, the play therapy time provided Dionne a forum for exploring sensitive material related to her loss that may have been disruptive to other children if enacted in the classroom.

The following session recording will help the reader understand how the process of play therapy might unfold with a young child, and how unresolved developmental issues may be reworked when the relationship supports a heightened level of receptivity in the child.

BEGINNING PHASE

Dionne has been in the classroom program for 6 months and has undergone 3 months of treatment. At the moment, she is cooking for her baby. She speaks to the therapist in a demanding tone.

DIONNE: Sit down. You're the daughter. (*softly, to her baby doll*) Here, poo, here your food. You don't want more? Okay. (*She feeds in a very realistic manner, looks up and sees the therapist looking at her.*)
DIONNE: Don't look at me. I told you.
THERAPIST: You don't like me to look at you?
DIONNE (*loud and demanding*): I told you. Eat your food. (*The therapist eats and gives Dionne the empty dish.*) Go to sleep, then, there! (*Dionne points to a pillow on the floor. The therapist pretends to sleep by closing her eyes and lying on the floor. Dionne cuddles her baby and then softly puts her into bed and spends several seconds adjusting her blanket. She catches a glimpse of herself in the mirror.*)

You stupid! (*The therapist opens her eyes and looks up at Dionne.*)
Shut up, you're lookin' again.

THERAPIST: I woke up and I heard you call the mirror of Dionne stupid.
You don't like me to look at you, and you don't like to look at
yourself either.

DIONNE: Shut up.

Two Months Later

Dionne is calling Grandma and several of her cousins on the play telephone,
standing and talking in front of the mirror. She alternates between dialogue
with the party on the other end of the phone and her mirror image.

DIONNE: Hi, how are you doing? Yeah? (*to her mirror image*) You
disgustin'! You fucker, get out of here! (*to the phone*) Grandma, just
a minute. (*She looks at the therapist.*) I gotta pee.

THERAPIST: Okay, tell Grandma you'll be back in a minute. (*Dionne and
the therapist go out to the bathroom, where Dionne announces that
she needs to "doo-doo" as well. She is very ambivalent about the
therapist's presence in the bathroom, screaming, "Go away," but
instantly calling her back the moment she leaves.*)

THERAPIST: You want me to stay with you for the doo-doo, but you're
scared for me to see.

DIONNE: I'm scared. (*She finishes and returns to the room. She sees the
telephone off the hook.*) Oh, Grandma! (*She picks up the phone.*) Hi, I
came back, I didn't do no doo-doo, nope, okay, bye.

THERAPIST: You told Grandma you didn't do a doo-doo, even though you
did. Maybe you're scared for Grandma to know about that.

DIONNE (*very anxious*): I want Grandma, I want Grandma, come on.
[Dionne's grandmother is in the parent's room downstairs.] See
Grandma, see Grandma! (*Dionne starts screaming. She becomes
more and more agitated, and it is close to the end of the session.*)

THERAPIST: Okay, we'll find Grandma. But somehow I think you're scared
that doo-doo will make Grandma go away. (*Dionne pulls the door
open and rushes down the hall with the therapist close behind her.*)

Six Weeks Later

Dionne says nothing. She goes to the baby bed and awakens her baby,
getting several accessories from the shelf, including a brush, a pocket-
book, Pampers, and so forth. She brings it all to the other side of the room
as if she plans to use the closet for a make-believe destination. In passing,
her eye falls on the baby potty that has always been in the room.

THERAPIST: Is your baby big enough to use the potty? (*Dionne abandons her mommy role instantly, drops the doll and other items on the table, and plops herself into the potty seat, giggling.*)

DIONNE: I'm going to pee on myself.

THERAPIST: If you sit down, you feel like you have to pee?

DIONNE: For real, I'm going to pee in this potty. I can?

THERAPIST: You can if you want to; it's up to you.

DIONNE (*pulls her overalls off, sits down, and begins to urinate*): Oh, doo-doo, doo-doo's tryin' to come out, too.

THERAPIST: Do you want to make doo-doo in the potty, too?

DIONNE: It's coming, it's coming out.

THERAPIST: All right, we'll wait for it to come.

(*Dionne watches in amazement as she fills the potty. She becomes anxious about not having toilet paper but accepts tissues from the therapist, and then fixes her clothes. She stands staring at the potty.*)

THERAPIST: Let's take the potty to the bathroom like in the story of "Once upon a Potty." (*This is a story Dionne has often read. The therapist and Dionne do this and carry out the ritual of parting from its content according to the script of the familiar story.*)

DIONNE: I made doo-doo in your room. (*looks at the therapist with disbelief*)

THERAPIST: You made doo-doo in my room, and it was okay. I stayed right here; I didn't go away. (*Dionne shrugs, giggles, and is unsure of what to do next.*)

THERAPIST: Sometimes you play like you're a mommy of a little baby, and you take such good care of her. Sometimes you play the mommy of a bigger daughter, and you get angry and yell. Today you were little. You made doo-doo on the potty like someone very little who's just learning.

DIONNE: Yeah, yeah, I'm a baby, give me a bottle.

(*The session continues with Dionne playing baby and asking the therapist to nurture her.*)

ONE MONTH LATER

Dionne is looking in the mirror. She is always well dressed by her grandmother and seems to be seeing something pleasing to herself today. She smiles but says nothing.

THERAPIST: It looks like the mirror Dionne is looking good today. (*Dionne smiles.*) I've got some paper bags for puppet making. I brought these so we can make a story about Mommy K., Dionne, and

Grandma. (*Dionne looks suspicious. She takes a bag and lets the therapist show her how to make a puppet.*)

DIONNE: Make Grandma.

THERAPIST: Okay, I'll make Grandma and Mommy K., and you make Dionne.

DIONNE (*makes a face on the bag*): That's Tina. [Tina is Dionne's cousin.]

THERAPIST: We're not playing about Tina, only Grandma, Mommy K., and Dionne. You can make two Dionnes, though. Dionne like now, 4 years old, and little Dionne, only 2 years old.

DIONNE: I make little Dionne.

THERAPIST: Let's pretend little Dionne is in her crib, waiting for Mommy K. to change her diaper.

DIONNE: Oooh, she made doo-doo?

THERAPIST: I don't know.

DIONNE: Yep, her did.

THERAPIST: But, remember, little Dionne is only a baby. She doesn't know about the toilet yet. She needs her mommy to help her.

DIONNE: Why her mommy ain't coming?

THERAPIST: I don't know. Dionne needs a new diaper, and Mommy's not coming.

DIONNE (*pointing to little Dionne*): Her disgustin'.

THERAPIST: Maybe you think Mommy didn't come to take care of little Dionne because of the doo-doo. But Grandma says that Mommy K. forgot things sometimes. This time she forgot about little Dionne. Dionne is sad and worried.

DIONNE: She worried. Where's Mommy K.?

SOME WEEKS LATER

The therapist has made a doorway from cardboard to use with the puppets.

DIONNE: What's that?

THERAPIST: We need this to try to understand about what happened to Mommy K.

DIONNE: Mommy K.? No, Mommy Grandma.

THERAPIST: Mommy K. was your mommy, and later after Mommy K. died, Grandma came to take care of you, and now she takes care of you like a mommy.

DIONNE: Mommy Grandma.

THERAPIST (*using puppets*): Look, Dionne and Mommy K. are in the doorway, walking through the door.

DIONNE (*screaming*): No, no! (*She hugs Mommy K.'s puppet.*) No, no, it's blood! (*She is agitated.*)

THERAPIST: The gun went bang and shot Mommy K., and there was blood, and it was so scary for Dionne. Look, some people are coming to call the ambulance to take Mommy K. to the hospital.

DIONNE (*gets the doctor bag*): Her better.

THERAPIST: The doctor tries to make Mommy K. get better, but they can't. It was so sad.

DIONNE: Mommy K. died, but then the doctor made her better, and now she's Grandma.

Clearly, at this point Dionne still has major confusion about the death of her mother and will need to keep working on sorting out her complex emotional experiences. However, play therapy illuminated some of the personal meaning that Dionne had attributed to her loss and allowed her to rework developmental issues that were paralyzing her. She was able to separate past from present enough to feel secure in the school setting, and the panic attacks diminished. As issues of self-image, nurture, autonomy, and loss received more therapeutic attention, they preoccupied Dionne less completely in the classroom setting, and she became a more verbal, more receptive child. Dionne's IQ was 30 points higher when she left the program at age 5 than it was when she entered the program at age 2½.

CONCLUSIONS

When play therapy takes place within the context of the early childhood program, children are able to experience attention to their dependency needs and use relationships to deepen their symbolic capacities. This allows them to use play to resolve difficult developmental and life experience issues, and to do so in the company of an attuned adult who can bear witness to their struggles and their growing integration. Parents may feel relieved to know that their children's emotional difficulties can be addressed in the trusted and familiar school setting. Indeed, given the lack of mental health care options for most young urban children, play therapy made available to preschool students may constitute a powerful form of preventive intervention, giving children a crucial opportunity to heal potentially paralyzing psychological wounds before the heavy doors of elementary school are pulled open.

REFERENCES

Alpert, A. (1963). A special therapeutic technique for prelatency children with a history of deficiency in maternal care. *American Journal of Orthopsychiatry, 33,* 161–182.

Axline, V. (1964). *Dibs: In search of self*. New York: Ballantine.

Bratton, S. C., Ray, D.. Rhine, T., & Jones, L. (2005). The efficacy of play therapy with children: A meta-analytic review of treatment outcomes. *Professional Psychology, Research, and Practice, 36*(4), 376–390.

Brody, V. (1978). Developmental play: A relationship focused program for children. *Journal of Child Welfare, 51*, 591–599.

Brody, V. (1993). *The dialogue of touch*. Treasure Island, FL: Developmental Play Training Associates.

Donovan, D., & McIntyre, D. (1990). *Healing the hurt child*. New York: Norton.

Freud, A. (1965). *Normality and pathology in childhood*. New York: International Universities Press. (Original work published 1926)

Greenspan, S., & Wieder, S. (2006). *Engaging autism*. Cambridge, MA: Da Capo.

Klein, M. (1932). *The psychoanalysis of children*. London: Hogarth.

Koplow, L. (1985). Premature competence in young children, a false declaration of independence. *Beginnings, 2*(3), 8–11.

Mann, D. (1996). *Serious play. Teachers College Record, 97*, 446–469.

Meade, A. (1999, November). *Schema learning, and its possible links to brain development*. Paper presented at a seminar at the Children's Hospital of Michigan, Wayne State University, Detroit, MI.

Pavenstedt, E. (Ed.). (1967). *The drifters*. Boston: Little, Brown.

Siegel, D. J. (1999). *The developing mind: Towards a neurobiology of interpersonal experience*. New York: Guilford.

Slade, A., & Wolf, D. (Eds.). (1994). *Children at play*. New York: Oxford University Press.

Stern, D. (2000). *The interpersonal world of the infant*. New York: Basic Books. (Original work published 1985)

Weil, A. M. (1972, December). *Ego strengthening prior to analysis*. Paper presented at the annual meeting of the American Psychological Association.

Westby, C. (1980). Assessment of cognitive and language abilities through play. *Language, Speech, and Hearing Services in Schools, 11*, 154–168.

Winnicott, D. W. (1977). *The piggle*. London: Penguin.

Winnicott, D. W. (2005). *Playing and reality*. New York: Routledge. (Original work published 1971)

Zelman, A., Samuels, S., & Abrams, D. (1985). I.Q. changes in young children following intensive long term psychotherapeutic intervention. *American Journal of Psychotherapy, 39*(2), 215–227.

CHAPTER 6

Therapeutic Technique: The Tools of Preschools That Heal

Lesley Koplow

TEACHERS AND CLINICIANS who are committed to acknowledging the meaning in children's behaviors face the task of adhering to their psychological principles while managing groups of very difficult children. Therapeutic techniques can be employed not only by individual therapists who are working with children on a deep level but also by teachers and other clinicians who are working on developmental and socialization issues within the group setting. Therapeutic techniques are available to all staff members who work in preschools that heal for use at appropriate moments. These are moments when traditional management strategies and intervention models fall short of what is meaningful for emotionally fragile children.

The therapeutic techniques suggested in this chapter will give the early childhood professional a repertoire of responses that can be used to address emotional and social issues expressed on verbal and nonverbal levels. The techniques will help the teacher or clinician to act effectively and attend to the emotional lives of children within the therapeutic milieu.

THERAPEUTIC LANGUAGE

Therapeutic language is a main vehicle for setting the emotional tone in a therapeutic milieu. Therapeutic language is distinctive in many ways: It is clear, spoken with genuine affect, and does not convey moral judgment. Therapeutic language is spoken with real communicative intent. It is not an exercise in politeness or a request for performance, but a dialogue of meaningful expression. While teachers and clinicians using therapeutic language may want to question a child or group of children during conversations, therapeutic dialogues do not consist of a series of questions from adult to child. Rather, questions are used in conversation as they would be in typical verbal exchanges between adults; one person asks something of the other in order to obtain the other's perspective or needed information.

The examples of therapeutic language in Figure 6.1 may serve to clarify its purpose and demonstrate its use. The examples are juxtaposed with more typical language patterns of preschool personnel in order to contrast therapeutic and traditional language modalities.

Therapeutic language requires fewer questions as initiators of conversation, relying instead on the adult's use of observational comments to help children make emotional and conceptual connections.

REFLECTIVE TECHNIQUE: LANGUAGE AND STORY

Therapeutic language is partially informed by client-centered psychotherapy approaches, which advocate the use of reflective techniques to help clients clarify and connect to their own thoughts and feelings. Reflective techniques can be employed with children on verbal as well as nonverbal levels.

Verbal reflections can range from literal repetition of what the child has said to more selective reflections of content or affect. For example, a child huddles in the cubbies outside of the classroom, refusing to enter. When the teacher tries to coax him in, he says, "I don't want to come to school." They have the following interaction:

TEACHER (*regards child empathically*): Sounds like you didn't want to come to school today.
CHILD: Ana didn't go to school!
TEACHER: Oh! Ana stayed home with Mommy?
CHILD (*nods*): I want to stay with Mommy, too. (*He sounds angry.*)
TEACHER: Ana stayed home and you had to come to school. You sound angry about that. Do you want to write a letter to Mommy to tell her how you feel?
(*The child nods, takes teacher's hand, and enters the room.*)

In this instance, the use of reflective technique helps both teacher and child to clarify the situation at hand. The teacher uses both literal reflection and selective reflection of affect to intervene effectively. The reader will note how readily the child was able to give salient information even though, or perhaps because, the teacher does not demand answers from the child.

FIGURE 6.1 Examples of Therapeutic Language

Situation	Traditional Response	Therapeutic Response
1. One child intentionally hurts another.	"No, Samuel! That's not nice! Why did you do that?"	"No hitting, Samuel. If you're angry at Donna, use words."
2. Child abruptly pinches the teacher.	"Marie! Don't do that! Don't you want to be Ms. Lillian's friend?"	"Ouch! That hurts me. It's not O.K. to pinch. If you're angry, tell me."
3. Several children playing in the sandbox have arranged various colored cups in one corner of the box.	"Oh look! What color cups did you use for your design?" *Children's response:* "Red, blue, yellow..."	"Oh look! You put all different color cups together in the corner." *Children's response:* "That's the fort. Now the bad guys can't come in."
4. Teacher is handing out cookies at snack.	"Miguel, if you want a cookie, say 'please'!"	"Miguel, here's your cookie. Do you want juice?"
If child remains unresponsive to the above:	"Oh well, I guess you don't want any snack today!"	"If you decide you want a cookie, I'll leave it right here for you."
5. Child has wet her pants and is crying. She has never done this before in school.	"Oh Mandy! You know how to use the bathroom! Next time, be a big girl!"	"It's alright Mandy. Kids forget sometimes. Let's go get dry clothes for you."
Mandy's crying escalates as the teacher proceeds to change her.	"Let's sing the new song we learned in circle today."	"Are you worried about what Auntie will say?"
6. One child is left waiting for her bus at the end of the morning. The teacher is waiting with her. The child says, "I'm not coming to school tomorrow!"	"Sure you are! Tomorrow is only Wednesday! Do you know what day comes after Wednesday?"	"Maybe you're worried about being left in school, because it's taking the bus a long time to come."
7. Child has put a large puzzle together independently.	"Good boy!"	"Hey look! You know how to put the whole thing together!"
8. Child is taking playdough from the table and putting it on the rug.	"Why did you put that playdough on the floor?"	"Ronnie, no playdough on the floor. The children might step on it."
9. Child is intent on painting every available space of his piece of easel paper.	"Why don't you start with a new piece of paper, Tyrone? You'll have more room."	"It looks like you really want to cover up all the spaces on your paper!"
10. Children are taking small dolls from the dollhouse and putting them into the back of a play garbage truck.	"Why are you putting those babies in the garbage truck? Don't you want them in the house and cook them a nice dinner?"	"Oh no! The babies are getting thrown into the garbage? Maybe they're crying!"

Another example of reflective technique is demonstrated in the following interaction with a parent who has come in upset. The assistant summons the teacher from the supply closet, as a mother is demanding to know her child's whereabouts and is speaking in a loud and angry voice.

TEACHER: Good morning.

PARENT: Good morning. I would like to know why my daughter came home yesterday with paint all over her clothes.

TEACHER: Well, we did some painting yesterday . . .

PARENT: Well, I can't afford to be letting her ruin her clothes every time you do an art project! It's not like I'm in any position to keep expanding her wardrobe!

TEACHER: You sound really upset. I guess you're thinking that if it happened one time, it can happen again.

PARENT: She might want to paint every day!

TEACHER: She might. Do you have any old shirts that you could send in so that she could put them over her outfits? We do have smocks for the children, but they don't cover their sleeves.

PARENT: Well, I do have some clothes my sister gave me, but they look so raggedy! I don't like to send her to school looking like that!

TEACHER: You like her to look nice when she comes to school. How about if you keep dressing her the way you have been, but send the old clothes to cover her outfits when she paints. Then we just have to figure out how to deal with outdoor playtime! That's when the kids really get dirty!

PARENT: Oh Lord! I guess it doesn't pay to get her too dressed up, does it?

In this interaction, the teacher reflects both affect and content to create a greater degree of receptivity to her suggestions and to help the parent to come to some conclusions about the problem on her own.

Many reflective techniques used with young children are nonverbal. The use of *bibliotherapy* materials in early childhood programs recognizes the power of reflective technique. Bibliotherapy is the classroom use of books with stories that reflect a range of cultural issues, developmental concerns, life experiences, and emotional dilemmas. Reading a book about comings and goings to a group of children experiencing separation anxiety acknowledges the children's concerns as part of human experience. Reading a book about what makes kids feel afraid may be soothing to a group that has just been badly startled by a noise coming from outdoor construction and may promote a more organized behavioral response to the feelings of fear.

While use of available children's literature can be an effective means of reflecting and addressing children's issues, teachers and therapists may want to make books for children in order to address the particulars of their unique issues and circumstances. For example, there are many books about the responses of children to the birth of a sibling. However, when a teacher in a therapeutic nursery became pregnant, the staff decided to make a book that would reflect the issues that faced the children who would be affected by her pregnancy. Using photographs, drawings, and cutouts from magazines as illustrations, they made a book to address the children's concerns as a group.

When a foster child in a preadoptive home was suddenly prevented from visiting her biological mother due to the legal termination of her mother's maternal rights, her teacher and therapist made a book for her about the confusing changes that were occurring.

As young children cannot rely on language alone to clarify abstract and complex issues, reflective techniques that include a visual representation of the content are often highly effective. Books can be made that reflect affective events as well as experiential ones. Teachers may want to identify common issues that the children in their class are concerned with and make books about those issues. Curriculums about affects can be augmented with teacher-made books about things that make the children feel afraid, angry, sad, or worried.

Teachers and clinicians who are interested in employing this therapeutic technique may use the following guidelines in creating their own books:

1. Define the parameters of your topic. Don't include extraneous material.
2. Assess the developmental and language levels of your audience, and reflect that level in your choice of words, storyline, and pictures.
3. Make sure that illustrations or photographs correspond to the content of the page.
4. Use illustrations that reflect personal features of the children's physicality, affects, environment, and cultural identity. Avoid drawing stick people, which may give children confusing feedback about body image.
5. Make sure content reflects or addresses children's developmental reality, experiential reality, or both.
6. Include only one photo or illustration per page to ensure that the group focuses on the desired content.
7. Use oaktag instead of paper to increase durability of the books. Cover the oaktag with clear contact paper or laminate it to prevent tearing or water damage.
8. Secure the pages with notebook rings or large paper fasteners.

Books made by teachers and clinicians can be read to groups as well as individuals; read-alouds should be followed by an open-ended invitation to discuss the content of the story. Teachers can ask the children what they thought about the story or what the story reminded them of. The teacher mentioned earlier read the story about her pregnancy during circle time. When she finished, she left time for the children to respond and followed this with an activity that allowed children to work on their feelings about the subject (see Chapter 9). The teacher then gave the book to the play therapist treating a child who seemed very concerned about the pregnancy topic. The use of the book in the individual session then yielded further information about the meaning of the experience for this particular child.

It is good practice to invite children to make their own books that hold symbols about experiences that are meaningful to them. When teachers allow children to tell their own stories through dictation, drawing, drama, and other ways of creating narrative, they are engaging in a powerful form of intervention. By facilitating this form of self-expression, the teacher is providing the child with a variety of symbolic opportunities to communicate his emotional and actual experience as well as stimulating brain functions that support memory and higher-level thinking (Siegel, 1999). Teachers can also model and invite storytelling about experiences that have affective significance. Studies have shown that young children who have had opportunites to co-construct narratives with their attachment figures are more capable of regulating their emotions and their behaviors (Oppenheim, Nir, Warren, & Emde, 1997).

Finally, the use of mirrors in the early childhood classroom may be considered a form of reflective technique. It is important for young children to learn about themselves and to get feedback about their physical presence, affects, and actions. Mirror play allows children to gather that feedback, both independently as they regard their images changed by the donning of dress-up clothes, or as initiated by the teacher who holds the screaming child before the mirror to remind her that she is still whole.

Techniques That Invite Expression

Teachers often worry that extending open-ended invitations for self-expression will result in anxious, explosive behavior on the part of emotionally troubled children. Learning specific techniques that invite self-expression within a structured context may allow staff to feel more confident about working within this emotional territory.

Opportunities for symbolic play, drawing, painting, and playdough or clay use must be built into the curriculum in preschools that heal. These same activities can also be used to facilitate children's expression regarding particular issues or anxiety-provoking events. While this concept underlies the method of curriculum development advocated in Chapter 9, it is the combined use of therapeutic language, curricular activity, and therapeutic technique that constitutes an integrative force for emotionally fragile children.

Spontaneous drawings are highly valued and well protected in preschools that heal. Teachers may ask the child if there is a story to go with the drawing and write the story down exactly as dictated. She may then mount the drawing or help the child place it in a folder of drawings that he has made. Often, consistent themes will emerge as children draw over time. Staff may learn to recognize the meaning of the metaphors as they become familiar with a child and her concerns. A 4-year-old boy who frequently became lost in fantasy and seemed to be in his own world often drew elaborate under-the-sea drawings, rendering the features of this "other world" in great detail. Other times, metaphors may be unclear to the teacher or clinician. The following exchange, which occurred just after the child had drawn and dictated a story about a mountain—his sixth mountain story that week—helped the teacher to get more information about a child's representation:

TEACHER: You like to draw about mountains.
CHILD: I like a lot of mountains.
TEACHER: Can you tell me more about that?
CHILD: Because when the water's all gone, then you have to go to the mountain so more snow can melt.

There are a number of ways the teacher can chose to respond to this. A teacher in a preschool that heals would go beyond the scientific concepts expressed in the child's comment and assume that it had some particular relevance to him. She might simply acknowledge his comment, reflect the concern about the water being all gone, reflect the positive features of the mountain as a resource, or simply make a mental note of the dialogue in case the child decides to elaborate at a future time. The issues that the child raises can be followed up in more depth if the opportunity arises, but the initial dialogue is valuable whether or not this occurs. The teacher's invitation to elaborate communicates her conviction that the child's expressions are meaningful and important, whether the meaning remains private or is shared. The context of the comment will help the teacher or clinician to understand its relevance. For instance, those close to the child might feel that the metaphor had a distinct message if the child were in the process of being weaned from the breast, was watching an infant sibling begin to nurse, or had suddenly been left in the care of his grandmother due to a serious maternal illness.

By providing children with the tools for self-expression and inviting elaboration, teachers and therapists convey their willingness to listen and to "hold" the child's metaphoric explorations while they are in process, allowing the child to return to these inventions of the mind at intervals to further develop and articulate feelings and thoughts.

Containing Techniques

Allowing emotional life a place in the preschool classroom will feel unsafe to children unless they are secure in the knowledge that the environment is strong enough to contain their feelings. Certainly, the process of addressing emotional issues will feel overwhelming and dangerous to the staff themselves if they feel at a loss to contain emotional responses or to manage emotionally charged behavior.

There are several features of the preschool milieu that serve containing functions. The first is the implementation of stable daily routines. Preschools that heal should take care to protect the children's rights to experience school as a dependable environment. Playtimes, snacktimes, meeting times, and so forth should always occur in spite of an individual child's inability to comply or in spite of a group's disruptive behavior. While preschools that heal are responsive to the individual child's distress and leave room for the expression of inner life in the curriculum, children need to know that the school structures are strong enough to survive their outbursts. Teachers can empathize with the child's distress about some aspects of the routine, but the routine itself should be carried out.

Clinicians who work with children individually should adhere to their treatment schedules and help children anticipate their sessions by using picture charts and other learning aids. While some children are too young to understand the days of the week and cannot organize themselves according to the calendar, if therapists are consistent these children will begin to feel the rhythm of their session patterns. This will help the child to feel more organized and less anxious.

While children need to know that they are not going to destroy the fabric of the school routine, they must also be sure that their relationships with significant adults at school are strong enough to survive angry interactions and tumultuous feelings. Children are ultimately reassured by the adult's ability to be firm and containing as long as the adult is not punitive and does not disconnect from the child in response to difficult behavior. For example, a little boy suddenly decides he had forgotten to paint during playtime and jumps up from the lunch table to retrieve paints from the closet. The teacher tells him that he can paint again tomorrow. The child becomes agitated and begins to pound and kick the latched closet door. The teacher tells him that she knows he is angry but he needs to stop as he is in danger of hurting himself and damaging the door. He is also disrupting the group, which is eating lunch. The child continues to pound and kick. The teacher comes from behind him and holds him, wrapping her arms around his hands and thus immobilizing him.

CHILD: Let go of me! You're hurting me!
TEACHER: I'm not hurting you. I'm holding you. I can't let you pound and kick the door. That's not safe.
CHILD: Let me go!
TEACHER: When you can stop pounding, I'll be able to let you go. Right now I need to hold you.
(*The child attempts to extricate himself, but the teacher's hold is firm. He eventually begins to sob, stops resisting the hold, and turns to cling to the teacher, who provides comfort at that point.*)
TEACHER: It's hard for you at the end of the day. Maybe we can think of a way to make it easier.
(*The little boy leans against the teacher, taking a deep breath, recovering.*)

The teacher's use of a holding technique involved holding the child by sitting or standing behind him and helping to contain his aggression. This helped to facilitate the expression of emotion that was being masked by the boy's driven behavior. The teacher's words were clarifying and supportive and announced her intention to stay with the child through his struggle. If the child's behavior warranted removal from the group because it was too disruptive and was taking a long time to resolve, the teacher or assistant involved with the child during the altercation would have accompanied him into the hallway or other containing space and stayed with him throughout the process.

A teacher who wants to communicate her ability to contain a child should avoid threats to reduce contact with him. For instance, telling the child that he will have to stay at home gives him the message that indeed the teacher is not strong enough to survive his difficult behavior, which he may be likely to escalate in order to test her commitment. Teachers may need to give the following message to difficult children again and again: "I know you're angry with me right now, but I won't let you hurt me. I'm still going to be your teacher, even if you get angry."

Modifying Behavior Modification

Many programs use behavior modification techniques both to motivate learning and to extinguish negative behaviors in preschool children. Programs that routinely use rewards or reinforcers to motivate learning should beware. Evidence shows that continual use of external rewards may interfere with the intrinsic motivation that underlies successful learning in early childhood (Greenspan & Wieder, 2006; Katz, 1985). Children who organize themselves around earning rewards may become less involved in the actual learning activities and processes. Programs that routinely use behavior modification techniques to extinguish negative behaviors may neglect to address the source of the difficulties and may find that the child finds another undesirable means of expressing his or her distress after the target behavior has been extinguished.

Behavioral techniques are sometimes useful in preschools that heal, but they are generally considered ancillary to more developmentally salient approaches. A language therapist may implement a sticker reward system to entice reticent children to participate in language-based activities so that they will ultimately experience themselves as achieving mastery through the treatment process. Once the children can participate in the treatment activities and express pride in their accomplishments, the stickers may be eliminated or used as part of a language routine instead of a reward.

Children who continually hurt others and subsequently disconnect from their aggressive behavior may be good candidates for a "modified" behavior modification program. The goal of this particular system is to increase the child's awareness of her hurtful behavior as well as increasing her awareness of her own socially appropriate behavior. The system involves obtaining a small notebook for the child who is hurting others in which each of her classmates' names are listed. Following periods of the day when the child is at risk for hurting, a teacher takes the child aside and together they recall whether the child has hurt any of her classmates during that period. The child involved must consider each classmate individually and recall her interactions with that classmate. If the child has not been aggressive toward the child being considered, she can put a sticker next to that child's name. If the teacher and child recall that the child involved hurt someone on the list, the teacher explains that because of the hurtful behavior, they cannot put a sticker next to that child's name. A reward can be given either at school or at home if the aggressive child refrains from hurting all of her peers during the schoolday. However, the process of recalling the behaviors and acknowledging her aggressive actions is the essence of the intervention.

Sticker books may help teachers perceive patterns in children's behaviors over time as they look back at a week's worth of stickers. They may then make the child aware of the patterns and offer her alternatives to striking out. For instance, a teacher might say, "Every day, right before cleanup time, you hurt somebody. Today, when it's almost time to cleanup, I'm going to come and find you. Maybe I can help you so you don't hurt anyone." She may have a dialogue with a child such as this one:

TEACHER: Whenever you play near Rhonda, you scratch her.
CHILD: Rhonda took my Barney.
TEACHER: You can tell Rhonda you don't like that, but it's not okay to scratch even if Rhonda takes Barney. Remember, if you scratch, you have to stop playing and leave the classroom. Maybe if you feel like scratching Rhonda, you can say, "Jill! Help me!" and I'll come to help. Can you remember?

The Art of Interpreting

Educational staff members may shy away from using interpretations as a therapeutic technique, feeling that interpreting is the province of the mental health professional. While mental health clinicians are certainly more familiar with the art of interpreting, other psychoeducational staff members may find it to be a useful tool in their intervention repertoires. Indeed, if interpreting is seen primarily as a vehicle for accessing unconscious material, it may be an intimidating prospect for the early childhood educator. Use of interpretations to address deep psychosexual conflicts is clearly the domain of the psychotherapist. However, there are other ways to use interpretations that are appropriate and effective outside of the individual session (Ivey & Authier, 1978). Interpretations are used by teachers and other early childhood staff as a way of reframing the child's experience, a way of increasing the child's insight about his behavior, and a way of elaborating social-emotional cause and effect (Greenspan & Wieder, 2006).

Often interpretations are useful when a child or group of children is highly anxious about an event or an activity but cannot articulate the source of the anxiety. For example, a teacher who was out sick for some time noticed that some of the children who had been the closest to her prior to her absence were maintaining their distance and acting wild and silly when she approached them. She decided to interpret their behavior in light of her absence, saying the following:

TEACHER: I wonder if you got worried when I was sick for so many days. Maybe you thought I wasn't coming back. Now I *am* back, but it's hard for you to come to me. You run around the room when I come to talk to you.

CHILD 1 (*is silent for a moment*): The caterpillars were worried they wouldn't get no food!

TEACHER: Oh! That must have been scary for them!

CHILD 2: My mommy said the doctor wouldn't let you come to school. I'm gonna punch him and throw him in the garbage!

TEACHER: You sound pretty angry about that! Maybe some of the kids thought I stayed home because I didn't want to come to school. Maybe they felt like I was throwing the whole class in the garbage!

CHILD 2: Cocoa [class rabbit] went in the garbage yesterday! (*other children giggle*)

TEACHER: How about if you guys draw me a picture about the things that I missed when I was sick.

The teacher's timely use of interpretative technique helped her to reconnect to the children, whereas reprimanding them for their wild behavior would have reinforced their feelings of rejection.

Another example of a teacher's use of interpretation helped ameliorate a child's difficulties with lunchtime. He had been refusing juice and then grabbing other children's juice and dumping it on the table. Although he had been punished for this behavior several times, he would repeat it if he got the opportunity. This caused havoc, of course, as the other child involved would scream in protest and the spilled juice made a mess on the table.

TEACHER (*takes child out to the hallway*): I don't think you like it when anyone has something to drink. You never want to drink in school, and you don't let the other kids drink either. It seems like when the kids have something to drink, you get angry.

CHILD: I don't get angry, my mommy does. My brother says Mommy's angry because she drinks. That's why she hit me.

The teacher chose to relate this incident to the child's therapist so that she could help him sort out the issue and look more closely at the family situation. Soon he stopped dumping the other kids' drinks and began to drink some water at snacktime.

Interpretations can be offered to children, but never imposed. If interpretations are imposed, children who are not ready to become conscious of the issue at hand may become more defensive and less receptive to intervention.

This distinction makes it important to be aware of the manner in which the interpretation is delivered. When offering an interpretation, the early childhood professional can use several constellations that leave the child room to consider the material presented. Interpretations can be preceded by phrases such as: "Maybe . . ." "I wonder if . . ." "That makes me think about . . ." "Sometimes children . . ." or "It sounds like . . ." These phrases frame the interpretation as something children can either accept, ignore, alter, or elaborate on. The teacher or clinician's voice tone should be genuine, gentle, and supportive. If children reject, deny, or ignore the interpretation, the professional involved can simply stop using the technique or reflect the child's emotional response. She might say, "You don't think so" or "You don't like that idea. Do you have another idea about what happened?"

THE TEACHER'S "PURPLE CRAYON"

For years, children have been intrigued by the story of *Harold and the Purple Crayon* (Johnson, 1955), in which a boy's drawings bring his fantasies to life. While early childhood professionals allow children to represent their fantasies by offering opportunities for them to draw, paint, and sculpt, preschools that heal also train teachers and clinicians to use drawings as an intervention technique when children seem detached from or muddled about their own real and emotional experiences.

For instance, a child may throw a tantrum when he discovers another boy wearing a hat similar to one he has at home. He may become convinced that the other child has somehow acquired his prized possession. The teacher attempts to explain the situation, but the child is too upset to listen and can only be contained and comforted during the tantrum. He shouts at the teacher, whom he perceives as depriving him in the moment. Later, when the tantrum is over, the teacher may invite the child to sit down with her.

TEACHER: Let's make a picture about what happened when you were worried about your hat.

CHILD: I was crying.

TEACHER: Yes. Here, I'll make you crying on the floor, and this is me sitting next to you.

CHILD (*regards with interest*): Make my Mickey Mouse shirt. Now make my pockets.

TEACHER: Okay. Now, look, I'll make Jeremy with an angry face. He was mad because you were trying to take his hat. Look! This is what I was thinking when you were too upset to listen. I was thinking, "This looks just like your hat that you have at home. When you go home, you will see the hat in the closet, and then you will know that there can be two hats." Let's make a picture of the one on Jeremy's head and the one in the closet in your house.

CHILD: Make my house with my own hat inside. Now make me a happy face.

TEACHER: Okay.

CHILD: Tomorrow I'll bring my hat to school.

TEACHER: You can bring it tomorrow so we can see the two hats together. Maybe you'll be able to remember about the two hats, even when it's home and you can't see it.

CHILD: Even in my house.

The teacher's drawing allowed her to bring up the upsetting issue apart from the context of the actual event so that the child could reflect on his perceptions and emotional reactions and take in the adult's intervention while in a more receptive state.

In another situation, the teacher used drawing to help a child connect to emotional responses that had previously seemed difficult for her to access. This little girl became sullen and withdrawn each day when it was time for outdoor play. The teacher managed to coax the child into the play yard, but she would stand silent and motionless in front of the door until it was time to go back inside. One day, the teacher brought paper and crayons to the yard and drew a picture of the girl standing in front of the door looking unhappy. She included details of the child's clothing, hairstyle, and affects. The child looked at the drawing process out of the corner of her eye. She was given the drawing to hold, and she eagerly took it.

The next day the teacher offered to draw again, making a similar drawing and asking the child for input.

TEACHER: Should I make anything else in the picture today?

CHILD (*whispering*): Keys.

TEACHER: Who should have the keys?

CHILD: Me.

TEACHER: Okay. (*draws the child with keys*) There. Now you have keys. Are you worried about not being able to get back inside?

CHILD (*bursts into tears*): If I don't have no keys, I can't find my mommy!

TEACHER (*offering her lap, which the girl accepts*): Oh. You were really worried about Mommy not knowing where to find you when we're outside. Let's write that right here on the picture.

This exchange helped the teacher to understand why outdoor playtime was troubling her student and then allowed her to address the child's separation anxieties, both by getting her a set of play keys to carry outside and by giving the child's mother a tour of the play yard in the child's presence. These measures gave her the security she needed to run and play with the other children during outdoor playtime.

Early childhood professionals may have concerns about using drawing techniques, fearing that they will inhibit the children's own artistic expression, as children may feel that they are unable to produce adequate representations in comparison with the adult model. Indeed, teachers and clinicians who use drawing techniques must be specific with children about when and where adults draw. Adults should avoid drawing directly on a child's paper. Adults should never instruct children in drawing technique or content, as this makes the diagnostic value of children's productions invalid. Children's own spontaneous drawings should be highly valued and well cared for, and children should be invited to articulate their metaphors as they see them. Captions and dictations should be recorded exactly as the child offers them. When used carefully, drawing technique can offer children a model for symbolizing both internal and experiential reality, and can invite instead of inhibit spontaneous expression.

Drawing techniques are valuable for the individual therapist as well as for the classroom teacher. The treatment of preschool children demands that the clinician be creative about the ways of making interventions meaningful to young children. Clinicians who rely solely on verbal modalities may be missing opportunities for deeper communication with children whose capacity for processing abstractions may need help to emerge more fully.

CONCLUSION

The early childhood professional who develops her repertoire of therapeutic techniques will feel more empowered in the presence of emotionally needy children. Children who are fortunate enough to be educated and cared for by staff members comfortable with therapeutic techniques will have many opportunities to process and integrate their experiences throughout the schoolday. They may ultimately become familiar with the techniques themselves and associate relief with selected interventions.

A 4-year-old sat looking sadly out the window following a play session in which he was told of his therapist's coming vacation. His teacher wondered aloud if he might be feeling sad about the therapist being gone for a while. "Say more about that," the child responds with interest.

A 3-year-old girl who had been attacking her teacher during an outburst approached her later in the morning, holding a box of crayons. "Draw me upset," she requested.

These children have learned a most powerful lesson. They have learned that behavior is meaningful and that they can rely on adults in the preschool setting to help them find meaning in their interactions and activities. Therapeutic techniques can assist them in their process of self-discovery.

REFERENCES

Greenspan, S., & Wieder, S. (2006). *Engaging autism.* Cambridge, MA: Da Capo.

Ivey, A., & Authier, J. (1978). *Microcounseling: Innovations in interviewing, counseling, psychotherapy and psychoeducation.* Springfield, Il: Charles C. Thomas.

Johnson, C. (1955). *Harold and the purple crayon.* New York: Harper.

Katz, L. (1985). Dispositions in early childhood education. *ERIC/EECE Bulletin, 18,* 1–3.

Oppenheim, D., Nir., A., Warren, W., & Emde, R. (1997). Emotion regulation in mother–child narrative co-construction: Associations with children's narratives and adaptation. *Developmental Psychology, 33*(2), 284–294.

Siegel, D. J. (1999). *The developing mind: How relationships and the brain interact to shape who we are.* New York: Guilford.

The Meaning of Curriculum

CHAPTER 7

Playing for Keeps: The Value of Open-Ended Play

LESLEY KOPLOW

TRAUMATIZED AND DEVELOPMENTALLY ARRESTED preschool children are often unable to play productively. Prior chapters have included discussion about the developmental evolution of play symbols and the need for play therapy when the language of play does not develop spontaneously. Yet the therapeutic preschool must go beyond the provision of play therapy as a form of individualized early intervention. Preschools that heal must allow a prominent role for play in the classroom.

Typically, high-quality preschool programs for healthy children encourage free play by providing motivating symbolic play materials and by allotting a portion of the day for open-ended activity. In spite of some parental fears about children "just playing" in school, developmentally oriented preschool programs protect the child's right to learn through self-initiated exploration and collective experiences with peers.

Early childhood professionals have protected young children's right to play for years based on their knowledge of child development and their own observations of children playing that have demonstrated its value. Recent research supports our clinical observations and shows that by playing, children activate synapses in their brains that allow them to think in increasingly sophisticated ways, thus improving their potential as learners (Greenspan & Wieder, 2006; Siegel, 1999). Indeed, there is evidence that play improves overall brain capacity in young mammals, who had larger and more developed brains if they played than their counterparts who did not play (Mann, 1996).

People who observe young children at play over time find that most children move through a sequence, initially characterized by isolated play, subsequently

This chapter was a collaborative effort. Anecdotal material was contributed by Virginia Hut, Tania Prybilski, Beverley Dennis, and Judith Ferber.

evolving to parallel play, and eventually moving toward more cooperative play. While the individual player must find a way to use toys to represent his inner world and his experiential reality if he is to move beyond the sensorimotor stage, the cooperative player must employ play metaphors that are meaningful to peers as well as to himself. The well-functioning child uses play as a way to interpret experiences and to integrate concepts, as well as to communicate his understanding to others. Children who lack play skills and play opportunities lack a crucial means of integrating their learning experiences. They are also at a loss for communicating their experiences to peers. Indeed, without play as a tool, these children may appear disorganized and without the capacity to interact constructively. There may be a temptation for the teacher to circumvent the play arena entirely and to develop a curriculum that relies heavily on teacher-directed activity, rote learning, and highly structured interaction routines. Sadly, children in these kinds of early childhood programs may not be able to compensate for their symbolic deficits without help. Integration and communication abilities may remain limited. Preschools that heal assume that play has the same value for traumatized, fragile, or arrested children as it has for healthy children. In fact, the development of symbolic play may be even more crucial for children whose life experience has been confusing and overwhelming, because these children need tools that will allow them to make sense of their experiences. Play becomes a primary avenue for helping these children to accomplish unfinished developmental tasks and to share their triumphs with others in social and growth-promoting ways.

CAUTION: CHILDREN AT PLAY

Teachers attempting to give play a more important role in their classrooms of young, emotionally needy children may want to proceed with caution. They can anticipate that children without well-developed play skills who are not used to open-ended activity may initially be wild, unfocused, or perhaps even destructive. Children who are unrelated or marginally verbal may initially use free playtime to withdraw or to engage in perseverative activity or to enact unusual rituals. Those children who do welcome play opportunities may seem driven to bring up frightening material that intimidates the other children and causes the teacher to watch the clock anxiously for cleanup time.

Certainly, helping nonplayers to play productively in a group requires low adult–child ratios. Children must be able to make contact with adults in order to feel more organized when difficult themes arise, and teachers must feel that they can use their usual management techniques in order to help children socialize and contain their play when necessary. Integrating the therapeutic techniques described in Chapter 6 may help teachers expand their resources and intervene effectively when play requires adult input. However, even when play and interaction are proceeding well, classroom staff are advised to remain present and available during free-play periods. While it may seem tempting to attend to classroom tasks while the children are occupied with one another, the teacher's quiet presence during these times is at least as salient as her more active presence during teacher-directed activities. It is the child's feeling that he is being well cared for and well protected that ultimately allows play to occur (Winnicott, 1971/2005). The teacher's attention, accessibility, and scaffolding may increase the fragile child's potential to engage, stay focused, and develop her play symbols.

Given the difficulties that at-risk children are likely to have during free-play periods and the need for intensive teacher supervision and availability, some readers may wonder whether the value of the interactive play experience is worth the cost. To address that question, this chapter will present a series of play scenes that were documented during free-play hours in a therapeutic nursery serving the populations we have described. Many of the children featured were initially unable to elaborate in play or to sustain playful interactions with others. Their evolving play themes are described here, along with their teacher's interventions and their classmates' responses. Each play anecdote will be preceded by a brief description of the child featured and will be followed by an analysis of the play themes and interactions.

PLAY SCENES

Darryl's Wife

Darryl is a 4-year-old African American boy who lives with his young, single mother. The family lives in a project in a densely populated urban area known for street violence and drug activity. Darryl is an alert, sensitive child with many fears. He was initially unable to allow other children to touch "his" playthings. Therefore, early play sequences took place with teachers only.

SCENE ONE

Darryl, in oversize clothes, pretends to be a daddy.

DARRYL (*in a low voice, barely audible*): I'm the daddy. It's time to go to the corner. . . . Gotta get my jacket.
TEACHER: What should I do?
DARRYL: You the wife. You stay home. You hear? You stay home.
TEACHER: Is there a baby?
DARRYL: Yeah . . . there's a baby. Take care of the baby while I go pick up the package.
TEACHER: What kind of a package are you picking up?
DARRYL: Shut up and take care of the baby. It's none of your business. I got to go to the corner and get the package.

TEACHER: That sounds kind of scary. I wonder if the baby is scared as
well. I'll stay here and keep him safe. (*Teacher cradles baby doll.
Darryl becomes silent and gets absorbed in looking at his mirror
image, which is dressed in the oversized clothes. He repeats his
mission about the package over and over again to his mirror image.*)

DARRYL (*pretending that he is back from his errand, picks up the baby*):
Don't cry. Don't cry. (*He hugs the baby, then suddenly disengages
from the play.*)

SCENE TWO

Darryl approaches the dress-up corner and puts on a policeman's shirt. He
asks the teacher to help him button it.

DARRYL: I'm the cop and you be the boss.

TEACHER: What does the boss do?

DARRYL: You get the bad guys.

TEACHER: Okay. Where are they?

DARRYL: There! Over there! (*points*) They got drugs! Let's go! (*Teacher
and Darryl walk over to where the "bad guys" are.*) Now we take
'em to jail. (*pulls out imaginary gun and aims at the bad guys*)
You're under arrest. Let's go! Get in the cop car. They gotta put their
head down! (*Darryl shoves imaginary perpetrator into car.*) We have
to lock them up. Where's the key? (*At this moment, Cheneka, who
has been watching the play, chimes in.*)

CHENEKA: I know where the key is at!

TEACHER: Maybe Cheneka can be a cop, too, and help lock up the bad
guys.

DARRYL: Yeah! Come on. We got work to do.

CHENEKA (*goes to a toy shelf and gets toy keys*): Here. (*She and Darryl
mime locking the jail doors.*)

DARRYL: C'mon! There's more bad guys! We got a get all of 'em.

SCENE THREE

With some prompting from the teacher, Darryl, Wendy, and Cheneka decide
to play a game of house. Darryl is the daddy, Wendy is the mommy, and
Cheneka wants to be the baby. Wendy spreads a blanket on the floor and sits
there with Cheneka and a collection of baby dolls. Darryl pretends that he is
going to work. He disappears for a few minutes and then returns with three
bags stuffed with play clothing, jewelry, and plastic fruits and vegetables.
Cheneka and Wendy look up at Darryl from their position on the blanket. At
this point, Pierre wanders onto the blanket that has become "home." Pierre

is an autistic child with an infantile level of functioning, and he does not seem aware that he is disrupting something.

DARRYL: I have presents for everyone. . . . I did the shopping.
TEACHER: It looks like Daddy is bringing lots of things for his family. He's taking care of them.
DARRYL: I'm not the daddy—I'm Santa Claus!
WENDY: Ooooh! Santa!
DARRYL (*takes Pierre by the hand and sits him down on the blanket*): He can be the baby, too.
WENDY: Give the baby food!
(*Darryl reaches into one of the bags and pulls out an apple and an orange. He hands one to Pierre and one to Cheneka. Cheneka pretends to eat, and Pierre sits holding his fruit and staring at Cheneka.*)
TEACHER: Look! Santa is feeding the children. They're so happy to get something special from Santa.
(*Darryl puts on a Santa hat from the dress-up corner and begins to give all of his goodies to Wendy, Cheneka, and Pierre. Darryl then carefully takes out the jewelry from his bag and fits necklaces over Wendy's head. She looks at him gleefully. Cheneka is gathering all of her presents into one big pile. Pierre, who seems oblivious to the proceedings at this point, walks away. A few minutes later, Wendy and Cheneka skip off and the play ends.*)

SCENE FOUR

Darryl and Wendy are in the dress-up corner. Wendy dresses up in a silver dress, satin hair ribbons, and a wide, decorative belt. Darryl is watching her closely.

DARRYL (*approaching the teacher*): I want to get married to Wendy.
TEACHER: Did you tell her that?
DARRYL: No, I can't. You tell her.
TEACHER: I'll help you. Wendy! Come here. Darryl wants to play getting married, but he's shy about telling you. Do you want to get married to Darryl in this game? (*Wendy nods.*) Okay. What happens when you get married?
DARRYL: You have to walk, hold hands, and then you kiss the bride.
TEACHER: All right. You can walk down here. Do you want to wear something special? It looks like Wendy is all dressed up. (*Darryl nods, goes to the dress-up corner, and returns wearing a policeman shirt. He asks the teacher for help with buttoning.*) There. You're all ready.

> (*Darryl and Wendy run to the other side of the classroom and then walk slowly, holding hands, over to where the teacher is sitting.*)
> TEACHER: You two are special friends, and now you are married.
> DARRYL: Can I kiss her?
> TEACHER: You have to ask.
> DARRYL: Can I kiss you? (*Wendy nods and Darryl kisses her on the cheek.*)

Darryl's play initially showed preoccupation with adult activity that he had observed but not understood emotionally. Indeed, the play indicates that Darryl's real-life experiences are difficult for him to sort out. His history includes information that several male relatives have been arrested and some imprisoned. Some of these men were present during Darryl's early life, and he felt attached to them. This gives Darryl the task of reconciling what he knows about "good" and "bad" with his need for identification with important people. Play helps Darryl to work on all of this. His ability to symbolize these experiences in play with peers is encouraged so that he does not remain isolated with his conflicts.

Darryl's Santa identity gave him a chance to take a giving, nurturing role that could be integrated with his image of what it is to be male. For a boy who frequently acts out the macho role and refers to himself as being "bad," seeing himself in a different light through play may be very powerful. After this, he is able to express age-appropriate Oedipal desires and "marries" Wendy.

Without the opportunity to engage in free play where these themes could be expressed, Darryl would probably be driven to act out his conflicts through aggressive and ambivalent behaviors toward others. Indeed, this sometimes occurred, but the information that Darryl gave through his play gave teachers valuable insights into the conflicts motivating his behaviors and, therefore, more tools for intervention.

Baby Wendy

Wendy is a 4-year-old foster child whose biological mother's rights have been terminated. Wendy's current foster mother is her third caregiver. Wendy has just been told that her teacher is pregnant and will stay at home to care for the baby when it is born. The teacher has made a book about the baby and the things that it will need as well as the children's possible reactions to the event. After this is discussed in a morning meeting and a group activity has been devoted to a "baby" curriculum, there is a period of free play, during which Wendy climbs up to reach an apron in the teacher's closet. She often likes to wear this to play the mommy.

> TEACHER: Are you going to play Mommy today?
> WENDY: No. You. (*She fits the apron over the teacher's head.*) I want to get in there (*pointing to the front pocket on the apron*).

TEACHER: Oh! It looks like you'd like to be like a baby inside of the mommy.

(*Wendy nods. She silently evaluates the space in the pocket and concludes that she cannot fit. Then she realizes that she can crawl under the apron, making the apron protrude like it would if the teacher were pregnant with her.*)

TEACHER: Oh, look! (*She is now seated in a rolling chair with Wendy in her lap under her apron.*) It looks like I will soon have a little baby! (*Wendy emerges, crying like an infant; she crawls up on the teacher's lap and lets herself be held like an infant.*)

WENDY: I want a bottle! I want a diaper!

TEACHER: You're thinking of all the things that the story said about what the baby will need when it comes out.

WENDY: I'm a baby, too.

TEACHER: You want to make sure that we take care of baby Wendy even after the new baby comes.

Open-ended play following the teacher's disclosure allowed Wendy to express her need for nurture as well as her competitive feelings about the teacher's baby. This opportunity was particularly important for Wendy, who had lost contact with her own mother and was often preoccupied by abandonment issues. The play about being inside and being born to someone responsive allowed Wendy to experience something precious even as she begins to deal with the loss of her departing teacher.

Bianca's Elevator

Bianca is a 4-year-old girl who is living in her second foster home. She has an ambivalent relationship with her second foster mother, who is a distant relative. The family lives in a crime-ridden and neglected housing project. Bianca often plays with her friend Juan at free playtime.

JUAN: Is this your house?

BIANCA: No, it's the elevator. Come in quick! The door is closing!

JUAN: We going up?

BIANCA: Oh, shit! We're stuck! Mommy's not here! We're stuck!

JUAN: Let's get out.

BIANCA: We can't. We're stuck. The door can't open and Mommy's not here! (*Bianca is becoming distressed.*)

TEACHER: That must be scary for you to be in a stuck elevator without Mommy! What can we do?

BIANCA: Get the firemen to fix it.

JUAN: Yeah! The firemen!

> BIANCA: Get me the phone! (*Teacher hands it to her.*) Hello, fireman?
> Help! We're stuck in the elevator!
> TEACHER (*picks up other toy phone*): Hello! I'm the fireman. It must be
> scary for you to be stuck in the elevator without your mommy, but
> I'm coming to help you right now!
> BIANCA (*smiles at Juan*): It's okay. The fireman is coming.
> (*After the children are "rescued" from the elevator, they continue their
> play by pretending to be the firemen helping needy dolls.*)

Bianca independently initiated this dramatic play scenario during free play with the cooperation of Juan. He seemed to identify with Bianca's play theme. Bianca began to reenact a recent experience of being stuck in a broken elevator in her building while also addressing a general concern about "who is going to keep me safe." Bianca did not require teacher intervention to initiate or organize her play, although the teacher's presence and participation helped Bianca avoid traumatic play where she is driven to keep repeating the frightening event without resolution.

Peter's Job Search

Peter is a 3-year-old boy with a language disorder. His parents are both professionals, but his father has recently had a change in his employment status. Peter and Bianca have decided to play house; Peter is the daddy and Bianca is the mommy.

> BIANCA: Let's make a house.
> PETER: Okay. I can help.
> BIANCA: I'm the mommy. Get the dress and the shoes.
> PETER: I'm Daddy. (*He puts on the hat and the coat and sits in a corner
> of the classroom looking sad.*)
> BIANCA: Why are you sad, Daddy?
> PETER: Daddy sad. Daddy sad.
> BIANCA: Did you get spanked?
> PETER: No. My job is lost. I can't find it.
> BIANCA: Your job is lost?
> PETER: Yes. I'm sad. I lost my job.
> BIANCA: Come on. I'll help you find it.
> (*Both children go off hand in hand in search of the lost job. They look
> around the classroom.*)
> BIANCA: I found it!
> PETER: No. Not that one.
> BIANCA (*smiling hopefully and holding up the doctor kit*): Is this your job?
> PETER: Yeah! That's my job! Daddy's happy now.

Peter is able to use dramatic play to represent complex issues, such as unemployment and despondency, that had recently been part of his familial experience. His limited expressive language would have prevented him from exploring these issues if he had had to rely solely on verbal means. He required no adult intervention in this play but used the cooperation and support of a peer to help him bring the play to resolution.

Michael's Monster

Michael is a 4-year-old boy who was referred by his Head Start program because he alternately terrified other children or screamed in terror for no apparent reason. His early life was spent on the street with a drug-addicted parent. Michael currently lives with his great-grandmother, who lives in a community plagued by violence.

SCENE ONE

Michael is running around the room making monster noises and causing the other children to scream in terror. The teacher intervenes.

TEACHER: That's too scary, Michael!
MICHAEL: No it ain't. I'm Freddy Kruger.
TEACHER: Freddy Kruger is too scary for the children.
MICHAEL: You be Freddy. You chase me and I'll scream.
TEACHER: It would be really scary if I were Freddy.
MICHAEL: No, it won't. I'm not a baby.
TEACHER: No, you're 4 years old. Maybe you'd like to pretend to be a baby who is afraid of Freddy. I can be the teacher and tell Freddy to go away.
MICHAEL (*looks intrigued, then curls up in a ball near the doll bed*): Waaaa! Waaa! Freddy's comin'!
TEACHER: It's okay, baby. I'm right here. I won't let Freddy Kruger hurt you.
MICHAEL: Say, "Go away!"
TEACHER: Go away, Freddy! Leave the baby alone. He's so little. He just wants to play!
MICHAEL: Give me somethin' to play with.
TEACHER: How about . . . this? (*hands Michael a set of nesting cups*)
MICHAEL: How about a gun?
TEACHER: No. That's too scary for a baby.
MICHAEL: All right. Give me those, then.

SCENE TWO

Michael, playing now with Adam, pretends that the "monster" has returned.

MICHAEL (*to Adam*): I think Freddy's comin' back.
TEACHER: Are you two pretending to be babies who are scared of
     Freddy?
MICHAEL: No. I'm Freddy. He goin' to be the baby.
TEACHER: No. Children can't be Freddy at school. It's too scary.
ADAM: We could be on television!
MICHAEL: Okay.
TEACHER: You could pretend to be on television but remember—no
     Freddy.
MICHAEL: We on TV and we the TV babies. Come on, Adam. (*They hide
     under a blanket, giggling. Then they start screaming.*)
TEACHER: What's happening to the TV babies?
MICHAEL: They see Freddy Kruger comin'.
TEACHER: Uh-oh. Who's gonna help them?
ADAM: Just turn it off. They're on TV. Okay?
MICHAEL: No! The TV lady has to come in and then take them away from
     here.
TEACHER: Okay. I'll be the TV lady. Come on, babies. Let's go. This
     show is too scary. (*Michael and Adam crawl away, still under the
     blanket, giggling.*)

Michael's spontaneous play was aggressive and terrified the other children. The
teacher's intervention helped him to abandon his identification with the aggressor and play out his own scared feelings, allowing him to receive comfort. Once
the rules about monster play were set, Michael felt safe enough to include another
child in his play. If monster play was simply outlawed, Michael might have lacked
an avenue for symbolizing his inner terror, and wild, aggressive behavior might
have continued to dominate peer interactions.

Ana's Doughnuts

Ana is a 3-year-old autistic girl whose play initially consisted of wandering around
the room and dumping toys. She frequently stayed on the periphery of the room,
tapping the wall with her fingers and repeating the names of television characters.

SCENE ONE

The teacher sits down at the playdough table in an effort to engage Ana in play.

ANA: That's Bert and Ernie. No, McDonald's. Later McDonald's . . . Bert
     and Ernie Good Night. No playdough.
TEACHER (*continues to play with the playdough herself*): Ana says "no
     playdough," but Peggy wants playdough. Look, cookies!

ANA: No cookies. Dunkin' Donuts. Time to make the doughnuts.

TEACHER: Okay. I'll make doughnuts with playdough. Look. (*Ana watches with interest as the teacher fashions the dough into doughnut shapes.*)

ANA: Two Dunkin' Donuts.

TEACHER (*makes another one*): See? I made two Dunkin' Donuts. We can make things with playdough. (*Ana giggles and skips away.*)

SCENE TWO

Ana is compulsively tapping shelves and walls and calling out in an unrelated manner. The teacher joins her in a reciprocal tapping game and then attempts to engage Ana.

TEACHER: Okay. Let's finish tapping and play with playdough. (*She gets the dough.*)

ANA (*with excitement*): Time to make the doughnuts!

TEACHER: Okay. I'll make doughnuts for Ana and doughnuts for Peggy.

ANA: No Ana. Bert.

TEACHER: Bert? Bert's not here.

ANA: Bert and Ernie. No Ana.

TEACHER: Okay. Let's make Bert and Ernie. Then we can give them doughnuts. (*She begins making Bert and Ernie from dough and articulates the process.*) Here's Bert's face, hair, . . . (*Ana watches, transfixed.*) There! That's Bert. Here's a doughnut for Bert. (*Ana silently hands teacher another clump of dough.*) What's that for?

ANA: Ernie.

SCENE THREE

The teacher and Ana are playing with playdough and have made Bert and Ernie eating doughnuts at Ana's request.

TEACHER (*mimes feeding a doughnut to Bert*): Hey, this tastes yucky!

ANA (*laughing*): Yucky!

TEACHER (*repeats the mime with Ernie*): This tastes good!

ANA: No good! Yucky!

SCENE FOUR

Ana is at the playdough table seated next to 4-year-old Raymond, a verbal and volatile child, and Jocelyn, a needy, demanding child. Jocelyn is trying to hoard all of the playdough, and Raymond is protesting loudly.

Ana is singing and tapping and seems oblivious to what's going on. The teacher intervenes and gives each child an equal amount of dough. Jocelyn begins eating pieces of the playdough.

RAYMOND (*pointing at Jocelyn*): Ewww! Look!
ANA (*looks and notices Jocelyn's activity; she becomes excited and animated*): Yucky! (*She begins flapping her hands.*)
JOCELYN AND RAYMOND (*laughing*): Yucky!
ANA: Yucky doughnuts!
JOCELYN: This ain't no doughnut. This is peanut butter.
ANA: No peanut butter. Doughnuts.
RAYMOND: I got doughnuts in mines. You want some?
ANA (*beaming*): Ernie! (*She calls out as if intending to engage the teacher, but the teacher is occupied elsewhere. Ana takes a clump of dough and presses it flat, pinching small pieces off and whispering.*) Ernie's nose. Ernie's eyes. . . .
(*Jocelyn and Raymond look on with interest. Jocelyn finally grabs the clay and Ana runs to the other side of the room to play with the xylophone.*)

Ana's teacher used Ana's autistic interest in television characters to entice Ana into representational play with playdough. Her ability to develop a play routine with the dough allowed Ana to make a meaningful play connection with her peers.

Natalie's Rabbit

Natalie is an extremely intelligent 3-year-old child who has developed minimal social skills and rarely interacts with peers. She is fearful and frequently aggressive. One morning a visitor arrives at school to observe the class.

NATALIE: Get out of my class. (*She picks up a small doll house and tries to hurl it at the intruder.*)
TEACHER (*stopping her*): Maybe you're worried because there's a new person in the class today and you don't know her. It's okay. She's not going to hurt you.
NATALIE: I don't like her. I don't want her here. I'm going to cut her up with a scissors.
TEACHER: It's scary for you when someone new comes into the class. Maybe we could make something from playdough that also feels afraid when we have visitors.
NATALIE: Yes. I'm going to make a very scared rabbit. He is scared and doesn't like her either. Now she should leave our room.

TEACHER: It's scary for the rabbit to have a stranger in the classroom. What can we do to make him feel safe?

NATALIE: I'm going to build a safe house for him to hide in! (*She works intently on building a playdough house, intermittently looking over at the visitor. She places the rabbit carefully inside the house.*)

TEACHER: Maybe the rabbit can ask the visitor her name and what she is doing in our class.

NATALIE: I'll ask. (*looking at the visitor*) Why are you in my class?

VISITOR: I wanted to see what the children do in your school.

NATALIE (*continues putting finishing touches on the playdough house, then looks back to the visitor*): Do you like rabbits?

VISITOR: Yes! I like rabbits.

NATALIE (*brings dough over and gives the visitor a handful*): Make another one. (*Natalie retrieves her rabbit from the house and the two rabbits interact cautiously.*)

Natalie's overwhelming stranger anxiety and sense of vulnerability was masked by her aggressive behavior. Her teacher helped her to connect with and express her anxiety through play, lessening her need to attack the visitor and promoting a dialogue with her.

Peter's Crocodile

Peter is a 3-year-old boy with a developmental language disorder and difficulty with impulse control. This play took place following a 2-week school vacation, and began with Peter sitting at a table feeding the toy crocodile puppet a diet of assorted animals, wooden pegs, and playdough.

PETER: Yum!

TEACHER: It looks like the crocodile is hungry.

PETER (*in deep crocodile voice*): I want lots! (*Peter makes the crocodile gobble everything on the table and then come toward the teacher.*)

TEACHER: Uh-oh. He ate the pegs and the animals, and now he's eating me!

PETER: Yum yum. I'm gonna eat you up.

TEACHER: Maybe you want to make sure I'm inside you, crocodile.

(*Peter makes the crocodile accelerate his eating behavior and become somewhat ferocious. He "bites" the teacher several times.*)

TEACHER: I think the crocodile is angry, too. Maybe you are thinking about the vacation. Maybe you wanted us to be here and we weren't and that made you angry and hungry!

PETER: You went to the doctor and you got a shot and you died.

TEACHER: You were worried that we died and could never come back?

PETER: Yes.

TEACHER: That must have made the vacation hard for you. Now you came back and we came back, too. That's what happens on vacations. (*The crocodile stops eating and goes to sleep.*)

Peter's teacher recognized that his eating play was an important expression of his feelings regarding the break from school. She used therapeutic techniques that allowed Peter to communicate his worries and thus lessen the need to act out because of them.

Sarah's House

Sarah is a 3-year-old girl who has lived with her sisters and great-aunt for all of her life. The court has decided that she will be returned to the custody of her father and her sisters will remain with her great-aunt. During free playtime Sarah went to the toy shelves and pulled out a bin of miniature people. She then dragged a large, two-story doll house to the center of the room. She took dolls out of the bin and named them, using the names of her sisters, herself, her father, her father's girlfriend, her great-aunt, and her great-aunt's boyfriend. The teacher was setting up an easel nearby and heard the names; she decided to make herself available to Sarah by sitting close to her but not interfering.

SARAH: There's Daddy, Auntie, Kiki, Dee. . . . There's Auntie, Sarah, Dee, Daddy, Kiki. . . . There's Dee, Auntie, Sarah. . . . (*Suddenly, Sarah grabs handfuls of dolls and stuffs them into the dollhouse together.*)

TEACHER: It looks like you want all the people in the family to stay together.

SARAH (*sighing with relief and settling against the teacher*): Read me a story.

Sarah is powerless to change her family situation or make decisions about her living arrangements. However, her ability to use free playtime to represent her needs shows resilience, and her teacher's ability to validate her wishes promotes connection and receptivity.

Anita's Doctor

Anita is a 3½-year-old girl who is overidentified with fantasy characters but lacks the symbolic play skills necessary for elaborating her fantasy play. Peter is the 3-year-old boy who was described earlier. Their play started with Anita alone in the dress-up corner. She put on a gold lamé dress, high-heeled shoes, a shower cap, and some beads. Then she wandered around the room with a distant look in her eyes, occasionally pausing to admire herself in the mirror.

TEACHER: Anita, who are you pretending to be?
ANITA: Cinderella!
TEACHER: Oh! I see you're wearing a beautiful dress.
ANITA: And shoes! (*She lifts her dress up to show the shoes.*)
TEACHER: And a necklace, too.
ANITA: I Cinderella. (*She wanders off, talking softly to herself. The teacher can hear fragments of a dialogue not meant to be shared. Some minutes later, the teacher notices Anita is still wandering and talking to herself.*)
TEACHER: Are you still being Cinderella? What is Cinderella doing?
ANITA: Go to the ball.
TEACHER: Okay. Should we make a castle for the ball? (*Anita does not reply.*) Anita?
ANITA: Shut up. Leave me alone. (*She walks off in a huff and resumes her wandering and mumbling.*)
PETER: I got no one to play with.
TEACHER: Maybe you could see what Anita is playing.
PETER (*joining Anita*): Hey. What you doing?
ANITA: Cinderella.
PETER: Oh, you are silly. (*He puts on some policeman clothes and sunglasses.*) Look. I'm police.
ANITA: You police? You silly. I wanna play police. (*She removes her outfit and puts on a jacket, hat, and sunglasses.*) Look, I police, too!
(*The two children stand side by side and giggle as they watch themselves in the mirror. Peter notices the reflection of the doctor toys in the cubby behind him. He turns and exchanges the police hat for a white doctor hat and picks up the red doctor kit.*)
PETER: Now I the doctor. You be sick, Anita. Good idea! Cough!
ANITA (*complies*): I need a blanket! (*She is covered by the teacher. Peter carefully listens to Anita's heart and takes her blood pressure. He gives her some medicine as well.*) I better. Now the baby's sick.
PETER: Oh! The baby sick! He got to go to the hospital!
ANITA: Give him a shot!
PETER: Okay. I give the baby a big shot.
ANITA: Waaa! Waaaa!

Both of these children have a limited play and language repertoire and need help to extend their play themes. When the teacher brings them together, they are able to help each other to develop themes at a level more typical for 2- to 3-year-olds.

Like younger children, they light on several themes before they can find one that is truly salient to them. Eventually, doctor play organizes them enough to develop a more elaborate play dialogue. This seems like a natural play theme for two children who still lack an age-appropriate sense of body integrity. This experience of developing and sharing play content with a peer promotes relatedness for these two children and allows them to build a foundation for more advanced play schemes.

CONCLUSION

A free-play period gives preschool children an opportunity to address developmental and experiential issues through their play themes. Children engaged in spontaneous play with peers and teachers are actively working on integrating experiences and communicating these experiences to others. By playing, the children increase their ability to connect and interact with one another and decrease their risk for remaining emotionally isolated with overwhelming emotional experience. Since many fragile children seem initially to be limited in their capacity to integrate and communicate, the evolution of these play capacities may greatly improve their prognosis for emotional well-being and learning potential.

Healthy children thrive if given the provision of time and space for open-ended play. However, the mere allotment of playtime is seldom enough to ensure productive play for emotionally fragile children. Teachers must make themselves available so that they can respond to children's play needs when appropriate, facilitate interactions with peers in play sequences, and help to organize children at times when they are unable to organize themselves. The reader will notice that the teachers described often used the therapeutic techniques explained in Chapter 6 in order to facilitate meaningful play. These techniques may help teachers feel more resourceful when children's play themes include drug pick-ups and police arrests, as well as job searches and doughnut making.

How can the reader analyze the learning that occurred in these play anecdotes? Indeed, the learning is not quantifiable and cannot be charted on a skill chart. Yet it is learning that can never be forgotten or discarded when the play period ends. Once children are able to use symbolic play as a means of representing their experiences and connecting with one another, their minds keep growing and are no longer completely reliant on an adult for moment-to-moment direction. Players develop their own learning agendas.

These themes that came from the children in the sequences above included themes born of their experiences as well as themes salient to developmental issues that still seemed to require negotiation. The themes that come from open-ended play must be noted by the preschool teacher, because they include the children's own learning agendas. These agendas constitute the basis for the development of the curricular themes elaborated in Chapter 8.

REFERENCES

Greenspan, S., & Wieder, S. (2006). *Engaging autism.* Cambridge, MA: Da Capo.

Mann, D. (1996), Serious play. *Teachers College Record, 97,* pp. 446–469.

Siegel, D. J. (1999). *The developing mind: How relationships and the brain interact to shape who we are.* New York: Guilford.

Winnicott, D. W. (2005). *Playing and reality.* London: Tavistock. (Original work published 1971)

CHAPTER 8

Affect Meets Cognition: Building a Curricular Bridge

LESLEY KOPLOW, VIRGINIA HUT, AND JUDITH FERBER

THE THERAPEUTIC CURRICULUM is an indispensable feature of preschools that heal. While a predictable schedule, open-ended play periods, and relationship-oriented teacher–child interactions are all essential components of the therapeutic preschool, the content of curriculum itself must be meaningful and highly motivating in order to promote ego development in at-risk children. Certainly, curriculum must meet the preschool child's need for stimulation and mastery. A therapeutic curriculum must also allow children at various cognitive levels to address unresolved developmental issues that are precursors to academic learning.

A therapeutic curriculum, also called an emotionally responsive curriculum (Koplow, 2002), is distinctive from a conventional curriculum in many ways. It is designed to help children bridge the gap between their internal and external worlds. On the one hand, progressive early childhood educators may have evolved curriculums that correspond to the demonstrated interests of well-developing preschool children, but teachers may have difficulty applying these curriculums to students who seem highly disorganized and dependent on teacher input. On the other hand, more structured, conventional curriculums tend to emphasize the accomplishment of specific tasks without regard for the child's own agenda. This often requires children to detach from compelling internal experience in order to focus on external inputs. When children are unable to do this, it is frustrating for children and teachers alike. For example, a separation-anxious child who cries throughout the teacher's lesson loses access to her ability to learn and is disruptive to the group.

A therapeutic curriculum does not leave learning completely in the hands of needy and fragmented children, nor does it encourage children to abandon their inner experience for the purpose of maintaining an external focus. Rather, a therapeutic curriculum seeks to strengthen the connection between affective and cognitive domains, helping the child to make sense of her own experiences as a basis for broader conceptual development.

EMBARKING ON A THERAPEUTIC CURRICULUM

Where does a teacher begin if she wants to embark on a therapeutic curriculum? The answer is threefold: First, she looks at the themes expressed in the children's spontaneous play; then she looks at the children's behaviors for manifestations of unresolved developmental issues; finally, she looks at the children's life experiences. An in-depth exploration of each of these areas will clarify the purpose of the teacher's threefold inquiry.

Spontaneous Play Themes

In Chapter 7, several play scenes involving emotionally fragile preschool children are recorded. A myriad of themes unfold in these anecdotal accounts, giving us insights into both the developmental and environmental realities of the participating children. For example, it is likely that Darryl had some real experience with adults purchasing drugs and some firsthand opportunities to see police at work. Most likely, Peter's father had lost his job or had feared losing it. It is probable that Bianca had a frightening experience in a stuck elevator. As these and other themes repeat themselves in the children's spontaneous play, the teacher makes note of the children's apparent interest in the topics. She looks at these specific, experientially motivated themes in the context of a broad range of compelling play material. For instance, while Bianca is the only child playing about problems with the elevator, several of the children are playing about themes related to breaking and fixing or injury and healing. The use of spontaneous play to express concern with themes regarding injury indicates receptivity to curriculums focusing on this theme. Indeed, injury is a developmentally salient theme for young children who are preoccupied with their own body integrity during the toddler period.

If the teacher concludes that Bianca's emphasis in her play scene was the experience of being alone in the elevator and thus separated from her adult caregiver, certainly a curricular theme organized around separation issues will be relevant to Bianca as well as to many of her peers. Separation issues are expressed in many of the recorded play scenarios and are clearly important to every child's developmental process. Children who are preoccupied with this issue will be able to attend to a curriculum that focuses on and allows them to master their worries.

Behavioral Clues

In Chapter 1, the essential developmental tasks of early childhood were reviewed. Issues of body integrity were seen to be paramount for the toddler, who must struggle to achieve a sense of whole self in a context that includes separation from his own body products, the intrusion of piercing vaccination needles, and the snipping of the barber's scissors. The toddler's sense of self-constancy is easily threatened. A broken toy may bring sobs of despair, expressing the child's conviction that what is lost or broken can never be repaired, or it may be handed silently to the adult in the belief that she possesses the magic necessary to bring even the wilted balloon back to life.

Developmentally arrested preschool children show many behaviors indicating difficulty with body integrity in the school setting. One child may scream when she sees a doll whose plastic arm has come off, as if this indicates that her own arm may also be severed or lost. Another child may seem to break things compulsively, disassembling whatever crosses his path and destroying his own products when they are close to completion. Another child may need to assemble toys compulsively, seemingly unable to relax until every hole is filled with a peg and every piece of train track is joined with another. He then may become inconsolable if he suffers even a minor injury from a fall or an altercation with another child. All of these behaviors indicate that issues of body integrity and self-constancy are still unresolved in these children. A curriculum addressing these unresolved developmental issues would then be in order.

Consider those children whose separation reactions remain extreme long after the usual "phase-in" period has passed. There are always children who scream as though they fear the temporary separation from parents will be permanent. They seem to experience a daily abandonment in preschool, while other children may feel empowered by the caregiver's confident goodbye. There are children who become so distraught that they vomit or fall asleep to seek refuge from intolerable feelings. There are also children who cannot acknowledge separation at the time of goodbye but never seem to be able to invest in the school environment. They remain silent, physically constricted, and seemingly preoccupied until their reunion with parents at the end of the schoolday. A curriculum addressing separation issues would be logical for a group of children with these behaviors.

Often, teachers analyzing children's behaviors focus on antisocial behaviors and the many ways that children find to act out within the group. Traditionally, analysts have seen acting-out behavior as a way of avoiding feelings. Children who act out are discharging or "getting rid of" emotions that are unwanted and overpowering. Instead of owning and experiencing their own sad, angry, and fearful feelings, children often act in ways that evoke these feelings in the other. Indeed, antisocial and destructive behaviors are important to understand, as their impact on the milieu is strong. Children who act out in intrusive ways may prevent other children from feeling safe in the school environment.

Traumatized and developmentally arrested children frequently lack the emotional foundation for experiencing a healthy range of feeling responses. They rarely possess the resources necessary for spontaneously expressing strong emotions in acceptable ways. They may hit another child if irritated by competition for the same toy, throw toys in anger when the teacher announces cleanup time, preemptively attack a peer whom they fear, or smash their own wood collage to the ground before the unkind words of an older brother destroys its worth. While examples of acting-out behaviors are infinite and could fill an entire chapter of a book, all examples can be seen as an indication that children need more help to tolerate their feelings, to understand emotional cause and effect, and to express their affects clearly. Therefore, curriculums focusing on identifying affects, predicting emotional responses, and expressing feelings through language, play, and drawing are appropriate for groups containing many acting-out children.

Valuing Psychosocial History

Psychosocial histories indicated that several of the children had experiences involving injury either to self or someone considered essential to their well-being. The teacher's access to this important common experience allows her to integrate body integrity themes into her curriculum plan and to design caregiving routines for the children that support a sense of physical as well as emotional well-being. Many teachers lack access to children's psychosocial stories because their preschools do not have a structure for the kind of parent meetings that facilitate sharing on that level. While mental health staff or consultants may have interviewed parents and have valuable information that could inform the teacher's practice, issues of confidentiality may prevent them from sharing what they know. Teachers and clinicians need to collaborate in order to hold the histories of young, fragile children and need to work together to use their knowledge to enable growth and learning in the classroom. Teachers and directors may want to organize "Story Gathering Days" to invite parents to tell their children's important life stories directly to their child's teacher (Koplow, 2002).

Strengths and Abilities

There are many ways that emotionally fragile children are atypical when compared to their agemates, but there are also many ways in which they demonstrate age-appropriate interests and abilities. For example, Darryl's preoccupation with street violence made him anxious, aggressive, and hypervigilant at school, yet it did not prevent him from developing an interest in "marrying" Wendy. "Marriage" play frequently emerges in groups of well-functioning 4- and 5-year-olds who are overflowing with Oedipal interests. Ana's autism limited her social behavior and made her communication idiosyncratic, but her ability to follow recipe charts during cooking activities was impressive.

These children's age-appropriate strengths and interests can and should be employed to explore early developmental issues through the curriculum. While body integrity may be an issue that is usually paramount in toddlerhood, the curriculums addressing body integrity may involve age-level concepts—such as

breaking and fixing, whole and part—that would be unavailable to the young toddler. The theme may generate discussions of cause and effect, "science-type"
experiments, and sequential learning activities that would be beyond the level of
most children under the age of 3.

The fact that the emotionally fragile preschool child may be able to use art
and collage materials constructively and creatively will enable participation in
complex projects that not only foster mastery of the curricular theme but also
provide the experience of being successful with a variety of materials and activities. Without the organizing influence of the therapeutic curriculum, the child might
be unlikely to discover her own capacities and talents.

THE ABCs OF THERAPEUTIC CURRICULUM

After the teacher completes the threefold inquiry previously discussed, she is ready
to choose a theme that will address the difficulties she observes. She then designs
a series of activities that incorporate the children's strengths and allows them to
work on the designated theme during various periods of the day (see Chapter 9).
Often themes are introduced at the morning meeting via song and story. A group
activity elaborating on the theme follows. Subsequently, materials that are particularly relevant to the explored theme are added to the usual selection of materials available at free play and outdoor playtime.

Curricular themes are generally planned to be carried out over the course of a
week, although some themes may require more time to be sufficiently explored.
Often, teachers may decide to rework a theme when a renewed sense of concern is
expressed by the group or when events occur that give a theme particular relevancy.

The assessment of a theme-based curriculum is made on the evidence that
children have retained and internalized the material presented. Evidence of integration is sought in the children's own spontaneous play, language, drawing, and
social behavior. Therefore, evidence of a successful separation curriculum may
be seen in a lessening of anxiety during arrival and dismissal, or in a separation-
anxious child's newfound ability to play about comings and goings, or in an aso-
cial child's spontaneous conversation with a peer about a baby kangaroo's sadness
as he watches his mother hop away.

DEVELOPING EARLY-LEVEL CURRICULUMS

This section will take the reader through the process of developing therapeutic
curriculums. The initial examples will focus on the development of curriculums
for children who are functioning on an early level. The teacher's attention to the
children's expression of developmentally relevant issues through spontaneous play

and behavior will be illustrated. The teacher's process of organizing and presenting themes related to the issues expressed will be demonstrated in the anecdotal material.

"Go Away–Come Back": Handling Routine Separations

Observations. It is 9:30 A.M. and Miranda, a 3-year-old girl, enters the gross motor play area. She covers her face with her hands and refuses to interact with other children. As the teacher moves closer to her, she can hear Miranda repeating to herself, "See Mommy soon. See Mommy soon. After lunch, see Mommy."

Miranda's classmate Peter spends his play time repeatedly opening and closing the classroom door. He exits the room and reappears seconds later, only to reenact this routine several more times.

Two 4-year-olds, Camilla and Preston, play together in the dress-up corner. Camilla pretends to cook, and Preston announces that he will drive to the store to buy her more food. He leaves the area for his make-believe destination, when he hears Camilla burst into tears screaming, "No! Come back! I want my daddy!"

At dismissal time, Camilla, Preston, and Miranda become increasingly disruptive. They run around the room, open and close the refrigerator attempting to grab more food, and finally cling tearfully to the teachers, resisting departure although they have wanted to be reassured about going home all day long.

Through observation, the teacher begins to recognize behavior patterns that reveal the children's shared developmental preoccupations. Although the children demonstrate a range of ability in the areas of cognition, communication, and social functioning, none of them seem to have achieved a solid degree of object constancy and thus cannot negotiate routine separations. Their difficulties prevent them from maintaining an external focus and disrupt their ability to sustain productive learning. Therefore, the teacher decides to design a curriculum called "go away–come back." Her goal is to help the children to cognitively and emotionally integrate the knowledge that important people continue to exist, regardless of whether or not they are out of sight.

Implementation. The teacher introduced the theme of "go away–come back" in morning meeting, using a music and movement activity. Each child used a cloth to hide himself, while the rest of the group sang a song about hiding and finding him. The song, to the tune of "Ten Little Indians," went as follows:

Where oh where is Preston hiding?
Where oh where is Preston hiding?
Where oh where is Preston hiding?
Underneath the cloth!

The hiding child was then uncovered. The teacher then read the story *You Go Away* by Dorothy Corey,* following the story with an activity in which each child was given a bin of sand and some small plastic bears to hide and then recover.

During gross motor playtime, children were provided with large cardboard boxes, hollow tumble forms, and tunnels to play out "disappearing and reappearing" games.

Several other activities were planned for subsequent days, including more elaborate stories about hiding and finding, tabletop fingerpainting (in which children made designs that could then be erased and redrawn), and circle games, where children hid and then came back to sit in their seats. Throughout, staff used the curricular focus to verbally organize cognitive and affective learning, even for the youngest or most developmentally arrested children. Language levels were determined by the developmental level of the child. For example, an autistic child's sand play with bears may have been articulated by the adult as follows: "Bears go away, bears come back!" However, the language used to communicate about the activity to a verbal 3-year-old who had experienced several traumatic separations due to changing foster placements was more personal and elaborate: "I see the bears are hiding so far down into the sand! Do you think they're worried that they won't be able to see us again?"

Assessment. Miranda runs to the mirror, looks at herself, grins, and runs away again. She eventually becomes involved in a turn-taking game with Peter, who is also interested in playing peek-a-boo with the mirror. After Peter spies his mirror image, he laughs and runs into the teacher's arms, then returns to his mirror image.

Camilla and Preston engage in making a sandcastle for bears "for hiding." Preston calls out, "Bear, where are you?" Camilla responds, "Here! In the basement!"

After lunch, Preston gets the book *You Go Away* and hands it to the teacher. All the children listen attentively as she reads. When the story is over, Camilla and Miranda are able to take the teacher's hand and allow themselves to be escorted to their cubbies to get their coats. Preston waves goodbye from the bus window.

In this case, the teacher clearly saw the children using the therapeutic curriculum input to master their worries about separation. She may decide to extend the curriculum another week or to revise or amend it by designing activities that might be especially meaningful to her particular group of children.

---

*Most of the children's books mentioned in this chapter are listed in the bibliography in Chapter 9.

"My Special Animal": Making Transitions

Observation. The children are coming off the school buses and entering the play-room. Camilla stands with her coat buttoned up tight and will not remove it. Wendy begins to whine for crackers and throws a tantrum when told that snacktime comes later. Preston stands frozen on the lobby steps, refusing to walk by himself but also refusing help from the teacher.

Eventually, everyone enters the room and becomes involved in play. How-ever, an hour later, when it is time to go down to snack, the children are distressed once again and require much staff attention in order to move on.

Children who have difficulty achieving inner representations of self and sig-nificant others are at a loss during transitions. They must rely on external sources of comfort and therefore become disorganized when the externals of a situation change. The children need help to develop their abilities to internalize comfort-ing feelings. A therapeutic curriculum was evolved to help the children begin to use transitional objects to self-comfort during transitions and thus foster autonomy and growth.

Implementation. Each child was asked to bring a favorite stuffed animal to school. If a child did not have an animal at home, one was provided from the class-room. The child was permitted to bring the school animal home each day, with parental agreement to ensure its safe return.

The special animals were given two primary functions. One was to comfort children in times of distress and to accompany them through transitions, thus re-maining a constant in periods of change. The other was to act as alter ego for children whose ego development was very much in process. Thus the teacher encouraged the children to use their special animals in every part of the daily rou-tine. Animals were given seats at snack, and children were asked to voice their animals' food preferences. Children were asked to decide how old their special animals were and what their special animals would like to have for their birthday parties, which were then celebrated by the class as a group activity. Teachers took pictures of the special animals as children used them for self-comfort and to bridge routine transitions, and they made books for each child about the genesis of his special animal and how he could use it to feel better.

Ongoing interactions between special animal and child and special animal and teacher in the context of the daily routine helped the animals to be endowed with properties of self and of comforting other, and also heightened the animals' ability to function as transitional objects.

Assessment. Miranda walks to the playroom door, hesitant about beginning her morning at school. She is clutching her stuffed green dog, saying, "Doggie's all right. He'll be all right." She puts the dog on the top of the slide and says, "Doggie's turn to go on the slide." At drawing time, Miranda asks the teacher to draw Doggie, who is feeling sad because "his mommy is at the store."

Wendy brings her stuffed bunny rabbit to the teacher and announces that her bunny is hungry and wants snack right away. The teacher suggests that she feed her bunny some pretend food until it is time for snack. Wendy takes her bunny to the sandbox, where she, Preston, and Camilla begin a game of cooking rice for Bunny.

Peter screams when the teacher turns the water off in the sink, where he has been washing his hands for several minutes, oblivious to the line of waiting children behind him. He jumps up and down squealing and does not respond to the teacher's words. When given his stuffed puppy, he quiets momentarily but then pulls toward the sink and as his distress escalates. The teacher gets a bin and fills it with soapy water, suggesting that Peter give his puppy a bath. Peter smiles in delight and begins soaping the puppy in a focused way instead of putting his face into the bin or splashing wildly, as he usually does in water play.

Watching the ways that the children used their special animals allowed the teacher to assess whether the curriculum helped them to better manage transitions and enabled them to develop their self-concepts and autonomy behaviors. For Miranda, Wendy, and Peter, the curriculum was quite successful. It allowed Miranda to bridge the gap between home and school more successfully and gave her a symbol for expressing her feelings about transition. Wendy was able to use her special animal to help her delay gratification and wait, without feeling deprived and getting into a power struggle with the teacher. Peter used his special animal for comfort and to promote more organized behavior. The "special animal" curriculum was a valuable tool through which each child expanded his ability to be more autonomous and to interact with the world in a more productive manner.

"Mine": Boundaries and Possession

Observation. Peter looks at his mirror image without seeming to recognize that he has control over the movements of the boy he sees in the mirror.

Miranda walks over to Camilla, who is playing with blocks on the rug. Miranda grabs Camilla's blocks and seems stunned when Camilla reacts by throwing herself on the floor and sobbing. Miranda then takes refuge in the lap of the nearest adult, where she stays for several minutes.

Preston and Shaneka are playing in the dress-up corner. Preston, who is being Batman, demands that Shaneka come over to him. He then proceeds to hug her in an intrusive and sexual manner. She pushes him away, and he slaps her for resisting.

At lunchtime, Miranda and Peter have difficulty staying seated in their own chairs. They need help from the teachers to stop taking food from other people's plates. Camilla doesn't want her own food but wants to be fed a bag of potato chips left over from someone else's birthday party. She cries when told that she needs to decide about eating her own food.

The children's behaviors suggest to the teacher that they are confused about personal identity, boundaries, and ownership. To address these unresolved developmental issues, the teacher evolves a curriculum based on the concept "mine." She plans activities that she hopes will enable the children to conceptualize and internalize a sense of themselves as separate individuals with control over their own bodies and a right to their own feelings and possessions.

Implementation. Teacher-directed activities for the "mine" curriculum were introduced in morning meeting. The group sang songs delineating body parts and differences in dress.

Teachers made individual books about each child at home and in school, using photographs to illustrate what was unique about each child's constellation.

Group activities included the assembling of a "this is me" puzzle, individualized to resemble each child. Children painted shoeboxes as "that's mine" boxes that could hold all personal items that they wished to keep inaccessible to other children. Each child was given a series of blank books entitled "My_____" to explore and represent issues of ownership that were personal to him or her.

Gross motor activities and free playtime offered infinite opportunities for teachers to help children appreciate and respect each others' boundaries and to help them verbalize their own rights to individual body integrity, as well as to participation in group games and sharing of group toys. Teachers emphasized the children's modeling of language, which would help children effectively communicate their claims; for instance, "No, that's my toy." "I want a turn next." "Don't squeeze me like that; it hurts." Games where children were given visual representations of their own physical boundaries, such as personal seat mats, individual bins, or individual clay trays, helped children feel acknowledged, protected, and clear about where they begin and end.

Assessment. Shaneka approaches Preston and begins tugging on his sweater. "Stop," says Preston. "That's my body."

Camilla is folding up green squares of construction paper and stuffing them into her "that's mine" box. "That's my money," she says proudly.

Miranda sees Wendy working at a puzzle at the table. She reaches out to grab a piece but is stopped by the teacher. "Not mine?" Miranda says with questioning intonation. She then answers herself: "Soon Miranda's turn."

Peter is blowing bubbles in front of the mirror. He is gleeful as he watches his image blow bubbles simultaneously. The teacher verbalizes the connection. "That's Peter. Peter's bubbles." Peter smiles broadly.

By going back and examining the children's spontaneous play, language artwork, and other activities, the teacher is able to monitor the extent that "mine" is being internalized as a cognitive and affective concept. The teacher is able to help the children move closer to claiming ownership of possessions, affects, and accomplishments. A successful "mine" curriculum may precede the development of a curriculum about sharing, mirroring the evolution of normal developmental processes.

METHODS FOR DEVELOPING PRESCHOOL-LEVEL CURRICULUMS

The process of developing therapeutic curriculums for children whose cognition is at or above age level but who have not worked through important emotional issues is much the same as the process of developing these curriculums for children arrested at early developmental levels. Often children with unresolved emotional issues have not developed in an even, integrated fashion. A 4-year-old, for example, might be able to do puzzles at an 8-year-old level or memorize the words to a story, while at the same time relating to others much as a toddler would. Another 4-year-old might be cognitively intact but unable to attend to typical learning activities because of pressing emotional preoccupations. The therapeutic curriculum taps into the child's emotional energies to provide investment in his cognitive explorations, and it appeals to the child's cognitive strengths to help the child understand and resolve important emotional issues.

The "Pumpkin" Curriculum: Exploring Affect

Observation. Melinda walks stiffly into the room at the beginning of the day with a wooden expression on her face and intones mechanically, to the teacher, "Hi, Judy, how are you?" Throughout the course of the day, her affect shifts very little. At meeting time, she reads, with no emotion, the words she has memorized from a book about feelings.

Sam speeds around the playroom on a tricycle. He suddenly tips and falls over, the heavy metal tricycle falling on top of him in a tangle of arms, legs, metal, and wheels. Quickly, he jumps up and laughs, insisting when the teacher rushes over and voices concern, "I'm not hurt, I'm not hurt."

Vanessa plays with the baby doll. She begins to cook for the baby but quickly begins to become hurtful instead, mashing food on the doll's face then hitting her repeatedly. When the teacher suggests that this must make the baby sad and pretends the baby is crying, Vanessa begins to laugh and says, "Okay, I'm leaving then. Goodbye," and abandons the play.

Tony wanders around the room during free play provoking the other children. He knocks over one boy's building. He takes a pegboard another child has been using when she is not looking. When challenged by the other children, he lashes out at them aggressively. When the teacher takes Tony aside and reflects that it seems as if he is feeling angry this morning, he begins to cry and screams, "I'm not angry . . . I'm happy! I'm happy!"

Through observation and evaluation, the teacher assesses that these children are all cognitively able to identify affects. However, they have not accomplished the important developmental task of integrating their own affects. They are either disconnected from their affects, show a narrow range of emotion, deny real feelings, or display false affect. The teacher thus designs a curriculum that will allow the children to explore affect on a variety of levels and help them connect to and express their own affects. A "pumpkin" curriculum around Halloween provided the perfect vehicle for this exploration. At the same time, it captured the children's natural excitement and curiosity about a popular holiday theme and addressed it in a meaningful way.

Implementation. In implementing the "pumpkin/affect" curriculum, the teacher introduced a variety of materials and activities related to the theme of pumpkins and affect and used them to both (1) model symbolic representations of affect and (2) offer children opportunities to explore affect through their own symbolic play, art, and language activities.

At meeting, the teachers used books and songs about both affect and pumpkins to introduce the themes of the group activities. Group activities included: making orange playdough to fashion personal pumpkins; cooking pumpkin Jell-O jigglers with raisin faces, pumpkin muffins with icing faces, and pumpkin pie; walking to the store to buy a large pumpkin and small individual ones; carving a jack-o'-lantern; making pumpkin face puppets; creating a collage of small paper pumpkin faces with varying affects; and taking turns creating expressions with a large pumpkin face with movable features. Finally, the children made masks and used them to dress up and go trick-or-treating in the school.

These activities provided important learning experiences (e.g., learning about the features of a face, cooking, exploring the neighborhood on a walk to the store) while at the same time offering a metaphor (pumpkin faces) through which the children could work on affect. Throughout, the activities emphasized choosing different kinds of affects to depict on the pumpkin faces, according to the emotional state of the "pumpkin makers." Emotional cause and effect was explored through play with the puppets. The teacher would ask the children such questions as, "Vanessa, what is making your pumpkin sad today?"

During free play, many of these materials were reintroduced and set out on the table so that children could play with them spontaneously. The large pumpkin face made of orange poster board and covered with contact paper could be arranged into a happy, mad, scared, or sad face, depending on how a child chose to stick on the movable features. The teachers modeled different affects by cutting pumpkin shapes out of the orange playdough the group had made and making faces on them; children were free to change these and create their own. Children also practiced creating faces on the feltboard by manipulating felt features. Books about feelings were easily accessible on the bookshelf, as were photograph books of the children, which focused on how they felt in different situations. On the playground, the teacher drew pumpkin faces on the wall with chalk and modeled different affects, then let the children draw their own.

As Halloween drew near, the holiday theme was explored more closely: A "pumpkin/affect" curriculum evolved nicely into a dressing up curriculum, where the children continued to play about affect as they made different kinds of masks and where issues of real and pretend were also examined.

Assessment. By observing the children's spontaneous language, art, and drawing representations over a period of time, the teacher can evaluate the extent to which the children are internalizing the concepts.

Vanessa sits at the table during free play, manipulating the features on the large pumpkin face. She puts tears on the face but turns the mouth upward in a smile. The teacher suggests that maybe the pumpkin is crying on the inside but feels like it has to smile outside. Vanessa glances up at the teacher, then turns the mouth down. Vanessa says, "He's sad." "How come your pumpkin is sad?" the teacher asks. "Because his mommy hit him," Vanessa replies softly. "That must have hurt the pumpkin," the teacher says.

Melinda is intently watching a conflict between two other children, staring in particular at a little boy who is crying. She walks over to the feltboard and quickly makes a sad face out of the felt features. "Look—Raul is sad!" she observes.

Tony becomes enraged when he has to take turns with a material he has been hoarding. The teachers stop him from hitting the other child and suggest that maybe he can draw an angry picture instead. Tony draws a mad pumpkin face, saying, "I'm angry at you. I don't want to share the trains!"

Through these observations, the teacher concludes that the "pumpkin/affect" curriculum has successfully been integrated and has helped to make children more connected to their feelings and able to communicate about them.

"Big and Little": Balancing Dependence and Autonomy

Observation. At snacktime, Vanessa jumps up excitedly and grabs the juice bottle to pour juice for a younger child in the class. When the teachers remind her that the grown-ups are there to help the other children and that the other child might like to pour the juice herself, she insists angrily, "Mommy says I'm bigger!" Vanessa has difficulty accepting limits set by teachers and frequently engages in power struggles with them.

Rosa arrives at the beginning of the day, clinging like a monkey in her father's arms. She begins to whine and whimper as he attempts to put her down and leave. Throughout the day, she relates to adults in a soft-spoken, compliant manner. When confronted by other children, Rosa is unable to assert herself and just withdraws quietly. When she is hurt, she assumes an infantile position and clings to the teachers as she sobs and sobs.

During cleanup time, Tony runs around the classroom jumping on furniture, shouting, "Look at me! I'm Batman!" He sees two children fighting over a toy and rushes over to intervene. Highly anxious throughout the morning, Tony is unable to seek comfort or reassurance from the teachers. When they offer him a lap to sit on at meeting, he adamantly refuses.

It is clear from these descriptions that the children in this group have not resolved the important developmental task of establishing an age-level self-concept and an appropriate balance between their dependency and autonomy needs. Some of the children, who may have been parentified or unprotected by adults, feel they must act as if they are "bigger" than they actually are; other children, who may have been infantilized by adults, have not achieved age-appropriate levels of autonomy or self-assertion. The teacher thus designs a "big and little" curriculum in order to allow children to move closer to a more appropriate developmental position of being both little and dependent and at the same time achieving increasing levels of autonomy and mastery over their environments.

Implementation. The teacher chose an array of materials and activities to represent the themes of big and little. The theme was introduced at first on a more conceptual level and later explored through activities that were more personally relevant to the children.

At meeting, books such as *Big and Little, Mama's Little Bears, Little Gorilla,* and *Peter's Chair* were read. Songs representing the theme of big and little, such as "Three Little Ducks," were sung. Later, the teacher made a "birthday cake" chart depicting their ages and measured the children on a height chart. During group time, children made big and little handprint pictures, big and little shape collages, cooked big and little pancakes or cookies, drew in big and little drawing books with big and little markers. Later, they pretended to be little and "grow big" to music. One day, the children played in the dress-up corner and were encouraged to be "little." The next day, they dressed up to be "big." A birthday party was held with playdough birthday cakes, in which each child got to choose to be little or big and select the number of candles for their cake. Another day, a similar birthday party was held with real cupcakes that children had cooked and decorated, and real candles were used.

During free play, children explored the concept through their play. They filled and emptied big and little bottles with water; drew with big and little markers; built big and little buildings with big and little blocks; played with big and little animals, toy people, pegs, stacking cups, and Russian dolls; cut out big and little shapes out of playdough—the possibilities are almost endless. Children were also encouraged to dress up in "big" clothes or to pretend to be little, like a baby.

Teachers helped children make connections to their own feelings about being little and being big. For Vanessa, a child who behaved in a parentified manner and experienced intense ambivalence about her dependency needs, a photograph book was made depicting her being "big" and being "little." Again, it was stressed that she could also do lots of 4-year-old things and grown-ups would still take care of her.

Assessment. Rosa comes into the room, and the first thing she does is walk over to the bookshelf and select *Little Gorilla*. She wants to hear again and again the part about how even though Little Gorilla gets bigger and turns 5 years old, everybody still loves him. She stands up and says, "That's like me. I'm 5. I'm getting bigger, right?" She measures herself against the height chart. "That's right," the teacher responds, "and even if you act like a 5-year-old girl, grown-ups will still take care of you." The next day, Rosa wants to walk, rather than be carried, into the classroom. At snack, when asked if she wants help pouring her juice, she says adamantly, "No! I want to do it myself!"

Vanessa plays with the big and little giraffes. "This one's little . . . this one's big." She pretends the mommy giraffe says to the baby, "I said, 'Clean up your room right now!'" The little giraffe responds, "I don't want to clean up. I want you to help me. I'm little!" At snacktime, instead of jumping up to pour the other children's juice, she asks to sit on a teacher's lap and wants help pouring her juice. She looks up at the teacher, "I'm little, right?"

Tony sits at the table making a collage out of big and little circles. He glues one large circle and lots of little circles surrounding the big one. "That's Grandma," he says, "the big one. That's me. That's Alicia. That's Michael. The little ones. 'Cause they like us—little." In the playroom, Tony pretends to be a kitten and crawls around, meowing. "Meow, I want milk."

During an activity where the children dressed up and pretended to be little, Sam gets inside a large blue laundry bag and cries like a baby. He wants to be carried up to the playroom this way. "I a baby," he says happily. Once in the playroom, he wants to be pushed in the carriage. A few minutes later, he pops out of the bag to ride the tricycle for awhile. "Before you were being little, like a baby," the teacher observes. "Now you are riding a bike like a 5-year-old boy." Sam continues to go in and out of the bag during the rest of playroom time, alternately playing and interacting with his peers at a 5-year-old level and pretending to be a baby. At lunchtime, he hands the bag to the teacher to hold and goes to wash his hands at the sink. "I'm going to be little again tomorrow," he says.

From her observations, the teacher concludes that the children in the group have not only integrated a conceptual understanding of the theme of big and little, but they have also explored the issue in relation to themselves and come closer to achieving a middle ground with regard to an age-appropriate balance between their autonomy and dependency needs.

"Boats and Bridges": Working Through Separation

Observation. It is summertime, and the end of the schoolyear is drawing near. Several children will be graduating and moving on to new schools in September. The teacher notices a lot of behavioral regression and an increase in the overall anxiety level of the children.

During free play, Tony runs around the room, unable to focus his attention on his play. Whenever the door is opened, he shoots out and runs down the hall, hiding from the teachers when they come after him. At goodbye time, he becomes angry and destructive, knocking things off the shelves, kicking the teachers angrily when they stop him, yelling, "Shut up, stupid. I'm not coming back to this school ever again."

Vanessa plays with the toy people. She puts a little girl in the school bus and drives it away from the teacher she is sitting with.

TEACHER: Where is the little girl going?
VANESSA: Away. To her new school. She's not coming back.
TEACHER: Who is going to be with her?
VANESSA: No one. She's bad. She is going to be all by herself.

At snacktime, Vanessa resumes some of her former parentified behaviors; when the teachers offer her help, she turns on them angrily, saying, "I'm 5, stupid. I'm going to a new school."

Rosa's eyes follow the teacher around the classroom. Each time the teacher goes out of the classroom, she quickly rushes over, asking the teacher if she can go with her. During transitions, Rosa lies down on the floor helplessly, wanting a teacher to pick her up and carry her like a baby. At goodbye time, she stands steadfastly by the bookshelf, her glaring eyes and silent expression declaring, "I'm staying right here." When she is helped to leave, she breaks down and sobs.

The teacher assesses that many children in the group are preoccupied with the upcoming separation and their feelings of anxiety, loss, and anger. Separations are particularly problematic for the children in the therapeutic nursery, many of whom have experienced traumatic separations in their lives and are insecure in the knowledge that adults will consistently keep them safe and cared for. The teacher designs a curriculum about boats and bridges, which provides a perfect metaphor for children to work through their feelings about the transition and be reassured of continued connection. The curriculum is in keeping with a summertime interest in water and lends itself to cognitive explorations of this and related themes.

Implementation. The curriculum was initiated at the beginning of the summer session, as the weather was growing hotter and the wading pool was introduced.

At meeting, books dealing with the themes of water, boats, journeys, and bridges were read, including *Where the Wild Things Are, The City, Jenny's Journey, The Story of Ping, Harold and the Purple Crayon*, and *The Little Red Lighthouse and the Great Grey Bridge*. Songs representing these themes were plentiful and included "Row, Row, Row Your Boat," "Down by the Bay," "Michael, Row the Boat Ashore," "A Sailor Went to Sea, Sea, Sea," "London Bridge," and "Baby Beluga."

There were numerous materials and activities that could be used to represent and play with the theme of boats and bridges. Children played with toy plastic boats in the water, making them go away and come back. They made soap boats with toothpicks and paper sails and sailed them back and forth in bins of water and in the wading pool. They made boats out of celery stalks and watermelon rinds. They painted oaktag boats in watercolors, as well as fish, and attached them to a large ocean mural they had created by painting a large sheet of Kraft paper blue. The group rocked together in a wooden boat to the tunes of "Row, Row, Row Your Boat," "A Sailor Went to Sea," and other boat songs.

The group took a walk to the river to look at the boats and bridges and then made a photo album about the trip. The whole school took a tram ride to a nearby island. When they came back, the children painted milk cartons and pretended to slide them back and forth along a string over the river they had crossed with the tram. On another day, the group read *The Little Red Lighthouse and the Great Grey Bridge* and built bridges out of wooden blocks, connecting one water bin to another, and had people and cars go back and forth across the bridges. In the playroom, the children pretended that the floor was an ocean and used large toys and furniture to connect one island of "land" to another. The grand finale of the curriculum was a parent–child activity that involved making and floating ice cream–banana boats in a tub of water, and then, of course, eating them.

Throughout, the themes of bridging separations, of moving back and forth across a gulf, and of being apart but remaining connected were highlighted. As the end of the summer drew near, the "boats and bridges" curriculum evolved into a "new school/old school" curriculum through which children addressed the issue of the school transition more directly. By this time the children were ready to do so, as they had already had ample time to explore their feelings on a metaphorical level.

Assessment. In the playroom one day, Tony announces, "Hey? I have an idea. Let's pretend the floor is water, like we did yesterday." Sam responds, "Yeah, that's a good idea. This is a boat [referring to his bicycle]. Watch out for the sharks. Yikes!" Sam shuttles Tony back and forth across the shark-infested waters from one teacher to another. When they arrive at the couch where one of the teachers is sitting, they jump on her lap, breathless. "Yeah—a safe island!" says Tony, "We was scared, right, Sam?"

During free play, Vanessa plays with a small blue plastic boat in a bin of water. In the boat, she places a little girl. "The boat's going away . . . now it's coming back. Uh-oh, it's sinking." She submerges it in the bubbles. "It's lost!" The teacher queries, "Hm, I'll bet that is scary for the girl—to feel so lost and all alone. Is there anyone who can help her?" Vanessa says, "Yes—here comes the rescue boat. Don't worry, little girl. I'll help you!" She steers another boat toward the submerged blue one.

Rosa plays next to Vanessa. She has constructed a wooden bridge out of blocks, connecting one bin of water to another. She lines up several little plastic people along the bridge. They include the children in her class.

TEACHER: I wonder where those children are going?
ROSA: They're going over there—to the other water. They're 5 now.
TEACHER: How do they feel to say goodbye?
ROSA: They sad.
TEACHER: Maybe they can come back for a visit sometime, or call on the telephone.
ROSA: They gonna come visit tomorrow.
TEACHER: That sounds like a good idea.

The teacher observes that the children are not only engaged in the teacher-directed group activities, but that they are also playing about the theme of boats and bridges spontaneously and using this play to address feelings about separation. Once given this channel through which to work through feelings about the separation, their overall level of anxiety diminishes, as do their acting-out behaviors.

CONCLUSION

A curriculum that is designed by teachers to address unresolved developmental issues is compelling to children and allows them to stay connected to their internal experience while maintaining receptivity to external input. A therapeutic curriculum discourages rote learning and encourages children to build a conceptual framework for their own personal experiences. This framework bridges the domains of cognition and affect, as teachers introduce symbols that can be used to express and elaborate both thought and feeling. This "curricular bridge" gives children a stronger foundation for understanding and embracing the more abstract symbols that come their way during the primary school years. An emotionally responsive curriculum gives children an early message that school is a place that offers them a mirror for important issues and life experience and also helps them create symbols to hold meaning, enhance communication, and decrease emotional isolation. That is an offer that young children cannot refuse.

REFERENCE

Koplow, L. (2002). *Creating schools that heal: Real life solutions.* New York: Teachers College Press.

Lesson Plans
for Emotional Life

Virginia Hut, Beverley Dennis,
Lesley Koplow, and Judith Ferber

THIS CHAPTER PROVIDES the reader with actual "lesson plans" that promote mastery of emotional and social issues relevant to preschool children. This may be welcome input for many teachers embarking on the creation of a therapeutic curriculum, because the plans offer specific ideas for projects and activities. However, in order to be used effectively, these suggested plans must be adapted to address the developmental issues expressed by the group for which they are being designed (see Chapter 8). Classroom staff must recognize the ways that children are expressing the nature of their developmental and experiential realities through language, play, and interactions before they will be able to design curriculums that address these realities.

Each lesson plan is organized around a theme. The themes were chosen by teachers because they allowed children to focus on unresolved developmental issues that were being expressed through spontaneous behaviors. The order in which the lesson plans are presented is neither arbitrary nor rigid. For example, the beginning and end of the schoolyear always bring up separation issues for young children. Therefore, themes dealing with separation issues are presented in the lesson plans at the beginning and end of this section. These same themes, or related themes, may also come up at intervals throughout the year, often precipitated by unpredictable events. For instance, a child in the class may abruptly withdraw from school, a teacher may become pregnant, and so forth. Teachers should be creative in their use of these plans, and others like them, and adapt the order, themes, and actual activities to meet the needs of their particular population of children.

LESSON PLAN GUIDELINES

The reader may find the following guidelines helpful in implementing these lesson plans:

1. Note the theme at the top of the page. Look at the stated objectives listed underneath. Are these objectives relevant for your group? Do the children's language, play, interactions, and behavioral reactions indicate that the issues addressed by the theme remain unresolved?
2. Consider using your morning meeting to introduce the theme. This may require you to replace part of your current morning meeting routine with theme-related activities. (Adding activities to an existing meeting routine can make the meeting too long, causing children to become distracted and inattentive.) Using a "Surprise Box" will allow for the introduction of new aspects of the curricular themes and help sustain the children's focus.
3. Analyze your current repertoire of children's songs, noting the themes expressed in the lyrics. The songs that appear in these lesson plans are familiar children's songs that address the theme featured. Many can be found in children's songs and fingerplay books, and some are included on children's records by artists such as Ella Jenkins, Hap Palmer, and Raffi. Many other songs relevant to the theme in question can also be used.
4. Look at the books currently in your classroom library and organize them by theme. The books listed in each lesson plan are *some* but certainly not *all* of the children's books available that address the topic. Supplement the list with familiar resources. Choose books that are appropriate for your population and read them during meeting time to focus the children on the intended topic.
5. Talk about the theme in a direct, focused way. For example, if your theme is "hurt and healing," you might read the story *It Hurts* at meeting time. You can then say something like, "Sometimes kids get worried when they get hurt. In our class, kids get hurt sometimes. Does anyone remember when that happened?" After a brief discussion, you can introduce the activity. For example, "I see that [teacher's name] gave everyone a stuffed animal at their place at the table. We can go see if the animals got hurt and then we can use some Band-Aids and tape and cream and you can try to help them feel better. Later, we can write a story about it."
6. Follow each group activity by having materials available for exploration during the next free-play period. In the above example, stuffed animals, doctor toys, blankets, pillows, and other items might be made very accessible during free play.
7. Look for opportunities to allow children to work on lesson plan themes independently throughout the day. Again, using the previous example, if some children finish their lunch early and are unoccupied, the teacher may suggest

that they draw a picture about their animal and what happened: how the animal got hurt and how he got better. Children can tell their stories to their teachers, who can write them down verbatim on the same page as the drawing.

8. Present themes on a more basic level if your group is less verbal and not able to symbolize spontaneously. The story *It Hurts*, for example, is a very simple story. Songs such as "Miss Polly" may be helpful to dramatize the theme. Teachers may need to demonstrate issues using toys. For instance, the teacher may hold the stuffed bear, make him walk, and then "fall" and cry. The teacher might say, for example, "Uh-oh! Bear fell! He's crying." Lesson plans for lower-functioning children can be implemented through modeling if the themes are engaging and relevant to experience. While these children may be very engaged by the activities of bandaging the animals, they may be unable to elaborate on the activity during open-ended play, draw about it, or dictate a story about it. Therefore, the teacher can help them to recall and consider the theme by making a photograph book capturing the sequence of activities and highlighting the affective elements of the theme.

9. Create your own curricular materials. While conventional songs and stories are listed as tools for the therapeutic curriculum, invented songs and books are an indispensable feature. Photograph books and drawn books that capture children in action or represent emotionally important events or socialization processes are more powerful than any ready-made material. As a rule, teachers should try to present book formats that include a single drawing or photograph per page in order to minimize confusion for the child audience.

10. Assess the continuing relevance of each theme at the end of the week. Themes that are compelling to children may last longer than 1 week. Themes may return at intervals throughout the year as teachers sense a renewed need to focus on the topic. While these lesson plans are process-oriented as opposed to performance-oriented, there are certainly ways to evaluate their impact. Teachers should look at behavioral indicators, spontaneous representation of the theme or related topics in play, reference to or elaboration of them or related topics in language, or elaboration or personalization of themes or related topics in drawings for evidence that the material has been integrated. The effect of the therapeutic curriculum is accumulative: You may not see as immediate a result as you would from a performance-oriented curriculum, yet lessons for emotional life are enduring in impact and often provide the foundation from which other learning can be made meaningful.

Finally, each lesson plan theme presented in this chapter has a cognitive as well as an affective conceptual component. While the affective elements are stressed here for obvious reasons, creative teachers will recognize opportunities to address and explore cognitive aspects as well. For example, in the lesson plans for "things I like" and "things I don't like," children will discover that their own likes and dislikes may differ from their peers. This discovery provides the teacher with a way of introducing cognitive concepts of "same" and "different." It provides children with a way of learning these concepts in an organic, experientially based modality, which is likely to make a deep and lasting impression.

BIBLIOGRAPHY

Ache, Frank. (2001). *Good Night Baby Bear*. New York: Harcourt.

Aliki. (1996). *Hello! Good-bye!* New York: Greenwillow.

Avery, Charles. (1992). *Everybody Has Feelings*. Seattle: Open Hand.

Aylesworth, J. (1997). *Teddy Bear Tears*. New York: Atheneum.

Baby Faces. (1998). New York: Dorling Kinderley.

Bemelmans, Ludwig. (1940). *Madeline*. New York: Simon & Schuster.

Bonnett-Stein, Sara. (1974). *That New Baby: An Open Family Book for Parents and Children Together*. New York: Walker.

Bornstein, Ruth. (1976). *Little Gorilla*. New York: Houghton Mifflin.

Brandenberg, Aliki. (1982). *We Are Best Friends*. New York: Mulberry.

Brennen, Barbara. (1970). *Faces*. New York: Dutton.

Brown, L. M. (1998). *How to Be A Friend; A Guide to Making Friends and Keeping Them*. New York: Little, Brown.

Burningham, John. (1975). *The Blanket*. New York: Crowell.

Burton, V. (1942). *The Little House*. Boston: Houghton Mifflin.

Burton, V. (1967). *Mike Mulligan and the Steam Shovel*. Boston: Houghton Mifflin.

Butler, Dorothy. (1988). *My Brown Bear Barney*. New York: Greenwillow.

Cain, Barbara. (2001). *Double-Dip Feelings*. Washington, DC: Magination.

Calhoun, M. (1997). *Flood*. New York: Morrow Junior Books.

Carle, Eric. (1984). *The Mixed Up Chameleon*. New York: Harper & Row.

Carle, Eric. (1987). *The Very Hungry Caterpillar*. New York: Philomel.

Carle, Eric. (1996). *Little Cloud*. New York: Scholastic.

Carle, Eric. (2004). *A House for the Hermit Crab*. New York: Little Simon. (Original work published 1987)

Cheltenham Elementary School. (1991). *We Are Alike, We Are Different*. New York: Scholastic.

Children's Television Workshop. Cookie Monster books. New York: Random House.

Children's Television Workshop. Oscar the Grouch books. New York: Random House.

Clifton, Lucille. Everette Anderson books. New York: Henry Holt.

Coatsworth, E. J. (1974). *All of a Sudden Susan*. New York: Macmillan.

Cohen, Miriam. (1967). *Will I Have a Friend?* New York: Macmillan.

Cohen, Miriam. (1998). *Down in the Subway*. New York: D.K. Publishing.

Conrad, Pamela. (1995). *The Tub People*. New York: HarperCollins.

Corey, Dorothy. (1980). *Everybody Takes Turns*. Chicago: Albert Whitman.

Corey, Dorothy. (1980). *We All Share*. Chicago: Albert Whitman.

Corey, Dorothy. (1999). *You Go Away*. Chicago: Albert Whitman.

Cowell, C. (2003). *What Shall We Do with Boo-Hoo Baby?* New York: Scholastic.

Crary, Elizabeth. (1986). *Mommy Don't Go*. Seattle: Parenting Press.

Crews, Donald. (1986). *Flying*. New York: Greenwillow.

Crowe Kay Chorao, R. (1987). New York: Puffin. (Original work published 1967)

Curtis, Jamie Lee. (1995). *When I Was Little; A Four-Year-Old's Memoir of Her Youth.* New York: HarperCollins.

Curtis, Jamie Lee. (1998). *Today I Feel Silly.* New York: HarperCollins.

Curtis, Jamie Lee. (2002). *I'm Gonna Like Me.* New York: HarperCollins.

Curtis, Jamie Lee. (2004). *It's Hard to Be Five.* New York: HarperCollins.

Day, Ellis, Conlin, Susan, & Levine-Friedman, Susan. (1989). *My Feelings at Home.* Seattle: Parenting Press.

dePaola, Tommy. (1979). *Strega Nona.* New York: Aladdin.

Dijs, Carla. (1990). *Are You My Daddy?* New York: Simon & Schuster.

Dijs, Carla. (1990). *Are You My Mommy?* New York: Simon & Schuster.

Dorros, Arthur. (1987). *Splash, Splash.* New York: Thomas Crowell.

Dunbar, J., & Gliori, D. (1998). *Tell Me Something Happy Before I Go to Sleep.* Orlando, FL: Harcourt.

Eastman, Philip D. (1960). *Are You My Mother?* New York: Random House.

Erickson, Karen, & Roffey, Maureen. (1985). *I Can Share.* New York: Scholastic.

Feczko, Kathy. (1985). *Halloween Party.* Metuchen, NJ: Troll Associates.

Florian, Douglas. (1982). *The City.* New York: Thomas Y. Crowell.

Fowler, Susi. (1994*). I'll See You When the Moon Is Full.* New York: Greenwillow.

Frankel, Alana. (1980). *Once upon a Potty.* New York: Barrons.

Freeman, Don. (1968). *Corduroy.* New York: Viking.

Garland, Sarah. (1990). *All Gone.* New York: Viking Kestrel.

Giff, P. (1998). *All About Stacey.* New York: Doubleday Dell.

Ginsberg, Mirra. (1975). *Mushroom in the Rain.* New York: Macmillan.

Ginsberg, Mirra. (1980). *Good Morning Chick.* New York: Greenwillow.

Golembe, C. (1999). *Annabelle's Big Move.* Boston: Houghton Mifflin.

Gomi, Taro. (1979). *Coco Can't Wait.* New York: Puffin.

Granatky, H. (2000) *Little Toot.* New York: Grosset & Dunlap. (Original work published 1939)

Greenfield, Eloise. (1975). *Me and Neesie.* New York: Harper & Row.

Greenfield, Eloise. (1991). *Big Friends, Little Friends.* Publishers Group West.

Grobel, R. (2002). *Peek-a-boo You!* New York: Scholastic Books.

Hamm, D. J. (1991). *Laney's Lost Mama.* Morton Grove, IL: Albert Whitman.

Hanson, Joan. (1972). *I Don't Like Timmy.* Minneapolis: Lerner Publications.

Hatkoff, C., & Hatkoff, J. L. (2001). *Good-bye Tonsils!* New York: Viking Press.

Havill, Juanita. (1986). *Jamaica's Find.* Boston: Houghton Mifflin.

Havill, Juanita. (1998). *Jamaica, Tag Along.* Boston: Houghton Mifflin.

Hayes, Sara. (1988). *Eat Up Gemma.* New York: Lothrop, Lee & Shepard.

Henkes, Kevin. (1988). *Chester's Way.* New York: Greenwillow.

Henkes, Kevin. (1986). *A Weekend with Wendell.* New York: Greenwillow.

Henkes, Kevin. (1990). *Julius, Baby of the World.* New York: Greenwillow.

Henkes, Kevin. (1993). *Owen.* New York: Greenwillow.

Henkes, Kevin. (2000). *Wemberly Worried.* New York: Greenwillow.

Henkes, Kevin. (2002). *Jessica.* New York: Greenwillow.

Hickman, M. W. (1979). *My Friend William Moved Away.* Nashville, TN: Abingdon.

Hill, Eric. (1982). *Where Is Spot?* New York: G. P. Putnam's Sons.

Hines, A. G. (1985). *Bethany for Real.* New York: Greenwillow.

Hoban, Tana. (1987). *What's Inside?* New York: Greenwillow.

Hoberman, M. A. (1999). *And To Think That We Thought That We'd Never Be Friends.* New York: Dell Dragonfly.

Hutchins, Pat. (1997). *Titch.* New York: Red Fox Picture Books.

Jacobs, Paul DuBois, & Swender, Jennifer. (2004). *My Subway Ride.* Gibbs Smith.

Jonas, Ann. (1982). *When You Were a Baby.* New York: Greenwillow.

Jonas, Ann. (1984). *Holes and Peeks.* New York: Greenwillow.

Jonell, Lynne. (2002). *When Mommy Was Mad.* New York: Putnam.

Jungman, Ann, & Goffe, Toni. (1989). *The Day Teddi Made New Friends.* New York: Barrons.

Kachenmeister, Cheryl. (1989). *On Monday When It Rained.* Boston: Houghton Mifflin.

Kandoian, Ellen. (1990). *Maybe She Forgot.* New York: Cobble Hill.

Keats, Ezra Jack. (1962). *The Snowy Day.* New York: Puffin.

Keats, Ezra Jack. (1964). *A Whistle for Willie.* New York: Viking.

Keats, Ezra Jack. (1968). *A Letter for Amy.* New York: Harper & Row.

Keats, Ezra Jack. (1991). *Peter's Chair.* Weston, CT: Weston Wood.

Kinsey-Warnock, N. (2005). *Nora's Ark.* New York: HarperCollins.

Kline, Suzy. (1989). *Ooops.* New York: Puffin.

Koplow, Lesley. (1991). *Tanya and the Tobo Man.* New York: Brunner/Mazel.

Krauss, Ruth. (1945). *The Carrot Seed.* New York: Harper & Row.

Krauss, Ruth. (1987). *Big and Little.* New York: Scholastic.

Laken, Pat. (1988). *Don't Touch My Room.* Boston: Little, Brown. (Original work published 1985)

Leonard, M. (1988). *How Do I Feel? Scared.* New York: A Bantam Little Rooster Book.

Lindgren, Barbro. (1982). *Sam's Car.* New York: Morrow.

Lindgren, Barbro. (1982). *Sam's Cookie.* New York: Morrow.

Lindgren, Barbro. (1982). *Sam's Teddy Bear.* New York: Morrow.

Marcus, Irene, & Marcus, Paul. (1990). *Scary Night Visitor.* New York: Brunner/Mazel.

Mayer, Mercer. (1968). *There's a Nightmare in My Closet.* New York: Penguin.

McCloskey, Robert. (1948). *Blueberries for Sal.* New York: Viking Kestral.

McLerran, A. (1992). *I Want to Go Home.* New York: Tambourine.

McMullan, K., & McMullan, J. (2003). *I'm Mighty!* New York: Joanna Cotler.

McPhail, David. (1990). *Lost.* Boston: Little, Brown.

Meyers, S. (2001). *Everywhere Babies.* New York: Harcourt.

Mills, J. (1991). *Little Tree.* New York: Brunner/Mazel.

Mitchell, Edna Preston. (1976). *The Temper Tantrum Book.* New York: Puffin.

Murphy, M. (2001). *Some Things Change.* Boston: Houghton Mifflin.

O'Brian, Ann. (1992). *It Hurts.* New York: Henry Holt.

Ormerod, Jan. (1981). *Sunshine.* New York: Lothrop, Lee & Shepard.

Ormerod, Jan. (1982). *Moonlight.* New York: Lothrop, Lee & Shepard.

Ormerod, Jan. (1985). *Messy Baby.* London: Walker.

Oxenbury, Helen. (1981). *Dressing.* New York: Wanderer.

Oxenbury, Helen. (1983). *First Day of School.* New York: Dial Books for Young Readers.

Oxenbury, Helen. (1989). *Tom and Pippo Make a Friend.* New York: Aladdin.

Peck, J. (1998). *The Giant Carrot.* New York: Dial.

Pelletier, Andrew T. (2005). *The Amazing Adventures of Bathman.* New York: Penguin Books for Young Readers.

Prestine, Joan Singleton. (1995). *Sometimes I Feel Awful.* Columbus, Ohio: McGraw–Hill.

Prestine, Joan Singleton. (2001). *Someone Special Died.* Columbus, OH: Waterbird Books.

Rockwell, Anne. (1986). *Things That Go.* New York: Dutton.

Rockwell, Anne, & Rockwell, Harlow. (1982). *Sick in Bed.* New York: Macmillan.

Rockwell, Harlow. (1973). *My Doctor.* New York: Macmillan.

Rockwell, Harlow. (1975). *My Dentist.* New York: Macmillan.

Rose, Agatha. (1992). *Hide and Seek in the Yellow House.* New York: Viking.

Samton, Shiela. (1990). *Jenny's Journey.* New York: Penguin.

Savadier, Elivia. (2006). *No Haircut Today.* Roaring Brook.

Selsam, Millicent. (1980). *All About Eggs.* Reading, MA: Addison-Wesley.

Sendak, Maurice. (1970). *In the Night Kitchen.* New York: Harper & Row.

Sendak, Maurice. (1984). *Where the Wild Things Are.* Madrid: Alfaguara.

Seuss, Dr. (1949). *Bartholomew & the Oobleck.* New York: Random House.

Seuss, Dr. (1958). *The Cat in the Hat Comes Back.* New York: Beginner Books.

Seuss, Dr. (1987). *Green Eggs and Ham.* New York: Random House.

Sharmat, Marjorie. (1980). *Gregory the Terrible Eater.* New York: Scholastic.

Sharmat, Marjorie. (1983). *I Don't Care.* New York: Delacorte.

Sheppard, J. (1993). *I Know A Bridge.* New York: Macmillian.

Simon, Norma. (1969). *I Was So Mad.* Chicago: Albert Whitman.

Simon, Norma. (1969). *What Do I Do?* Chicago: Albert Whitman.

Simon, Norma. (1970). *How Do I Feel?* Chicago: Albert Whitman.

Simon, Norma. (1971). *I Know What I Like.* Chicago: Albert Whitman.

Simon, Norma. (1987). *Children Do, Grownups Don't.* Niles, IL: Albert Whitman.

Simon, Norma, & Lasker, Joe. (1970). *I Feel Scared.* Chicago: Albert Whitman.

Singer, M. (2002). *Boo Hoo Boo-Boo.* New York: Harper Growing Books.

Sis, Peter. (2000). *Madlenka.* New York: Frances Foster. (Original work published 1949)

Sis, Peter. (2002). *Madlenka's Dog.* New York: Farrar, Straus & Giroux.

Stinson, Kathy. (1983). *Big or Little.* Ontario: Annick.

Stoneway Books. (1990). *Things That Grow.* Southeastern, PA: Author.

Sturges, P. (1998). *Bridges Are to Cross.* New York: Putnam.

Swift, H., & Ward, L. (1942). *The Little Red Lighthouse and the Great Grey Bridge.* New
    York: Harcourt, Brace & World.

Tafuri, Nancy. (2002). *Mama's Little Bears.* New York: Scholastic.

Titherington, Jeanne. (1987). *A Place for Ben.* New York: Greenwillow.

Tompert, Ann. (1988). *Will You Come Back for Me?* Chicago: Albert Whitman.

Torres, Leyla. (1993). *Subway Sparrow.* New York: Farrar, Straus & Giroux.

Tresselt, Alvin. (1989). *The Mitten.* New York: Mulberry.

Viorst, Judith. (1972). *Alexander and the Terrible, Horrible, No Good, Very Bad Day.*
    New York: Atheneum.

Waber, B. (1991). *Ira Sleeps Over.* New York: Houghton Mifflin.

Waddell, M. (1998). *Can't You Sleep Little Bear?* Cambridge, MA: Candlewick Press.

Walthambury, Jane. (1989). *Mrs. Mustard's Baby Faces.* San Francisco: Chronicle Books.

Weiss, Nicki. (1990). *An Egg Is an Egg.* New York: G. P. Putnam's & Son.

Williams, Vera. (1984). *A Chair for My Mother.* New York: Greenwillow.

Williams, Vera. (1987). *More, More, More, Said the Baby.* New York: Greenwillow.

Wise-Brown, Margaret. (1942). *The Runaway Bunny.* New York: HarperCollins.

Wise-Brown, Margaret. (1947). *Goodnight Moon.* New York: Harper & Row.

Wise-Brown, Margaret. (1989). *Baby Animals.* New York: Random House.

Withall, Sabrina. (1983). *The Baby's Book of Babies.* New York: Harper & Row.

Wolde, Gunilla. (1974). *This Is Betsy.* New York: Random House.

Wolde, Gunilla. (1974). *Betsy's Baby Brother.* New York: Random House.

Wolde, Gunilla. (1976). *Betsy's First Day of Day Care.* New York: Random House.

Yabuuchi, Masayuki. (1940). *Whose Baby?* New York: Philomel.

Young, Ruth. (1987). *My Blanket.* New York: Viking Kestrel.

Zelinsky, Paul. (1990). *The Wheels on the Bus.* New York: Dutton Children's Books.

Ziefert, Harriet, & Brown, Rick. (2005*). All Dirty! All Clean!* New York: Sterling Press.

Zion, Gene. (1956). *Harry the Dirty Dog.* New York: Harper & Row.

Zolotow, Charlotte. (1987). *I Like to Be Little.* New York: Thomas Y. Crowell.

GO AWAY–COME BACK

Objective:
- To help children achieve a conceptual understanding of "going away" and "coming back"
- To allow children to explore and address issues of object constancy.

Population:
- Children who have a high degree of separation anxiety or who are oblivious to separation.
- Good beginning of the year curriculum for all children, which will need to be repeated during the year for children with separation anxiety.

Meeting (Surprise Box with cloth for peek-a-boo)

Songs

"Where Oh Where Is [child's name] Hiding?"
"Two Little Blue Birds Sitting on the Wall"
"Three Little Ducks Went Swimming One Day"
"Where Is Thumpkin?"
"The Bunny Ran Away"
"My Mommy Comes Back"

Books

You Go Away (D. Corey)
Where is Spot? (E. Hill)
Mommy Don't Go (E. Crary)
First Day of School (H. Oxenbury)
Will you come back for me? (A. Tompert)

Activities

- "Home" and "School" boxes are provided. Children choose where to place self-photos.
- Go away/come back games using scarves, mirrors, and bubbles.

Group Activity Time
- Children hide and find miniature bears in the sandbox.
- Children make individual peek-a-boo books (attach child's photo or small mirror to tagboard page, stick material flap over photo, and so forth).
- Children make erasable pictures using chalkboards, finger paints, Magnadoodle boards and so forth.
- Children take turns hiding and are found by peers.
- Children and teachers take walking tour of school to find all the places children and teachers go during the day when they leave the room.

Free Play Time
- Jack-in-the-boxes, pop-up toys, shape boxes, and hammer-and-ball toys will be available.
- Cloths, scarves, and hiding tents will be available.
- Chalk boards, marker boards and finger paints will be available.
- Small dolls, puppets, and toy animals will be available.

Outdoor/Gross Motor Play Time
- Large blanket or parachute can be draped over climber to make hiding place.
- Game of running to and away from teachers.
- Game of making balls roll away to other children in a circle.
- Modified Red Rover game (children are called and run to join the opposite line, then get called back by peers).

MORE / NO MORE

Objective:
- To help children achieve a working knowledge of concepts "more" and "no more."
- To help children express their need for gratification and constructively cope with their feelings when gratification is delayed.

Population:
- Children who have difficulty waiting, expressing needs, and controlling impulses.
- Children who hoard toys and food and children who do not seem to know when they are full.

Meeting (Surprise Box with brown paper bags)

Songs

"I want more ____, I want more ____.
Give me more. Give me more.
I have so many ____. I have so many ____.
I don't want any more."
(Tune of "Frère Jacques")

"Five Little Monkeys"

Books

More, More, More (V. Williams)
The Very Hungry Caterpillar (E. Carle)
All Gone (S. Garland)
What Do I Do? (N. Simon)
Cookie Monster books (Children's Television Workshop)
Teacher-made "We Want More" books using photos and drawings of children needing "more" and "no more."

Activities

- Children learn sign language symbols for "more" and "no more" to increase their awareness of use and meaning.
- Children are given small paper bags to fill with more and more items until they are full.

Group Activity Time

- Each child is given a bin of water with small pitcher and can add more and more water to the bin until it can accommodate no more.
- Each child invites a stuffed animal to the table for a snack of play food. Each child can decide if his animal wants more or no more.
- Group makes playdough from ingredients, children having their choice of adding more ingredients (double recipe), more and more ingredients (triple recipe), and so on.
- Each child gets a tray for fingerpainting, and chooses a few colors, more colors, no more colors, and so on.
- Group makes a shape collage on large brown roll paper. Children can paste more and more shapes until the collage is full.
- Teacher-acted puppet show about what happens if kids want more but there is no more. How do they feel? What can they do?

Free Play Time

- Playdough and cookie cutters for making animal food will be available with toy animals.
- Materials for personal collage will be available.
- Blank books entitled "____'s More/No More Book" will be available.
- Puppets used in puppet show will be available for children to use in elaborating their own "more" and "no more" themes.

Outdoor/Gross Motor Play Time

- Teachers swing individual children in a blanket with other children surrounding and helping to "hold" the child inside. The child who swings verbalizes or signs desire for more or no more swinging.
- Each child is given a bubble jar and wand with the group goal of making more bubbles than ever before.

THAT'S MINE

Objective:
- To facilitate children's ability to feel and express ownership.

Population:
- Children who have poorly defined self/other boundaries, unresolved autonomy issues and difficulty recognizing or expressing possession.

Meeting (Surprise Box with cardboards for placemats)

Songs

"Head, Shoulders, Knees, and Toes"

"No, don't touch that, No, don't touch that,
No, that's mine! No, that's mine!
No, no, no, no, no! No, no, no, no, no!
No, that's mine."
(Tune of "Frère Jacques")

Books

Sam's Car (B. Lindgren)
Sam's Cookie (B. Lindgren)
Sam's Teddy Bear (B. Lindgren)
My Blanket (R. Young)

Activities

- Children pass around a small mirror to focus on their own unique features, clothing, and so on.
- Teacher takes Polaroid picture of each child. Children find their own cubbies and attach pictures with clear contact paper.
- Teacher passes out small carpet squares or vinyl seat cushions for each child to sit on during the meeting, each having a distinctive color or feature that may be a special symbol for that particular child.

Group Activity Time

- Children decorate cardboards, making placemats that can be used to more clearly define their table space at meal time.
- Each child paints a shoe box–sized empty box to be used for storing his own personal treasures.
- Children paint their hands (and/or feet), making prints that are distinctive and belong only to them.
- Each child is given a blank book, entitled "My Drawing Book," to fill with drawings and dictated stories.
- Each child has a colored, cut-out teddy bear on the back of her chair and at her place at the table—each with her name written on top.
- Lotto-like game where the teacher has many small replicas of the bears and pulls them out of a bag one at a time to be claimed by the appropriate child.
- Teacher tape records children's vocalizations, singing, or language. Group listens to see if children can differentiate and recognize their own voices and the voices of their classmates.

Free Play Time

- Wooden boards are made available in the block area, on the playdough table, and so on so that each child has his own delineated play space.
- Mirror and dress-up props are made available to help children experience self constancy when removing added props.
- Teachers model use of the phrase "that's mine!" when children intrude on each other's play, possessions, or bodies.
- Manipulatives are made available for each child to build his/her own house.

Outdoor/Gross Motor Play Time

- Teacher uses chalk to outline each child on the playground wall or floor. Children play a game to see which child fits into which form.
- Teacher draws a large chalk circle around each child. Child can decide whether to stay in his space, come out, or invite another child to come in with him.

142

WE CAN SHARE

Objective:
- To increase children's social awareness by focusing on and promoting sharing behavior.

Population:
- Children who are able to claim and express ownership, but cannot yet tolerate sharing or taking turns.

Meeting (Surprise Box with play apples)

Songs

"I Have Three Apples"

"Sharing Song"

Books

We All Share (D. Corey)

Everybody Takes Turns (D. Corey)

I Can Share (K. Erickson)

Teacher-made *Sharing* book using photographs of children sharing toys, snack, and so on and captioned appropriately.

Activities

- Teacher uses play apples to demonstrate song lyrics and children join her.
- Teacher does mini-puppet show with sharing theme, children take turns sharing something with puppet character.

Group Activity Time

- Each child is given a piece of fruit to wash and cut up to contribute to group made fruit salad, which is then shared by everyone. Teachers comment on process.
- Each child is given a certain number of blocks for building. If they choose to collaborate, they can make their buildings longer or taller.
- Cooking activity which involved shared use of one special implement. (This may be an egg beater, or another utensil.) Each child gets a turn to use the beater, but must tolerate waiting his turn while others use it. A special turn-taking song can be sung during this process.
- Collective painting project on one long piece of paper, large box, and so on. Each child receives one or two colors and can chose to stay with those or trade with others to obtain new colors. The product is shared space; "our" box, house, school and so on.
- Each child is given a limited number of train tracks and can make his own small track or collaborate with others to make a long and more complex route for the train.

Free Play Time

- Teachers comment on and photograph sharing and turn taking behaviors as children play in shared spaces such as playdough table, water/sand tables, dress-up corner, and so on.
- Puppets from teacher-led puppet show will be made available for children to develop their own sharing and turn taking scenarios.

Outdoor/Gross Motor Play Time

- Ball game that requires children to share one large ball and wait their turn for the ball to come to them.
- Parachute play demonstrating that the children's collaborative energy and motion makes the parachute move in different, exciting ways.
- Parachute or blanket game where each child gets a turn to be swung or rocked with the others helping to hold the child in the center.

HOLES AND PEEKS

Objective:
- To help children address body integrity and self constancy issues, and master related fears of toilets, drains, darkness, and so on.

Population:
- Toddlers.
- Preschoolers who are preoccupied with concerns about their bodies and are fearful about toileting, bathing, haircuts, doctor visits, and darkness.

Meeting (Surprise Box with book *Holes and Peeks*)

Songs

"In a Cottage In a Wood"

"Taping, Taping, Taping up the Holes, Filling up, Filling up, Filling up the Holes…" (Tune of "Swimming, Swimming, in a Swimming Pool")

"The Bunny Ran Away"

Books

Holes and Peeks (A. Jonas)
Once Upon a Potty (A. Frankel)
Where Is Spot? (E. Hill)
Hide and Seek in the Yellow House (A. Rose)
The Haircut (A. Rockwell)

Activities

- Each child takes a turn filling a "hole" with flannel board forms.
- Each child takes a turn peeking through a hole made with one hand, two hands, or two arms, or by hiding behind meeting chair.
- Each child can take a turn filling a hole in large peg board with appropriate size peg.

Group Activity Time

- Children are given empty paper towel rolls to decorate for "peeking."
- Children and teachers walk through the school and "peek" at whatever children find interesting, or perhaps, intimidating, using cardboard peeks. Follow up with discussion, drawings, or dictated stories about the experience.
- Children can fill up bagel holes with cream cheese, peanut butter, or butter, then eat for snack.
- Children can find any papers, books, or photos with holes or tears and repair them with tape.
- Game with large net and small plastic animals. Children think of ways to make net safer so that animals will not fall through. Teachers provide various materials that may be used for the project.

Free Play Time

- Playdough and clay available for use and exploration.
- "Once upon a potty" dolls and pottys are made available.
- Doctor kits and hospital toys available in dramatic play area.
- Water bins and receptacles made available for water play.
- Large play house box with windows or peek holes made available.

Outdoor / Gross Motor Play Time

- Children hide in crawl tunnels, tumble forms, and so forth, peek out and then reemerge so others can see they are intact.
- Children bring their cardboard "peeks" out to the playground to look for holes in grass, pavement, walls, and so on. Is anything in there? Do they want to cover them, let them stay open, make them bigger or smaller? Is it safe?
- Haircut props available in dramatic play area.

THINGS I LIKE

Objective:
- To help children identify and express preferences in a variety of situations.
- To help children recognize and tolerate similarities between self and peer group.

Population:
- Children who need help with self–other differentiation and identity formation.
- Children with food-related anxieties.

Meeting (Surprise Box with book *I Know What I Like*)

Songs
"I Like Apples and Bananas"
"My Favorite Things" (Standard version and/or version tailored to children in classroom)
"Over in the Meadow" (what various animals like to do)

Books
I Know What I Like (N. Simon)
Gregory the Terrible Eater (M. Sharmat)
Green Eggs and Ham (Dr. Seuss)
The Mixed-Up Chameleon (E. Carle)

Activities
- In response to *I Know What I Like*, which children like the things discussed in the book? Which children like something different?
- Chart with each child's name at the top and various categories (food, toys, daily routines) at side with stick on symbols that depict desired content. Children participate in representing their own preferences and predicting preferences of peers. Do likes change?

Group Activity Time
- Group embarks on tape recording project to sing and record each child's favorite song.
- Teacher and children make a lotto game with construction paper squares having each child choose a favorite color to match on his board.
- Children will be given two-pronged choices at mealtimes and snacktimes and invited to indicate their preferences. (If they are unable, teacher or other children may voice what they suspect to be the case but ultimately child must decide what he will or will not eat.)
- Daily cooking curriculum featuring each child's favorite food. At the end of the week, teacher can make a chart of "Foods We Like" with movable pictures representing all foods that children have cooked and eaten. Kids can participate in assembling chart.
- Design activity to explore all the different ways to express preference. (Using words, pointing, signing, eating or playing more and more, drawing a picture, making up a song, whispering, and so forth.)

Free Play Time
- Containers from the ingredients used in "Things I Like" cooking curriculum will be made available in play kitchen area.
- Scarves of each child's favorite color will be added to dress up area.
- Charts will be available for individuals or small groups to work on or revise.

Outdoor/Gross Motor Play Time
- During physical play time, teachers will comment on children's favorite activities.
- During lunchtime, the teacher will ask children to recall and report activities enjoyed by themselves and their peers.

THINGS I DON'T LIKE

Objectives:
- To help children identify and express distaste for experience or stimuli.
- To help children identify and tolerate differences between self and others.

Population:
- Children who need help differentiating self from others and strengthening identity.
- Children who have food related anxiety.

Meeting (Surprise Box with ingredients for "Yucky Soup")

Songs
"The Babysitter Song"
"Don't You Push Me Down"
"Baby Bumblebee"
"Don't Put Your Trash in My Back Yard"

Books
I Know What I Like (N. Simon)
We Are Alike, We Are Different (Cheltenham Elementary)
On Monday When It Rained (C. Kachenmeister)

Activities
- Read I Know What I Like, focusing on the things children in the book did not like. Who feels the same? Different?
- Use of chart to sort out what each child does not like. Do these dislikes change?

Group Activity Time
- Children have a "juice fest." Class can prepare several different kinds of juice and each child who wants to participate can have a tiny cup of each. Teacher charts which kind each child dislikes.
- Children make "Yucky Soup" out of broth and several odd ingredients that the teacher provides. Children can suggest adding whatever they want to of the ingredients provided, then cook it. Each child can have a chance to taste the soup, or to feed it to a stuffed animal. Who likes Yucky Soup? Who thinks Yucky Soup tastes yucky?
- Children dictate story and make drawings related to the Yucky Soup project.
- Each child has a blank book entitled "Things I Don't Like" for representing personal dislikes in drawing, story, or collage formats.
- Children cut pictures of things they don't like from magazines. (Teachers must sort for appropriate possibilities beforehand.) Group creates a "things we don't like" collage.

Free Play Time
- Ingredients for "pretend Yucky Soup" will be available. (These might include large bowls with soap flasks, water, food coloring, etc. and large spoons for mixing.)
- Puppets will be made available for puppet shows about "things I don't like to do," "things that happen that I don't like."

Outdoor / Gross Motor Play Time
- Children are invited to pretend that bean bags are disliked items or activities (teachers can tag with pictures to make it clearer). Children can decide to keep the bags in baskets or to throw them far away.
- During lunchtime, teachers can help children recall experiences that they might have disliked during the day, then compare to the things they liked recalled from the week prior.

HURTING AND HEALING

Objective:
- To help children master concerns about body integrity and related fears about doctors and hospitals.
- To help children feel empowered by acknowledging and empathizing with their physical and psychologically painful experiences and helping them develop resources for healing.

Population:
- Children who have had traumatic medical experiences.
- Children who have been abused.
- Children who have unresolved body integrity issues.

Meeting (Surprise Box with Band-Aids)

Songs

"Miss Polly Had a Dolly"
"Five Little Monkeys Jumping on the Bed"
"Head, Shoulders, Knees and Toes"
"Chicks, Chicks" or "Los Pollitos"

Books

It Hurts (A. O'Brian)
My Doctor (H. Rockwell)
My Dentist (H. Rockwell)
Madeline (L. Bemelman)
Little Tree (J. Mills)
Sick in Bed (A. and H. Rockwell)

Activities

- Each child gets a doll or stuffed animal to bring to meeting corner. Make believe the doll/animal got hurt. Tell about how it got hurt.
- Repeat of activity above. This time tell about something that helped the doll/animal to feel better.

Group Activity Time

- Each child gets doll or stuffed animal to doctor, and several band-aids. If their dolls/animals have injuries, they use as many band-aids as they want.
- Children can make "doctor bags," each decorating a special bag to contain "feel better ingredients." These may be as band-aids, gauze, hand lotion, and so forth, or personal symbols which comfort the individual child.
- Children cook "Feel Better Soup" (chicken broth with noodles and another good tasting ingredient). They can eat "Feel Better Soup" themselves or feed it to dolls or animals.
- Each child receives a felt square to draw or make symbol of something comforting. Teacher sews the squares together to make "Feel Better Quilt" which distressed children can use to comfort themselves. (Teachers provide symbol of something they perceive to be comforting for nonsymbolic children.)
- Children make doctor and patient puppets and have small group puppet shows concerning themes of hurting and healing.

Free Play Time

- Doctor bags, hospital equipment, gowns, doctor tools, and other medical items will be made available in dramatic play area. (This should include plastic injection and a simulated I.V.)
- Playmobile doctor and hospital scenes and small playmobile people will be made available in block and doll house area.
- Play telephones will be made available in all areas for children to play out calling for help when needed. (Teachers can assist by helping children to play the role of responding to the other in need, or play that role herself.)

Outdoor / Gross Motor Play Time

- Teachers must empathize with children who become injured during play, not minimize painful feelings if child appears to be in pain or to have sustained an injury that is probably painful.
- Teachers can provide special nerf toys, balls, frisbees, nerf bats designed to promote physical activity but encourage safe play.

REAL / PRETEND (Halloween Curriculum)

Objective:

- To help children participate in Halloween rituals and activities without becoming frightened and overwhelmed.
- To help children develop and further differentiate their concepts of "real" and "pretend."
- To help children improve self constancy.

Population:

- Children who become fearful about putting on costumes or seeing others wear costumes.
- Children with poor reality testing, and less than age-appropriate means of differentiating fantasy and reality.

Meeting (Surprise Box with animal ear dress-ups)

Songs

"Do you know my friend
My friend _____, My friend _____,
Do you know my friend _____?
Whose wearing _____ ears."
(Tune of "Muffin Man")
"First you take a pumpkin"

Books

Halloween Party (K. Feczko)
Teacher-made Halloween books with photos of each child before putting on costume, with costume on, and after costume comes off.

Activities

- Children can take turns trying on animal ears and contrast their presentation with usual appearance. Teachers can add that "It is really _____ pretending to be a rabbit."
- Children can pretend to talk, walk, and act like the animal whose ears they are wearing. Group can talk about the contrast between this and the way each child really walks, talks, and acts.

Group Activity Time

- Children can experiment with using face paint on dolls and then washing it off to see that the doll is the same as before.
- Children can make masks with paper plates that are held in front of the face with attached popsicle sticks. They can experiment with holding the mask up to their face and looking in the mirror.
- Children can invent Halloween costumes from dress up clothes familiar to them.
- Children can play a special "Simon Says" game. Simon says to pretend to be _____. Simon says to sit, stand, talk, walk (and so on) like your real self.
- Teacher provides "real pumpkins" of all sizes. Class can explore their real attributes (size, weight, color, etc.). Group cuts top off, finds and removes seeds. The pumpkin really grew from seeds. Children plant pumpkin seeds in individual pots. Teacher comments that the pumpkins would have to get very big before they could use them to make pretend faces like in the song.

Free Play Time

- All dress-ups and costumes used for curriculum are made available as well as mirrors.
- All pumpkins are made available for exploration.
- Children are invited to carry the "real" "pretend" theme into all activities (For example, how do pretend playdough treats taste? How do the real foods taste?)

Outdoor / Gross Motor Play Time

- Children are invited to pretend that bikes, wagons, and so on are cars, buses, and police vehicles. When they are finished and park their vehicles they can talk about what they really are.
- Games like "Red Light–Green Light" and "Mother May I?" can be played with teachers commenting on how child leading game is pretending to be like a policeman, mother, and other adult roles.

PUMPKIN FACES (Affect Curriculum)

Objective:

- To help children internalize the constellation of a face.
- To increase children's awareness of communication via affects.
- To help children participate in Halloween ritual without feeling overwhelmed.

Population:

- Children who have difficulty tuning in to the affects of others, differentiating affects and expressing true affect.

Meeting (Surprise Box with a large felt pumpkin and assortment of features)

Songs

"First You Take a Pumpkin"
"Five Little Pumpkins"

Books

Faces (B. Brennen)
The Baby's Book of Babies (S. Withall)
Mrs. Mustard's Baby Faces (J. Walthambury)

Activities

- Large felt pumpkin is presented and each child has a turn to give him a face, deciding on desired affect.
- Children pass around a hand mirror, practicing making faces to match the affects they have given the pumpkin.

Group Activity Time

- Each child gets a construction paper cut-out pumpkin and an assortment of facial features and uses glue to assemble the features and create affects any way that he wishes. (Teachers should not correct.)
- After pumpkins dry and are displayed, each child can draw and/or dictate a story regarding the emotional cause of his pumpkin's affect, e.g., "The pumpkin is sad because…"
- Children take walking trip to fruit market to buy many small pumpkins and one large one. (Use photos or drawing to predict trip for children who are disoriented by change.)
- Each child uses a marker to give a small pumpkin affect and tape records a story about his pumpkin's affect. Nonverbal children listen to tape recording and are helped to focus on affects described.
- Group decides which affect teacher should carve on large pumpkin. Teacher uses sequence chart to help children predict steps and participate in hollowing pumpkin. Sing pumpkin song, save seeds for cooking.

Free Play Time

- Face puzzles, felt pumpkin faces, velcro feature toys such as Mr. Potato Head are available for exploration.
- Materials for creating hand held paper plate pumpkin masks are made available.
- American cheese slices and pumpkin cookie cutters are made available.
- Ingredients for making orange playdough are made available at table with teacher present. Children are invited to create playdough pumpkins and give them affects.

Outdoor / Gross Motor Play Time

- Children can collect leaves or crumble large amounts of newspaper to fill large orange plastic bag to create huge pumpkin. Use markers to decorate face, use as giant "beach ball," kick ball, rolling ball, and so forth.

149

ANGRY FEELINGS (Affect Curriculum)

Objective:

- To help enable children to express and respond to angry affects with-out becoming aggressive.
- To help children recognize the emotional cause and effect of their own angry feelings.
- To allow children to experience a holding environment where adults can acknowledge, affirm, and contain even negative emotions.

Population:

- All preschool children who need an opportunity for dialogue about angry feelings.
- Children with Pervasive Developmental Disorders who may lack a range of readable, appropriate affect.

Meeting (Surprise Box with angry pumpkin face)

Songs

"If You're Angry and You Know it."

"What do People do When They're Feeling Angry?"

Books

The Temper Tantrum Book (E. Mitchell)
I Was So Mad (N. Simon)
My Feelings at Home (E. Day)
Double-Dip Feelings (B. Cain)
Sam's Teddy Bear (B. Lindgren)

Activities

- Children pass around a hand mirror and practice making angry faces.
- Children practice using an angry voice with tape recorder.
- Teacher presents a chart with each child's name. Children recall experiences that made them angry in past weeks at school. Teacher represents with drawing symbols.

Group Activity Time

- Children make puppets with angry faces.
- Children compose and play an angry song using musical instruments.
- Teacher puppet show highlighting emotional cause and effect of angry feelings and strategies for expression and resolution. What made the angry feelings come? What made angry feelings go away.
- Children use their puppets in puppet theater to create show about angry feelings.
- Teacher will introduce teacher-made books which include photographs of the children expressing anger at school, highlighting the children's affects, emotional cause and effect, form of expression, resolution.
- Children will be given blank books to draw and dictate stories about what makes them feel angry.
- Class will compose song about what you can do when you're feeling angry at school, called "The No Hurting Song."

Free Play Time

- "Angry puppets" made by the children and teachers are made available.
- Art materials such as clay, playdough, and paints are made available.
- Teachers take the opportunity to comment about any incidents of anger that arise in the group, pointing to the emotional cause and effect in the situation, the form of expression, and the resolution. (This may include teacher intervention such as holding an out of control child.)

Outdoor / Gross Motor Play Time

- Punching bag is made available. (Large tumble forms can be used as well.)
- Colored chalk is made available for children who want to draw angry stories on the playground.
- Teachers remind children of strategies for nonaggressive expressions of anger, as physical play time can be difficult for impulsive children.

SAD FEELINGS (Affect Curriculum)

Objective:
- To enable children to express sad feelings using appropriate affect and respond to sad affects in others.
- To help children develop strategies for self-comfort, seek comfort from adults and provide comfort to peers.
- To help children recognize the emotional cause and effect of their own sad feelings.

Population:
- All preschool children who need an opportunity for dialogue about sad feelings.
- Children with Pervasive Developmental Disorders who may lack a normal range of readable affect and may miss affective clues from others.

Meeting (Surprise Box with crying doll)

Songs

"If You're Sad and You Know It"

"It's All Right to Cry"

"What do People do When They're Feeling Sad?"

Books

How Do I Feel? (N. Simon)

It Hurts (A. O'Brian)

Alexander and the Terrible, Horrible, No Good Very Bad Day (J. Viorst)

Everybody Has Feelings (C. Avery)

Double-Dip Feelings (B. Cain)

Activities

- Children pass hand mirror and practice making sad faces.
- Children practice using a sad voice talking into tape recorder.
- Teacher presents chart with each child's name. Children recall things that made them or peers sad in school in past weeks. Teacher represents.

Group Activity Time
- Children make puppets with sad affects.
- Teacher puppet show highlighting emotional cause and effect of sad affects expressed by puppets—What made the sad feelings come? How did the children know the puppets were sad? How did the sad feelings go away?
- Children have opportunity to enact scenarios about sad feelings with their puppets.
- Teacher presents teacher-made books capturing the emotional cause and effect of children's sad affects. Children are given their own blank books to draw or dictate stories about times that they felt sad.
- Children compose and play a sad song using musical instruments.
- Each child thinks of something that makes him feel better when crying. (Teachers can articulate what comforts the nonverbal children.) Each represents the comforting object or experience using art materials on a plain white pillow case. Children stuff case; teachers sew comfort pillows for each child.

Free Play Time
- Color fest with paints, food coloring, colored chalk, varied crayon, and marker shades available. Children encouraged to mix colors and equate them with *Double-Dip Feelings* concepts—Can you feel sad and angry at the same time? A little sad? Very sad?

Outdoor / Gross Motor Play Time
- Teachers highlight emotional cause and effect of sad affects that naturally occur during playground time.
- Chalk is available for drawing stories about sad feelings on playground.

SCARED FEELINGS (Affect Curriculum)

Objective:
- To enable children to express and respond to scared affects.
- To enable children to seek protection when feeling afraid at school.
- To help children understand the emotional cause and effect of their scared feelings.

Population:
- All preschool children who need a dialogue about their fears.
- Children who seem to defend against fearful affects by acting aggressively to demonstrate their strength and resilience.
- Children who seem to freeze when feeling afraid, and cannot express their feelings or seek comfort.

Meeting (Surprise Box with scared pumpkin face)

"If You're Scared and You Know It."
"What Do People Do When They're Feeling Scared?"

Songs

"Little Miss Muffet"

Books

How Do I Feel? (N. Simon)
I Feel Scared (Simon and Lasker)
There's a Nightmare in My Closet (M. Mayer)
How Do I Feel? Scared. (M. Leonard)

Activities

- Children pass around hand mirror and practice making scared faces.
- Children practice making *scary* faces. Contrast differences.
- Teacher presents chart with children's names. Children recall times when they or peers felt scared and teacher represents.

Group Activity Time

- Different things scare different people game. Teachers draw and present cards depicting scenarios that they know to be frightening to group members, or experiences that tend to be scary to this age-group (e.g., being alone in the dark). Children can stick scared faces on the cards representing scary experiences.
- What can you do when you're feeling scared? Group adds verses to the song and records it.
- Each child receives a blank book to draw and/or dictate stories about scared feelings or something scary.
- Teacher puppet show with theme of seeking comfort and protection when afraid. Who can help to keep you safe if you feel scared? Children use puppets to act out solutions for making scared feelings go away.
- Treasure hunt for items in room that can help when you're feeling scared. Each child gets sack to gather items such as stuffed animals, comfort pillows, "peeks," feel-better quilt, and other items.

Free Play Time

- Teachers comment on dramatic play themes that have scary elements, highlighting emotional cause and effect of fearfulness, mode of expression, and resolution in the play.
- Toy animals will be made available.

Outdoor/Gross Motor Play Time

- Large box can be provided for children to hide in if they see something scary, capture and contain scary image, and so forth.
- Teacher can reflect fearful affects expressed during climbing tasks, swinging play, and so forth.

HAPPY FEELINGS (Affect Curriculum)

Objective:
- To enable children to experience joy and use appropriate affect to communicate it to others.

Population:
- Children who have difficulty anticipating happy feelings and sharing them with others (especially children with PDD).

Meeting (Surprise Box with felt happy face)

Songs

"If You're Happy and You Know It"
"What Do People Do When They're Feeling Happy?"
"The More We Get Together"
"Sing, Sing a Song"
"I Love to Laugh"

Books

The Snowy Day (E. Keats)
A Whistle for Willie (E. Keats)
Everett Anderson books (L. Clifton)
Me and Neesie (E. Greenfield)
Double-Dip Feelings (B. Cain)

Activities

- Children pass hand mirror and watch themselves making happy faces.
- One thing that sometimes makes children happy is being able to do things. Each child gets a turn to complete simple task (such as fitting form in board) and others clap. Does that make the child who finished feel happy?

Group Activity Time

- Parachute game. Does being together make people feel happy? Whole group can play with parachute by all getting underneath together. Is it fun? Does it make you laugh? What makes *you* happy? Teacher will show photographs of the children with happy affects and each can review and speculate about what was making them feel happy.
- Children make happy sounds, using tape recorder.
- Each child gets a blank book with numbers on the top of each page to represent the different ages he has been. What made you happy when you were 1 year old? Two? Three? Children draw and dictate stories about their happy feeling in retrospect. (For nonsymbolic children, substitute an activity that makes them happy in the here and now, e.g., if a child loves to fingerpaint, have him fingerpaint in the "happy book.")
- What makes your friend feel happy? Children tape record their perceptions of what makes peers feel happy.
- Happy snacks. Children bake cookies or cupcakes and decorate with happy faces, sprinkles, happy colored icing, and so forth.

Free Play Time

- Playdough available for making pretend "happy snacks."
- Empty boxes, wrapping paper and tape made available for children to make pretend presents for self and peers.
- Teacher reflects on emotional cause and effect of happy affects expressed by children at play.

Outdoor/Gross Motor Play Time

- Children make giant bubbles with large wand and large pans of soap. Children are invited to run after bubbles, pop them, and so on. Does this feel good, and make them smile?
- Children and teachers play game of "jump your jiggles out" and other movement and music games with happy themes.
- Children do happy dance. Can other feelings come into the happy dance? Can you have more than one feeling at the same time? Can there be sad or angry parts in the happy dance? Children can demonstrate and label affects.

153

MY SPECIAL ANIMAL

Objective:
- To facilitate the productive use of transitional object as a symbol for relationship.
- To increase child's capacity to self-comfort during transition or other times of stress.

Population:
- Children who have difficulty during transitions and cannot self-comfort when in distress.
- Children who show impoverished symbolic functioning.

Meeting (Surprise box: Ira Sleeps Over)

Songs

"Where oh where is _____ bear?
Where oh where is _____ bear?
Where oh where is _____ bear?
Sitting in her lap!" (tune of "Where Oh Where Is Dear Little Suzie")

"Do you know my friend _____, my friend _____, my friend _____, do you know my friend _____ who has a very special *bear*?" (tune of "Do You Know the Muffin Man?")

Books

My Brown Bear Barney (D. Butler)
Whose Baby? (Yabuuchi)
Pippo (H. Oxenbury)
The Blanket (J. Burningham)
Ira Sleeps Over (B. Waber)

Activities

- Teacher makes and reads book representing children in group with their special animals.
- Special animals can be welcomed to meeting—children can decide whether to hold them on laps or give them their own seats.

Group Activity Time

- "Special animals" are requested from home or given to each child at school. Children are encouraged to have the special animal accompany them through the daily routine with teachers highlighting their participation.
- Children make jello jigglers using animal cookie cutters representing their special animals.
- Children can help special animals to play musical instruments to accompany songs about what each animal likes to do.
- Children draw or dictate in blank special animal affect books, that is, my special animal feels _____.
- Children can play doctor with doctor kit and make special animals feel better if they are sick.
- Class will have special animal birthday parties. How old is your special animal?

Free Play Time

- Children are encouraged to have special animals participate in symbolic play.
- Children are encouraged to have special animals dialogue with one another in dramatic play.

Outdoor/Gross Motor Play Time

- Children bring special animals to playground and demonstrate their own physical abilities for animals to appreciate.

154

BABIES: What Do They Need? What Do They Do?

Objective:
- To help children cope with teacher pregnancy.
- To help children anticipate and cope with birth of sibling.

Population:
- Children who have a pregnant teacher.
- Children who are anticipating birth of sibling.

Meeting (Surprise box: Baby Doll)

Songs

"If you're a hungry baby, you can *cry/ask for food*" (tune: "If you're happy and you know it").

"When ____ was a baby, a baby, when ____ was a baby, a baby, when ____ was a baby, a baby was he. He *went/said* [words or motion] this way and that way and this way and that way. When ____ was a baby, a baby was he" (tune: "Did You Ever See a Lassie").

Books

When You Were a Baby (A. Jonas)
Splash, Splash (A. Dorros)
That New Baby (S. Bonnetstein)
Betsy's Baby Brother (G. Wolde)
Helen Oxenbury books
A Place for Ben (J. Titherington)
The Baby's Book of Babies (S. Withall)
I Don't Like Timmy (J. Hanson)

Activities

- Children can take turns to talk about what they did or needed as a baby.
- Teacher uses photographs and drawings to assemble a book about her pregnancy, leave, and return. This will be read at meeting over the last 2 months of her pregnancy, allowing discussion and followed by free play where children play out their concerns.

Group Activity Time

- Children will make a variety of baby foods (soft/mushy) and feed baby dolls and selves. What do babies like to play with? Children can make rattle toys by filling cups with dry beans, and other materials and taping plastic wrap over the top.
- Children experiment with washing baby dolls with special baby soap, shampoo, sponges, and so on.
- Children experiment with diapering baby dolls using baby wipes, baby powder, and so on.
- Children make baby cradles from shoeboxes that they can paint and decorate (teacher can cut rockers from lid of shoebox). Blankets can be made to keep baby warm.
- What do babies do when they need something? Children take turns pretending to be babies that need something—use tape recorder for cries and baby talk.

Free Play

- All activity materials will be available so children can diaper, feed, wash, and cradle babies or express angry feelings in baby play.
- Children can use dress-up clothes and props to play baby, Mommy/Daddy, or sibling.

Outdoor/Gross Motor Play Time

- Large toy baby carriages will be available.
- Crawling tunnel and mats will be available.

MOMMY AND BABY ANIMALS

Objective:
- To help children identify and differentiate baby animals from adult animals.
- To increase childrens' self-esteem by fostering identification with emerging abilities of baby animals.

Population:
- Children whose dependency needs may not have been met in infancy and toddlerhood.

Meeting (Surprise box: Kangaroo and Baby)

Songs

"Three Little Ducks"
"Chick, Chicks, Cry, Cry" (Los Pollitos)
"Old McDonald"
"Where oh Where is Baby *Tiger*?"
"The Bunny Ran Away"

Books

Are You My Mother? (P.D. Eastman)
Are You My Mommy? (C. Dijs)
Are You My Daddy? (C. Dijs)
Baby Animals (M. Wise-Brown)
Whose Mouse Are You? (R. Kraus)
The Runaway Bunny (M. Wise-Brown)

Activities

- Children can match baby and mommy animal, felt pieces, making distinction verbally, if able.
- Children and teachers can enact story, "Are you my mother"? with toy mommy and baby animals.

Group Activity Time

- Children play game with animal sounds— how different baby animals cry, what they want, what mommies do to help them.
- Children can practice vocalizing their animal's needs using tape recorders.
- Children will make big and little animals from playdough or clay using cookie cutters.
- Children can use various building materials to build house for small plastic mommy and baby animals. Tell stories about what happens inside.
- Children cook for baby animals. Mommies can feed them or babies can learn to eat by themselves.
- Children can play with mommy and baby animals in water bins, mommies can bathe babies or babies can learn to swim or bathe themselves.
- Group or individual collages made with magazine photos or drawings of mommy and baby animals. Children tape record stories of what babies are learning to do and what they still need.

Free Play Time

- Animal families and props will be made available.
- Playdough food will be made available for animals.
- Group activity materials will be available (such as blocks on sand for houses or habitats, water, tape recorded animal sounds).

Outdoor/Gross Motor Play Time

- Children bring animals to playroom and build houses from large blocks and tunnels.
- Children use sandbox to play hide and find games with animals.
- Children can act out being mommy/baby animals—such as walking, noises, and interactions.

BABY MONSTERS

Objective:
- To facilitate children's feeling that their needs, fears and rages can be contained by adults.

Population:
- Impulsive, angry, acting out children who have difficulty accepting comfort or expressing needs.
- Children who are preoccupied with monsters.

Meeting (Surprise box: Monster Toys)

Songs

"If You're Scared and You Know It"

"I'm a baby monster, little and sweet, will you please feed me, I want to eat. Give me my _____, then some more. If you don't feed me, I'll scream: Roar!" (tune: I'm a Little Teapot)

"I Love Trash"

Books

There's a Nightmare in My Closet (M. Mayer)

Scary Night Visitors (I. & P. Marcus)

Where the Wild Things Are (M. Sendak)

Oscar the Grouch Books (C.T.W.)

Activities

- Children can help tell story of, *There's a Nightmare in My Closet,* using felt board pieces or baby monster soft toys.
- Children will talk about what makes baby monsters angry, scared, sad, and so forth.

Group Activity Time

- Children use monster dolls from Where the Wild Things Are to represent baby monsters.
- Children will tape record their monsters roaring their loudest roars and whispering their softest secrets.
- Children will decide what food their baby monsters like and feed them—do they like good food or "yukly" food? Cooking activity to satisfy monster tastes.
- Children can use flashlights to help 'scared' baby monsters to feel better by showing them what is hidden by the darkness.
- Children pretend that baby monsters are very angry. Where did the angry feelings come from? How can they take care of baby monsters when they're angry?

Free Play Time

- Children will have opportunity to represent baby monsters with the use of a variety of art/ sculpture media.
- Children will have opportunity to dictate stories about baby monsters.
- Group activity materials will be available for continued play with monsters.

Outdoor/Gross Motor Play Time

- Children will bring baby monsters to play-room, push them in carriage, take them for ride on bike, and so forth.
- Children can play hide and seek with baby monsters.

157

MESSY / CLEAN

Objective:

- To help children master unresolved issues about becoming messy or staying clean.
- To help children experience mess as a reversible state which does not alter their core selves.

Population:

- Children who have a developmentally appropriate interest in and concern about messes.
- Children who may have obsessive concerns about cleanliness.
- Children who have fears about getting wet or dirty while playing.

Meeting (Surprise box: Ingredients for Peanut Balls)

Songs

"Messy Baby"
"This is the way we wash our clothes…"
"You Brush Your Teeth"
"Peanut Butter"

Books

Messy Baby (J. Omerod)
This is Betsy (G. Wolde)
Ooops (S. Kline)
Harry the Dirty Dog (G. Zion)
The Cat in the Hat Comes Back (Dr. Seuss)
Bartholomew and the Oobleck (Dr. Seuss)

Activities

- Children will make mess of shredded newspaper while singing "Messy Baby" song and then clean it up singing "Clean Baby" song.

Group Activity Time

- Children will finger paint—making a "mess" with the paints and then washing their hands clean.
- Children will make messy peanut butter balls for snack.
- Children will cover table with shaving cream and then clean it with sponges.
- Children will let baby dolls "play" with shaving cream and then bathe the babies.
- Children will wash messy doll clothes and then hang the clean clothes on a line to dry.
- Children will use water table to make a "mess" using a combination of soap flakes, water, food coloring, etc. and then think of ways to make the table clean again.

Free Play Time

- Shaving cream, animals, and water will be available.
- Children will have opportunity to make messy paintings with liquid soap and food coloring or plastic trays and then clean them off.
- Children will have opportunity to cook with flour and water and then clean plates, and so on.

Outdoor/Gross Motor Play Time

- Children will make a mess by scattering blocks over floor and then clearing them up again.
- Children can clean up mess around sandbox by using brooms and dust pans.

SOME THINGS CHANGE, SOME THINGS STAY THE SAME

Population:
- Children who have experienced or will experience significant change in some aspect of their environment or life experience at home, in the community, or in school.
- Children who have experienced community trauma.

Objectives:
- To help children anticipate and acknowledge change.
- To help children recognize and connect to continuity.

Meeting (Surprise Box with a picture or artifact depicting something in the classroom that used to be different than it is now—room arrangement, color, toy or equipment, photo of teacher who used to have long hair and now has short hair, etc.)

Songs

"Eensy-Weensy Spider"
"I Had a Little Overcoat"
"Green Grass Grows All Around, All Around"
"Why, Oh Why, Oh Why?" (adapt lyrics from Woody Guthrie song)

Books

Some Things Change (M. Murphy)
A Chair for My Mother (V. Williams)
A House for Hermit Crab (E. Carle)
Annabelle's Big Move (C. Golembe)
When I Was Little (J. L. Curtis)
Peter's Chair (E. Keats)
My Friend William Moved Away (M. W. Hickman)
All of Sudden Susan (E. James)
The Little House (V. Burton)
Mike Mulligan and the Steam Shovel (V. Burton)
Nora's Ark (N. Kinsey-Warnock)
I Want to Go Home (A. McLerran)
Flood (M. Calhoun)

Activities

- Teacher asks if anyone remembers about the item in the Surprise Box: How was the classroom when _____ was there? (or before _____ happened?) How is it different now?
- Teacher reads a book that reflects an experience of change that many children have experienced. She asks if the story reminds them of anything. She gives them a chance to talk.

Group Activity Time

- Silly Shoes—All the kids take their shoes off and trade with other kids. They look at themselves in the mirror, and they look at each other. "What has changed about Michael?" "What has stayed the same about Michael?"
- The children each get a shoebox to make a pretend classroom. The teacher has drawn some stable classroom features inside (rug, door, light switch, etc.). Kids can use construction paper and cardboard pieces to make a classroom diorama. They can make their mini-classroom change or be the way it is or was before. What about the classroom has changed? What has stayed the same?
- The group is asked if they would like to make something all together that will stay up on the wall for the whole rest of the year. A group discussion takes place about what kids would like to include before doing the project. Mural paper and supplies are provided.
- Children are given wood pieces and glue to make sculptures. The next day, they are given the opportunity to decide whether to make changes to the sculpture by adding or removing pieces, or to leave it the way it is.
- The teacher presents flannelboard stories that are familiar to the children. The children have the opportunity to make the ending come out differently. What part of the story changed? What parts stayed the same?

Free Play Time

- Transportation toys will be available.
- Small suitcases or boxes will be available.
- Things to pack will be available.
- Community worker dress-up clothes and hats will be available
- Dolls and diaper bag accessories will be available.
- Puzzles will be available.
- Duplos and Legos will be available.
- Doctor and hospital toys will be available.

Outdoor/Gross Motor Play Time

- Large blocks to build and arrange environments and structures.
- Parachutes, play tents, and make-believe shelters that children can go in and out of.

LOST AND FOUND

Objective:
- To help children integrate concepts of lost and found on affective as well as cognitive level.
- To allow children avenues for mastery of concerns about being lost, lost objects, and so forth.

Population:
- All preschool children who have lost treasured items and have fears about being lost themselves.

Meeting (Surprise box: Something that had been missing in classroom and is now found)

Songs

"A Tisket, A Tasket"
"Where Oh Where Is _____ Hiding?"
"The Bunny Ran Away"

Books

Are You My Mother? (P.D. Eastman)
I Don't Care (M. Sharmat)
Corduroy (D. Freeman)
Hansel and Gretel (Grimm) (use simple, less scary version)

Activities

- Act out lost and found story using miniature props.
- Act out lost and found story using dress ups.

Group Activity Time

- Children can paint large box that can be classroom "Lost and Found." If someone finds something that isn't his, he can put the item in. If someone loses something, he can check in the box.
- Children dictate stories to caption pictures about times when they were lost and then found (or pets, treasured items, and so on). How did it feel to be lost? How did it feel to be found?
- Everything (and everyone) that gets lost is still "somewhere"—each child gets large paper covered with cardboard "peek" flaps and can draw or paste shapes or figures to represent lost items or people and practice finding them.
- Group walk through the school looking down at the floor and behind doors and furniture. What can we find that was lost before?

Free Play Time

- Dress-ups and props from lost and found stories can be available to encourage pretend play on theme of lost and found.
- Children can hide, pretending to be lost. Others can look for them.

Outdoor/Gross Motor Play Time

- Treasure hunt for items that teacher has hidden (similar to egg hunt but use relevant item).
- Go on a walk to collect pebbles (each child can bring small bag to collect them), make trails to show the way back to school.

160

WILL I HAVE A FRIEND?

Objectives:

Population:
- All children in classrooms that include 4- and 5-year-olds.

- To address peer issues of acceptance and rejection that often dominate in groups of young children.
- To invite children to represent peer dynamics through play.

Meeting (Surprise Box with 3 paper or flannel dolls and books about friends to read. Teacher reads one of the books about friends each morning.)

Songs

"Playmate"
"One Elephant Went Out to Play"
"The More We Get Together"

Books

Will I Have A Friend? (M. Cohen)
And to Think That We Thought That We'd Never Be Friends (M. A. Hoberman)
How to Be a Friend (L. and M. Brown)
We Are All Alike, We Are All Different (Cheltenham Elementary)
Chester's Way (K. Henkes)
A Weekend with Wendell (K. Henkes)

Activities

- Teacher asks the children if they think the dolls are friends. What should the dolls' names be? Who is friends with whom? How can one tell if the other one is his friend? What will happen if one says to another one, "I'm not your friend"? Let children explore and tell make-believe mini-stories about the dolls.

- Teacher introduces language about community and friendship. The classroom is a community of children and teachers. Everyone belongs to the classroom community, and everybody has friends in the classroom community. Not all of the kids are friends with one another all the time. Sometimes kids are friends, but they don't want to play. Kids feel sad when other kids say, "You're not my friend." Because we are a community where everyone belongs, we try to care for each other and help each other feel good about being in school.

- What can you say when you don't want to play?

Group Activity Time

- Children make kid puppets and do puppet shows about things that happen with friends (positive and negative).

- Kids make paper dolls of themselves that the teacher laminates and puts up on an accessible Velcro board. When complicated dynamics happen between peers, kids can show what happened using the paper dolls.

- Guess who's missing? Children sit in a circle with their eyes closed, and teacher taps one child, who goes to hide. Children look around and call out the name of the missing child, who then runs back to join the group. Children play Red Rover and embrace the newcomer in this version.

Free Play Time

- Little people will be available.
- Velcro people will be available.
- Books about friends will be available.
- Puppets and puppet theater will be available
- Blank books about what happens with friends will be available.
- Toys that express changing affects will be available.
- Teacher uses language that has been introduced in group times to help children interpret and cope with peer dynamics that arise. "If you say 'I'm not your friend,' it makes Annie sad." "What's another way that you can tell Annie that you don't want to play?"

Outdoor/Gross Motor Play Time

- Red Rover game.
- Elephant song game.
- Can't Jump Josie game.
- Parachute game.

GIVING AND GETTING (Valentine's Day)

Objective:

- To help children find meaning in the experience of giving and receiving.
- To help children differentiate in relatedness to peers and acknowledge special relationships.

Population:

- Children attending pre-school during Valentine season. This curriculum can become a valuable experience for children who have neither sent nor received mail, helping them extend their sense of connectedness over time and distance.

Meeting (Surprise box: Several heart cut-outs)

Songs

"Hearts Are Special if You Give 'Em Away"
"A Tisket A Tasket"
"Do You Know My Friend _____?"
"Make New Friends"

Books

We All Share (D. Corey)
We Are Best Friends (A. Brandenberg)
Will I Have a Friend? (M. Cohen)
A Letter for Amy (E. Jack Keats)

Activities

- Children will sing "hearts are special" into tape and listen to it played back.
- Children will sing "hearts are special" and give each other cut out hearts.

Group Activity Time

- Children will make a Valentine mailbox.
- Children will make Valentine cards for their parents to be sent in Valentine mailbox during parent-child group.
- Parents will make Valentine cards for their children to be sent in Valentine mailbox in parent-child group.
- Children will make Valentines—for special friends—send in mail.
- Children will make heart-shaped cookies and give some to other class.
- Children will make playdough hearts and take turn with heart cookie cutter.
- Children will make group heart collage, filling large group heart with individual hearts.

Free Play Time

- Children will have opportunity to practice giving and receiving Valentine cards using mailbox.
- Pink and red playdough and Valentine cookie cutters will be made available.

Outdoor/Gross Motor Play Time

- Children can play mail delivery using vehicles and large mail box.
- Children will take walk to mailbox to send Valentine letters to themselves at home.
- Children will practice "giving and getting" turns on the bikes.

HATCHING

Objective:
- To help children identify with and participate in springtime rituals and holidays.
- To help children use metaphors for their own personality development.

Population:
- All preschool children—spring time curriculum.

Meeting (Surprise box: Plastic egg)

Songs

"Chicks, Chicks, Cry, Cry, Oh, Oh, Oh"
"Circle Song"
"Where Oh Where is Chick Hiding?
Where Oh Where is Chick Hiding?
Where Oh Where is Chick Hiding?
inside the egg"
"Way up in the Sky"

Books

Baby Animals (M. Wise-Brown)
What's Inside? (T. Hoban)
An Egg is an Egg (N. Weiss)
The Very Hungry Caterpillar (E. Carle)
Good Morning Chick (M. Ginsburg)
All About Eggs (M. Selsam)

Activities

- Hiding and finding baby chicks inside plastic eggs that open and close.
- Children will "hatch" from laundry bag "egg."

Group Activity Time

- If possible, children visit farm or children's zoo to see eggs hatching.
- Children can make sequenced hatching collage: egg, hatching chick, hatched chick, chicken/rooster. What is it like for chick inside of egg? What is it like to come out?
- Children can take walk to collect sticks, leaves, grass, etc., to make nests for pretend eggs/chicks (can also be done with strips of paper).
- Teachers send for caterpillar kit. Children observe stages of cocooning and transformation from caterpillar to butterfly. Children represent each stage, making egg-carton caterpillars, enclosing them in lunch bag cocoons, and hanging them from the ceiling, then attaching wings when they come out.

Free Play Time

- Children will have opportunity to continue inside/outside, hiding/finding games with plastic eggs.
- Children can use a variety of sensory art materials to simulate hatching.

Outdoor/Gross Motor Play Time

- Children can conduct "egg hunt"—looking to see what's inside eggs.
- Children can pretend to hatch out of tumble forms and cardboard boxes.
- Children can make cocoons from parachutes—use brightly colored wings to practice flying as butterflies.

163

TOGETHER / APART

Objective:
- To facilitate children's conceptual understanding of "together" and "apart."
- To help children maintain a sense of individual integrity even when apart from school.

Population:
- Children who have difficulty tolerating disruptions in program over vacation.
- Children who are extremely dependent upon routine and context bound in learning and social functioning.

Meeting (Surprise box: Duplos)

Songs

"The more we get together, together, together, the more we get together, the happier we'll be. There's [name children]...the more we get together the happier we'll be."

"Where is Thumbkin?"

"Two Little Blackbirds"

Books

Vacation Story—Teacher made book talking about upcoming vacation and depicting where each child will be during vacation, as well as their return to school.

Runaway Bunny (M. Wise-Brown)

Coco Can't Wait (T. Gomi)

Activities

- Each child will have a piece of puzzle to put into the puzzle board. Each piece will be a whole independent of the picture created (i.e, person, animal, and so on). Fantasy about what each does independent of the others, what they do together.

Group Activity Time

- Children will participate in together/apart musical concert with instruments—demonstrating sound of each individual instrument vs. sound when all are played together.
- Each child can be given duplo piece with group task of putting all pieces together to create a whole _____.
- Felt board or colorform game can be used to fashion a house or school consisting of several pieces to be contributed and arranged by each child in turn taking pattern.
- Children will each choose a fruit to cut up and put together to make fruit salad, tasting each individually vs. taste of whole salad.

Free Play Time

- Children can use velcro materials to make objects come together and apart.
- Children can use dolls, house and vehicles to play out "together and apart" scenarios.

Outdoor/Gross Motor Play Time

- Children can use rope to play together/apart structured games.
- Children will build with large interlocking blocks to reinforce together/apart concept.
- Children will play hide-and-seek.
- Children will play together/apart games using parachute.

164

LIGHT/DARK, DAY/NIGHT

Objective:
- Children will understand contrasting concepts of "light and dark" and "day and night."
- Children will explore night-time fears and develop ways to master them.

Population:
- Children who are having separation difficulties at night and are becoming aware of dreams.

Meeting (Surprise box: Several small flashlights)

Songs

"Twinkle, Twinkle"
"Birdie Song"
Recordings of lullabys from cultures that reflect ethnic make-up of class

Books

Dressing (H. Oxenbury)
Sunshine (J. Ormerod)
Tanya and the Tobo Man (L. Koplow)
In the Night Kitchen (M. Sendak)
Moonlight (J. Ormerod)
Goodnight Moon (M. Wise-Brown)
There's a Nightmare in My Closet (M. Mayer)
You Go Away (D. Corey)

Activities

- Teacher will compile book about nighttime and daytime routines of class members, using photos and information given by parent.

Group Activity Time
- Children will use flashlights to play out making it lighter when it seems dark.
- Children will enact going to bed at night and waking up in the morning when it's light.
- Children will make chocolate milk—contrasting light milk changing to dark when chocolate is added.
- Children will help make day/night collage—sun, stars, light, dark, etc.
- Children will draw with chalk on black paper or black crayons on white paper.
- Verbal children will be asked to draw or paint a dream of their own, after dream concept becomes familiar via stories.
- Teacher recalls material from Real/Pretend curriculum—How can you tell if something really happened or if it happened in a dream?
- Children will be offered blank books entitled "My Dream Stories" for drawing and dictation.

Free Play Time
- A variety of art media in light and dark colors will be available.
- Flashlights will be available
- Children can dramatize going to sleep and waking up.
- Both prisms and glow-in-the-dark materials will be available for children to experiment with light and darkness.

Outdoor/Gross Motor Play Time
- Children will use light switches in motor room to transform room from day to night.
- Children will take flashlights into motor room and explore dark areas.
- Children will use white chalk on black playground floor.

165

BIG AND LITTLE

Objective:
- To promote children's working knowledge of concepts "big" and "little."
- To help children stay connected to their own developmental process in order to improve self constancy.

Population:
- Children who have developmentally appropriate interest in "being big" but fears about moving away from babyhood.
- Children with disruptive early experiences resulting in hypervigilance, preconscious self care, and lack of age-appropriate identity.

Meeting (Surprise box: Book—*Big or Little*)

Songs

"Eensy, Weensy Spider"
"I Wonder If I'm Growing"
"Parents are People"

Books

Children Do, Grownups Don't (N. Simon)
Big or Little (K. Stinson)
Big and Little (R. Kraus)
Little Gorilla (R. Bornstein)
Big Friends/Little Friends (E. Greenfield)
When You Were a Baby (A. Jonas)
I Like to Be Little (C. Zolotow)

Activities

- Teacher assembles and then reads individual books about each child's developmental process; When _____ was little he liked to _____. Now he is 4 years old and he likes to _____."
- Children can choose big and little felt people to place on felt board, contrasting size.
- Children can practice starting little and then growing big to music.

Group Activity Time

- Teachers make big handprints, children make little handprints.
- Children play with popsicle sticks and playdough to make birthday cakes and children can decide what age to be and what kind of present they will need for that age.
- Children play with water bins using big and little containers.
- Children can cook big and little: pancakes, cookies, sandwiches, and so forth.
- Children can draw in Big and Little drawing books. Theme "What I will do when I'm bigger," "What I used to do when I was little," and "What I can do now."

Free Play Time

- Children have opportunity to use dress-up clothes to pretend to be bigger or littler than they are.
- Children have opportunity to use various building blocks to build big and little towers, houses, roads, and so on.

Outdoor/Gross Motor Play Time

- Big and little blocks are provided.
- Big and little balls are provided.
- Children play game of "Mother May I?" deciding whether to take giant steps or baby steps.
- Nerf basketball game is provided with one basket mounted high and one low.

EMPTY / FULL

Objective:
- To help children integrate concepts of "empty" and "full" on affective as well as cognitive level.
- To provide real experiences that support children's learned concepts of "empty" and "full."

Population:
- Children who are at an early developmental level and have an intrinsic interest in dumping and filling.
- Children who have been deprived of nurture and have difficulty "filling up."

Meeting (Surprise box: Empty container)

Songs

"Five Green and Speckled Frogs"
"I'm a Little Teapot"
(use visual aids while singing)

Books

The Mitten (A. Tresselt)
More, More, More (V. Williams)
The Very Hungry Caterpillar (Carle)
Blueberries for Sal (R. McCloskey)
Eat Up Gemma (Hayes & Ormerod)
Mushroom in the Rain (M. Ginsberg)

Activities

- Children will empty bookshelf and then fill it with books.
- Children will use felt pieces to fill and empty felt board.
- Children will examine empty container and each have several turns to pour cornmeal until it is full.

Group Activity Time

- Children will be given empty containers to fill with beans to make rhythm instruments.
- Children will fill an empty piece of poster board with glued paper shapes—making the poster board full.
- Children will fill the chalk board with drawing and then sponge it off to make it empty.
- Children will make mashed potatoes and feed to babies and selves and announce when babies or selves feel full.
- Children can play with water and containers—making them empty and full.

Free Play Time

- Water bins and containers will be available.
- Children will have opportunity to use sand and cornmeal to fill and empty containers.
- Children will have opportunity to use play-dough to make pretend food to fill empty pots, cups, and so on.

Outdoor/Gross Motor Play Time

- Children will take empty sacks to playroom/playground and fill them with leaves, dirt, sand, and similar materials.
- Children will use sand and dump trucks to fill trucks and empty them.
- Children will make giant playhouse with climber and all get in simultaneously to fill it up.

PLANTING AND GROWING

Objective:

- To give children experiences to explore their own capacities to nurture and support growth.
- To allow children to observe and record changes of state and growth sequence.

Population:

- All children who are attending preschool in the late spring/early summer. May be especially relevant for graduating children who can take their plants with them at the end of the year as a symbol of their own growth.

Meeting (Surprise box: Seeds)

Songs

"Carrots grow from carrot seeds"
"Inch by inch, row by row"
"I wonder if I'm growing"

Books

Things that Grow (Stoneway Books)
Carrot Seed Book (R. Krauss)
An Egg is an Egg (N. Weiss)
A Letter for Amy (E. Jack Keats)

Activities

- Children and teachers will enact "Inch by Inch."
- Children will enact "Carrot Seed Song."

Group Activity Time

- Take walk around block to look at flowers—that is, things that are growing.
- Children sprout lima beans, popcorn, and other things, place on paper towels in plastic containers—later children plant in soil.
- Children draw what they think their seeds will grow into—dictate text.
- Children will experiment with predicting which things will grow when offered a selection of small items (including seeds) to plant. They can plant anything they select and chart growth. Later teacher can chart things that grow and things that don't.

Free Play Time

- Children will have opportunity to take care of flowers and plants.
- Children will have opportunity to play with bins of soil, sprinkling can and small garden implements.

Outdoor/Gross Motor Play Time

- Children can plant seeds in soil outside, use child size garden tools.
- Children can pretend to plant seeds in sand box.
- Children can make growth chart or body tracings on outside walls to become aware of their own growth.

TRANSPORTATION

Objective:
- To give children a focused experience with available transportation modalities.
- To help children represent transportation experiences using symbolic means.
- To help children get in touch with and express feelings about separation.

Population:
- Children who may feel disoriented by ventures away from school building.
- Children with age appropriate interests in transportation.

Meeting (Surprise box: Transportation theme stickers)

Songs
"Wheels on the Bus"
"Sammy"
"Row, Row, Row Your Boat"
"Going in the car, car"
"I'm Going to School Today"
"Subway Song"

Books
Wheels on the Bus (P. Zelinsky)
The City (D. Florian)
Things That Go (A. Rockwell)
Subway Sparrow (L. Torres)

Activities
- Teacher will introduce concept of trips using transportation stickers and a chart of destinations.
- Teacher will take photos of group transportation experiences and make a book to read at meeting.

Group Activity Time
- Children will take walking trip to store to buy foods for cooking activity. Dictate story about how it felt to walk away from school.
- Children will take bus trip to neighborhood pet store and childrens' library, and other places. Dictate story about how if felt to take a bus away from school.
- Children will build a bus with chairs and enact bus trips.
- Children will take subway trip to visit former classmates in new school placements.
- Children will make drawing book about trips and how they got there. They will dictate text to be written by teacher.
- Children and teacher will make chart, remembering what they saw on trips and what mode of transportation they liked or did not like.

Free Play Time
- Children will have opportunity to explore concept of going to various destinations through play with toy vehicles and people.
- Children will have opportunity to use a variety of construction materials to make trains, cars, boats, buses, airplanes, and so on.

Outdoor/Gross Motor Play Time
- Children will take turns "sailing" self or doll in boats made from plastic bins in swimming pool.
- Children will use bikes and wagons to pretend about various modes of transportation.
- Children will build roads with large blocks.

169

NEW SCHOOL / OLD SCHOOL

Objective:
- To help children understand concepts of "new" and "old."
- To help children anticipate change in school placement.
- To help children express feelings and concerns regarding major separations.

Population:
- Children who are remaining in the preschool and will see some of their classmates leave.
- Children who are anticipating a change in school placement.

Free Play Time
- Children will have opportunity to use buses and people to enact who is going to a new school and who is staying at old school.
- Children will have opportunity to use play telephones to talk to each other and teachers in old and new schools.

Outdoor/Gross Motor Play Time
- Children are invited to ride in cart and pretend it's a bus going to new and old school.
- Children are invited to use climbing frames or play houses to represent new and old schools.

Meeting (Surprise box: School Bus Toy)

Songs

"_____ rides the bus to school…" (tune of "I'm going to school today")

"Do you know my friend _____, my friend _____, Do you know my friend _____, who's going to a new school/coming back to this school" (tune: "Do You Know the Muffin Man?")

Books

First Day of School (Oxenbury)

Betsy's First Day of Day Care (G. Wolde)

Will I Have A Friend? (M. Cohen)

Teacher-made book, telling who is going to a new school and who is staying at old school

The Day Teddy Made New Friends (Jungman & Goffe)

Activities

- Teacher makes old and new schools for felt board, and children place cutouts of themselves in new or old school. This activity can be accompanied by choice of affect stickers representing children's feelings about going or staying behind.

Group Activity Time
- Children will paint old school and new school using individual cardboard boxes. (Children who are leaving will need 2 boxes.)
- Children will make school buses from shoe boxes, paint them yellow, glue on windows, and affix tires.
- Children will paint small individual cereal boxes to make lunchboxes. Teacher will help to attach pipe cleaner handles.
- Children will make tiny sandwiches, and so forth for lunchboxes, put lunchboxes in buses, and drive them to their old or new school to eat lunch.
- Group will phone former classmate(s) or write letters asking them how they now feel about their new schools—contrast with their feelings about leaving prior to departure.
- Children can paint large refrigerator boxes to represent "new" and "old" schools and can play out sequences of separation and remaining connected.

BOATS AND BRIDGES (End-of-Year Curriculum)

Objective:
- To give children a working metaphor for the experience of moving forward yet remaining connected.

Population:
- Children who will be moving on to another class or another school at the end of the year.
- Children who are remaining in preschool but experiencing the departure of peers.

Meeting (Surprise box w/Scotch Tape)

Songs

"Row, Row, Row Your Boat"

"This is the way we make a bridge, make a bridge, make a bridge...so we can go across"

Books

Jenny's Journey (S. Samton)

Where the Wild Things Are (M. Sendak)

The Little Red Lighthouse and The Great Grey Bridge (A. Swift & L. Ward)

Homemade photo book of trips to the river where children observe boats and bridges

Activities

- Children and teachers can use lengths of tape to bridge distances between them in meeting circle.
- Children and teachers can pull plastic slinkys to bridge distances between them, and then fold slinkys to minimize distance.

Group Activity Time

- Children, teachers and parents take tram or boat trip across the water, return to school and make representations of tram, water, boats, and so forth.
- Children and parents take walking trip across a bridge.
- Children make a variety of boats from: soap bars, celery, watermelon rinds, toothpicks, and sails in water.
- Children will use long wooden blocks to bridge individual water bins or buildings they have made from blocks.
- Children can make water mural, initially painting large sheet of paper blue and gluing cut out boats and bridges.
- During last day party, children and parents make banana boats, eat contents and then sail "boat" in pool of water.

Free Play Time

- Children will have opportunity to use toy boats and people in water bins.
- Children will have opportunity to use a variety of building materials to make bridges. Little people will be available to enact separation and connectedness.
- Toy telephones, envelopes, play stamps, and other items are available.

Outdoor/Gross Motor Play Time

- Children can use lengths of tape, yarn, and so on to bridge long distances in play yard.
- Children can go across and under "bridges" constructed from various playground equipment.
- Children can sail boats in wading pool.

171

PART IV

Understanding Special Populations

The Traumatized Child in Preschool

Lesley Koplow and Judith Ferber

THE IMAGES OF VIOLENCE and disaster that fill our evening news programs both involve and are witnessed by a population too young to be interviewed by reporters. These youngest witnesses and most vulnerable victims may survive the dangerous experiences that assault them, yet they may also have to surrender the energy of childhood to the burdensome task of coping with trauma. Because this process of surrender is often a silent one, early childhood professionals must be vigilant for signs that trauma has become a deterrent to a child's development. Indeed, if left untreated, trauma may become an invisible but potent force, acting to diminish a young child's developmental potential.

How can the early childhood professional learn to recognize and effectively treat the traumatized preschooler? Certainly information gathered in the psychosocial interview may alert the teacher or clinician to traumatic history and help them assess the child in light of his traumatic experiences. Yet the child's history may leave many unanswered questions. What exactly constitutes trauma for a young child? If the history includes traumatic experiences but the child remains asymptomatic, should she be considered a traumatized child? If a child shows symptoms of trauma but has no known traumatic history, does it mean that he has been traumatized by events that have not been known or acknowledged?

WORKING DEFINITIONS

There are many ways to look at the issues raised above. The diagnostic manual of the American Psychiatric Association (APA) includes a diagnosis for persons whose functioning has been compromised by trauma. This diagnosis, known as postraumatic stress disorder (PTSD), defines a traumatic event as one that "the person experiences, witnesses or is confronted with that involved actual or threatened death or serious injury, or a threat to the physical integrity of self or others"; during the incident, "the person's response involved fear, helplessness or horror." In children, these responses "may be expressed by agitated or disorganized behavior" (American Psychiatric Association, 2000).

The National Institute of Mental Health (NIMH) (2001) explains the term *psychiatric trauma* as referring to "an experience that is emotionally painful, distressful, or shocking which often results in lasting mental and physical effects" (p. 2). The NIMH notes that extreme reactions to trauma are normal since traumatic experiences are usually extreme events. While the majority of children and adults exposed to single-incident trauma will recover in the weeks and months following the traumatic experience if they have a good support network, children and families who experienced ongoing trauma, have traumatic histories, or have poor psychosocial supports are more vulnerable to long-term mental health problems such as depression and PTSD. Children who reexperience traumatic events out of context, actively avoid reminders of traumatic events, or show hyperarousal symptoms and regressed behavior for longer than a month may be diagnosed with the disorder.

We are gaining a growing understanding of the physiology of trauma and its powerful effects on children's overall well-being. While the psychological effects of trauma are observable and often palpable to teachers and clinicians, the physiology of trauma may be invisible, working as a potentially devastating force within the traumatized child. Children who are traumatized are likely to mobilize stress responses in the brain that can become damaging if they are overstimulated. Stress hormones, including adrenaline and cortisol, are released at high levels in order to mobilize an adequate response to crisis. When trauma is not ameliorated by supportive relationships, or occurs for a child who already has a history of trauma, or occurs repeatedly, these high levels of stress hormones may not subside. Rather, they can leave the traumatized child in a constant physiologic state of high alert, making him vulnerable to impulsive behavior in response to perceived threat and inhibiting higher-level thinking. Abnormal levels of chemicals that negatively impact learning, behavior, and memory have been found in people with PTSD (DeBellis et al., 1999). Over time, this can result in chronic immaturity of the brain's development, diminishing attention and memory capacity and causing emotional and behavioral difficulties (Gunnar & Donzella, 2002; Lupien et al., 1998; McEwen & Sapolsky, 1995).

Trauma or Deprivation?

Although trauma and deprivation both impact negatively on a young child's development, they are not synonymous, nor do they necessarily manifest in identical ways. For example, a 3-year-old and her 1-year-old sister attend a day-care center in a homeless shelter. The 3-year-old survived an apartment fire that endangered the lives of her entire family and destroyed their home. This little girl awakens frequently with nightmares of the traumatic event. The 1-year-old was born after the fire, while the family was living in the shelter. She reportedly has no difficulty sleeping through the night.

While the 3-year-old's development should be considered in light of her traumatic history, the 1-year-old cannot be said to have experienced trauma. She may have been deprived of important developmental opportunities due to high levels of parental stress and inadequate living space, but her homelessness is not equivalent to trauma. However, this toddler is certainly *at risk* for traumatic experiences, as congregate shelters are known to have high incidences of violence and drug activity. The toddler's living situation makes it likely that she will be underprotected, increasing the likelihood of a traumatic event. The inadequate provisions for family life and the sometimes threatening environment may raise her stress levels if the family remains in shelters over a long period of time. In addition, the family's history will certainly come to be meaningful to this little girl as she grows, and she may develop secondary symptoms of trauma as she takes in the traumatic affects of the people she loves.

The Disguises of Trauma

When 3-year-old Juana entered day care, it was hard for the teachers to think of her as a traumatized child. Her behavior was quite destructive. She frequently broke the other children's possessions as well as her own. She came dangerously close to igniting a paper tablecloth at a birthday party after a parent had accidentally dropped a book of matches.

Then one day a team of firefighters came for the annual inspection of the day-care center premises. Many of the children were fascinated by the visit of firefighters wearing their uniforms and carrying their special equipment. But not Juana. She stood still as if glued to the spot where she happened to be standing at first sight of the firemen, trembling violently, crying silent tears, and urinating into her clothes, unable to respond to the teacher's comforting overtures.

Later that day, several staff members expressed surprise at Juana's ability to remember a fire that had happened more than a year earlier, when Juana was only 2. While adults often seem incredulous about a young child's ability to remember and be affected by very early trauma, research shows that the youngest victims are indeed affected. Terr's study of traumatized children from birth to age 3 confirms that although children under 28 months of age have no verbal memories of a traumatic event, children of all ages have behavioral memories of trauma. These are expressed in fearfulness, play, reenactment, and dreams (Terr, 1988). In studies of traumatized people of all ages, Terr found that single traumatic events tended to heighten memory capacity and were remembered in detail for a lifetime. However, children who were repeatedly traumatized used defenses to disassociate themselves from the traumatic experiences and therefore frequently lacked memories from that period (Terr, 1990).

While many children affected by trauma do not meet the necessary diagnostic criteria for PTSD, children with a traumatic history often show at least some of the symptoms described, even if some present quite differently from Juana.

Consider the child with a traumatic history whose symptoms of increased arousal include hypervigilance and difficulty concentrating. Preschool children who have difficulty concentrating often flit from one activity to the next, appearing incapable of sustaining attention. They may express their high anxiety level through increased motor discharge, mirroring the symptoms of attention-deficit hyperactivity disorder (ADHD). Sadly, a child like this may receive no treatment for the trauma if the problem is misdiagnosed.

Another salient feature of PTSD in childhood is the loss of previously acquired ego capacities, such as language skills and toilet training (APA, 1994/2000). What happens to the toddler who is in process of mastering these essential developmental achievements when the trauma occurs? Such children are sometimes the victims of a trauma-induced developmental arrest, which may appear organic in nature if it is not assessed in light of the traumatic history. The assumption of organic retardation may result in inappropriate intervention programs that neglect the child's emotional life and ignore the need for corrective experience in order to facilitate optimal development.

Then there is the child who actually appears to be traumatized. He is timid, wide-eyed, and vigilant; avoids experiences that other children take for granted; and startles easily in reaction to seemingly benign stimuli.

These children present the preschool teacher with recognizable clues to the nature of their experiences, as well as insight into the intrapsychic mechanisms that they use to cope with the assault of trauma. When children act out their external and internal worlds in the classroom environment, they present special challenges as well as emotional burdens to the classroom staff. This chapter will help early childhood professionals to recognize behaviors that may be indicative of traumatic history and will heighten staff awareness of their own responses to traumatized children.

DIAGNOSTIC INDICATORS OF TRAUMA IN THE CLASSROOM

Since the traumatized child might easily be mistaken for a child who has other types of developmental difficulties, it is important to tease out those behaviors and qualities that distinguish traumatized children. Accurate recognition and understanding are essential for appropriate intervention. Diagnostic indicators of trauma will be described in the text that follows, and examples of each indicator will be given.

Hypervigilance

Many traumatized children are perpetually on guard. They are anxious, wary, and preoccupied with monitoring the environment for potential sources of injury or loss. Hypervigilant children are frequently assumed to have an attention-deficit hyperactivity disorder since their activity levels are high and attention spans seem compromised. The hypervigilant child may not have a primary deficit in attention but cannot afford to abandon his "watch" in order to ensure his own survival. In this way, hypervigilant children are deprived of essential play, learning, and social interactions, as they must stay alert to their external surroundings.

For example, Marissa, 3½ years old, sits at the table, absently scribbling with a crayon. Her gaze is fixed on the teacher, who is helping another child to stop from climbing on the table.

MARISSA (*to the teacher*): You going to hit her?
TEACHER: No, I'm not going to hit her. I'm trying to help her stay safe.

Marissa continues to observe the teacher as she moves around the room. When she notices the teacher walking toward the door, Marissa abruptly drops her crayon, jumps up, and is by the teacher's side before she even has her hand on the doorknob. "Where you going? I wanna go with you!" she cries anxiously.

Preoccupied and Disassociated States

Children who have been traumatized may sometimes present as preoccupied, inattentive, worried, dazed, "spacey," and uninterested in what is happening in the here-and-now. Trauma may stay in their consciousness and occupy their minds in a way that makes it difficult for them to attend to new input and take in new learning. Since traumatized children may not be taking in what is being presented in the classroom, they are unlikely to remember their learning. Repeated traumatization may indeed diminish a child's capacity for memory, as high levels of stress hormones can negatively impact memory functions (DeBellis et al, 1999; Gunnar & Donzella, 2002). A preoccupied state is also debilitating to peer relationships, as children seem uninvested in peers who then loose interest in initiating play.

Children who disassociate are often less preoccupied with traumatic experience in a conscious way. However, they may appear to "go far away," or lose connection with the here-and-now when confronted with an experience that evokes the trauma. Since they are not conscious of the traumatic experience to begin with, they may appear disoriented and seem as though they are in a strange and altered state. Teachers may feel frightened as they watch a child who is verbal and capable suddenly seem disconnected and oddly distressed without obvious cause. Disassociated states may look like psychotic episodes at times, and early childhood programs may require psychiatric consult in order to sort out one from the other.

Hyperarousal Responses

The traumatized child will often be startled by stimuli that might be perceived as benign by most children. For the majority of young children, noise and movement in the environment do not necessarily signal danger. To a certain extent, children learn to screen out peripheral stimuli and tune in to what is salient to them. Traumatized children, on the other hand, are often hypersensitive to peripheral auditory stimuli and are easily frightened by loud or unexpected noises. For instance, a traumatized 4-year-old would tense with fear each time a heating pipe banged or knocked in the nursery. While these noises went largely unnoticed by the other children, Jerome would freeze each time the pipes sounded: "Who's that?" he would ask breathlessly, "I think it's a bad man!"

Traumatized children may react to routine experience as though it were potentially threatening, mobilizing stress responses at times when other children and adults feel safe and comfortable. Walking down a staircase, riding in the elevator, using the bathroom, or passing a police car during an outing may trigger hyperarousal responses in traumatized children who have some negative association to the activity in which or place where they find themselves. Children may become anxious, become frozen in their tracks, scream and refuse to participate, begin to cry, or try to hurry through or run away from the situation that they find threatening.

Hyperarousal responses may also make rest time extremely difficult for traumatized children who may not be able to relax and go to sleep. Since children often rely on a high activity level to fend off intrusions of traumatic memories or affects, the inactivity required of children at rest time is often untenable, and children tend to act out or resist the routine in some way. Without being able to move around, traumatized children may feel too vulnerable. They may be flooded by inner turmoil and simultaneously fear attack. Because rest time tends to be dark in many centers and is sometimes done without the classroom teacher present, young traumatized children who may not have resolved object constancy issues may feel alone and unprotected.

Flashbacks

Traumatized children sometimes experience flashbacks of a traumatic event. During a flashback, the traumatized child reexperiences the event as if it is happening to him in the present moment. The reality at hand is lost as the child becomes reimmersed in the traumatic experience. While this symptom has been described and documented in war veterans, it is often unfamiliar to the early childhood educator.

For example, Emmanuel, at age 4, had already been in three different foster homes. His social worker reported that when visiting him in his original home (just prior to removal), she had discovered Emmanuel and his siblings in a state of extreme neglect. They were sitting listlessly on the floor, clad in nothing but diapers, which were riddled with cockroaches. Emmanuel was nearly 2 years old at the time.

One day in Emmanuel's preschool, the children are changing into their swimsuits to go in the wading pool. Emmanuel suddenly looks at his underwear in horror and begins to scream, "Cockroaches! Cockroaches!" He scrambles to get the undergarment off, flings it away, and, sobbing, grips the teacher in fright. "Cockroaches, cockroaches in my pants," he moans again and again. The teacher checks Emmanuel's underwear and finds no roaches.

Panic Attacks

When a traumatized child has a panic attack, he seems to become lost in a flood of anxiety. During the panic attack, the child may lose access to many of his ego capacities and/or experience bodily manifestations of his emotional crisis. The child might cry or scream inconsolably, tremble, hyperventilate, urinate, defecate, vomit, or sweat profusely. He might recoil into a fetal position, flail, perseveratively yell out a demand, or pummel his comforter without seeming to realize her presence.

Panic attacks might resemble ordinary temper tantrums, but should not be confused with them. Temper tantrums, which are part of the normal course of a young child's development, occur and are usually resolved in the context of the young child's relationship with his caregiver. A temper tantrum may be seen as representing the child's current struggle to resolve his rage at his caregiver for placing limitations on his heretofore enjoyed omnipotence.

In contrast, a panic attack in a traumatized child seems to involve the resurrection of old terrors. These terrors are associated with former traumatic experiences that may themselves remain unconscious. During panic attacks, children seem to lose their connection with others and become emotionally isolated. Panic attacks can be triggered by seemingly mundane events in a traumatized child's daily life. A panic attack is usually not resolved quickly and can continue for a long period of time until the child is simply spent.

For example, 4-year-old Jerome had been removed from his home and placed in foster care when he was 1½. He had failed to thrive as an infant because his mother, a heroin addict, had been unable to provide him with adequate physical or emotional nourishment.

One day in his nursery classroom, Jerome stands frozen at the refrigerator, frowning, his eyes downcast. He has asked for a cupcake and been refused; the teacher has explained that the cupcakes are being saved for a birthday party later that morning. Suddenly Jerome bursts into tears. "Gimme it! Gimme it!" he begins to wail. He acts as though he is starving, although he ate 15 minutes earlier. His screams grow louder and higher pitched. He stretches his arms toward the cupboard again and again as tears, perspiration, and mucus stream down his face. The other children look on in amazement. When the teacher tries to comfort him, Jerome shrugs her hand away and seems oblivious to her words. This continues for a full 15 minutes until Jerome is finally exhausted and collapses in a heap on the floor.

Traumatic Play

Trauma can alter the quality of the young child's play in several ways. Some traumatized children are quite restricted in their range of play activities. Many traumatized children are initially unable to use play symbolically. Trauma may have interrupted developmental processes to the extent that symbolic capacities were not well developed. Early relationships may have been disrupted, preventing the child from using transitional objects and other toys as symbols for significant people and experiences.

Some traumatized children have developed their symbolic capacities, but at times the quality of their symbolic play is unlike that of most young children. Gone is the sense of joyful adventure, story, and spirited and imaginative discovery that is characteristic of childhood. Traumatic play is grim, businesslike, and driven; it often contains traumatic affects that belong to the experience of the trauma being played out. It tends to lack flexibility and becomes less and less collaborative if peers are involved. Disturbing themes develop but are not resolved in the context of the play. The traumatized child's play can become perseverative as the child is driven to play and replay his traumatic experiences in a compulsive attempt to master them. Traumatic play tends to alienate other children, who become upset by the content or traumatic affects and usually decide to play elsewhere.

Four-year-old Patrick had experienced sudden and multiple upheavals due to domestic violence. His play at school reflects this. One day, having fashioned a "house" out of furniture and blankets, Patrick turns suddenly to his playmate, Devon, and shouts, "Quick—the bad man is coming! He's going to kill us! Let's get out of here!" Frantically, he grabs the baby doll, collects his belongings, and moves them to the other side of the room. He yells at Devon, "Get the baby's things! Hurry up—the bad man is going to get us!" Devon tarries at the "house." "Come on, Devon! That's the bad house; this is a good house." Patrick begins to construct a "good house," using tables, chairs, a blanket, and tape. Perspiring heavily as he works, he sweeps the room with his eyes at intervals. He painstakingly orders the contents of the "house." He is intent upon his arrangement and will allow for no interruption. Patrick instructs Devon to help him barricade one of the openings with a chair, but Devon has lost interest. Patrick does it himself. "That's so the bad man can't get in," he whispers solemnly to himself.

THE DEFENSES OF TRAUMATIZED CHILDREN

Traumatized children may use defenses in the classroom in uncomfortable and challenging ways. One of the psychological mechanisms that children will employ to defend against the painful feelings brought on by traumatic experiences is called identification with the aggressor. In cases of physical or psychological abuse, the person who traumatizes the child is often a parent or other member of the family upon whom the child depends for care and security. Thus, the child's alliance with this person is one he cannot afford to lose, despite the conflict it creates. Identifying with the aggressor allows the child to maintain this alliance; however, preserving it requires a great emotional sacrifice on the part of the child. By identifying with the aggressor, the child drives underground his own very real feelings of injury, fear, and helplessness. He instead often embodies the powerful aggression of the adult. The child may behave in a sadistic manner toward others, show little empathy, and seem to be disconnected from his own hurt and fragility.

For example, 4-year-old Antonia looks quizzically at the lifelike monkey puppet before her. A sadistic gleam appears in her eyes. Skillfully, Antonia cuts a piece of masking tape and pins the monkey's arms behind its back.

> ANTONIA: I'm gonna tie you up, monkey. Now you can't move.
> TEACHER: Isn't that going to make monkey sad?
> ANTONIA: He's a bad monkey.
> TEACHER: Why is he bad?
> ANTONIA: He made a mess.
> TEACHER: All monkeys make a mess sometimes. That doesn't mean they're bad, even if some grown-ups get mad.
> ANTONIA (*ignoring her*): Monkey, I'm gonna whip your butt. (*She hits the monkey repeatedly.*) Now, I'm gonna lock you up—in the dark! (*She crams the monkey into the play refrigerator and closes the door.*) Ha, ha, ha! I'm glad you're cryin'! That's good for you.

Another defense mechanism often used by traumatized and abused children is called splitting. Splitting happens when children are not able to resolve object constancy issues in a positive way. A very important developmental task for the young child is the psychological integration of both the gratifying and the frustrating aspects of his parent or primary caretaker. In normal development, as the increasingly autonomous toddler confronts parental limits, he must come to terms with the fact that the very same person who nurtures him can also be the source of frustration. The toddler becomes able to tolerate this frustration, so long as it occurs in gradual and masterable levels, within the context of a positive relationship with his parent. He is certainly ambivalent about his parents but becomes able to integrate the "good" and "bad" feelings he has in response to them, and he develops a generally positive nurturing image to call upon.

The development of a unified image can be complicated for the traumatized child. When the parent is the source of either physical or psychological injury, the child is presented with unmanageable levels of frustration. Often, in order to preserve a positive image of the parent, the child "splits" off the very negative feelings aroused by the traumatic experience and projects them onto someone else. The child thus comes to see the parent as "all good" and the other as "all bad." This can sometimes occur with traumatized children even if the parent was not the direct source of the trauma but (in the eyes of the child) failed to protect him from the traumatic event. In this case, too, the parent engenders the child's rage, and the child splits off these negative feelings. This psychological split is frequently played out in the classroom in the context of the child's relationships with his teachers. The child who splits will characterize the limit-setting teacher as "all bad" and another teacher, in contrast, as "all good." For example, a child who splits may respond to limit setting in the following way:

TEACHER: Stephan, you need to stop throwing toys; it's dangerous. If
        you're angry, you can use your words and tell me why you are mad.
STEPHAN: Shut up, fucker. (*He throws a toy car, which narrowly misses
        the head of another child.*)
TEACHER: This is not okay. That will hurt someone. I'm going to hold
        your hands and help you stop.
STEPHAN (*kicking teacher*): Get offa me! Let go of me! (*He turns to the
        assistant teacher, who is sitting nearby.*) Elaine, help me! Save me!
        (*Breaking free, he runs to Elaine and jumps in her lap, clinging to
        her and glowering at the first teacher.*) See, that's why I hate you,
        you're stupid, you're ugly. You're a bad teacher. Elaine is a nice
        teacher.

COMMUNITY TRAUMA: LESSONS FROM 9/11
AND HURRICANE KATRINA

Recent tragedies affecting thousands and thousands of young children in America have brought us closer to issues of community trauma and their effects on individual children over time. The attacks of September 11, 2001, and the devastating experience of Hurricane Katrina in 2005 challenged early childhood programs to practice under frightening circumstances and to address issues of trauma and loss in the early childhood center. While children who suffer trauma within the privacy of the family system often show traumatic affects and other symptoms of posttraumatic stress in the classroom, the teacher frequently has little context for understanding where these affects have come from and what the exact nature of the traumatic experience has been until she can gain access to the child's psychosocial story. Community trauma offers the early childhood professional the opportunity and the challenge of acknowledging shared traumatic experience and thus diminishing the emotional isolation that is often an insidious outcome of trauma.

Studies of the effects of 9/11 on children in New York City offer some important lessons for practitioners and policymakers. The children most likely to experience symptoms of posttraumatic stress after September 11 were children directly exposed to the destruction of the towers, children whose parents were in harm's way, children who lived in close proximity to the towers, and children with traumatic histories (NIMH, 2001). Symptoms such as nightmares, fears, and separation anxiety were persistent for many affected children, continuing into the 3-year follow-up period measured (U.S. Government Accountability Office, 2004). Almost all directors of early childhood programs interviewed in 2001–2002 reported repeated play themes involving building and knocking down block towers with planes or toys symbolizing planes. Representations of this traumatic event predominated when children were allowed to draw and paint freely in early childhood and early-grade programs in New York City and surrounding communities. The descriptions of play and the dictations taken on the children's drawings included examples of both healthy, integrative play and traumatic play.

While there were many opportunities to help children sort out what they were seeing and hearing after September 11, there was a disturbing trend in early childhood and early-grade programs in New York City to "go back to business as usual" without acknowledging what had happened. Many teachers were told not to mention the World Trade Center unless children brought up the topic themselves. Children were therefore often left to fall back on their own resources to make sense of what they were seeing and hearing on TV, to process the traumatic affects on the faces of the adults in their world, and to deal with their reactions to that tragic day. Since many young children were unable to formulate questions about the attacks or express their fears directly, their fears were expressed in regressions in functioning and difficult behavior. Fortunately, Federal Emergency Management Agency (FEMA) funds made possible Project Liberty, a program of child mental health working with individual children in the downtown Manhattan public schools. One intervention professional reported needing to point out to teachers and directors again and again that the increase in children's regressive behavior in the winter of 2001 and spring of 2002 could still be related to their emerging reactions to the events of September 11.

While some programs provided the older children and families in their care with opportunities to communicate and symbolize their feelings, in many schools there was a pervasive institutional denial about the effects of this trauma on the youngest schoolchildren. There was a tendency for administrators to cling to the belief that young children should "hear no evil and speak no evil," in spite of what we know to be true about traumatic experience in childhood. Statistics show that the younger the exposed child, the more likely he or she is to develop posttraumatic stress disorder in response to trauma. The Center for the Advancement of Health (2001) finds that 39% of preschool children develop PTSD in response to trauma and compare that to 33% of primary school children and 24% of adults.

While trying to protect young children from an unthinkable event, early childhood professionals struggled to protect themselves from the secondary trauma of living through the children's emotional expression at a time when they themselves were shaken, overwhelmed, and often suffering effects of trauma. Paradoxically, the fact that teachers and parents were so traumatized by the attacks themselves often resulted in a need to imagine that their young children had not taken in what had occurred. Yet when a group of 4-year-olds in upper Manhattan were offered the opportunity to share their feelings about things going on in the city that they had seen on television or heard about 2 weeks after the attacks, all of the 20 children referred to the buildings at the World Trade Center that had been knocked down by planes (Koplow, 2002). The comments ranged from mentions of the televised footage of the attacks as "a scary movie," to references to people dying because they jumped out the window, to observations that "people were singing America's favorite song and holding the flag because they are sad that the bad guys had come."

At the time of this writing, the majority of children and families affected by Hurricane Katrina are still scattered, displaced from their communities and waiting for assistance with housing, jobs, education, and other basic needs. Those who have been attending to Katrina-affected children note the unprecedented scale of this disaster, which displaced 372,000 children (Crowel, 2005). Crowel notes that research predicts that 10% to 30% of people exposed to traumatic events on the scale of Katrina develop mental health problems, yet little funding has been released to address the special needs of Katrina-affected children. We know that the children most likely to develop posttraumatic stress symptoms and disorders are those who have had other traumatic experiences, who have poor psychosocial supports, and who have had disruptions in family relationships. Since the flooded communities of New Orleans were high-poverty areas with few social supports and an escalating problem of violence before the hurricane hit, it is likely that large numbers of the children and families displaced by Katrina are at risk. Currently, a study funded by the NIMH is underway in three communities in Louisiana where children's school performance and social adjustment pre- and post-Katrina will be studied (Kelley, 2002).

The National Institute for Mental Health notes that teachers can do a lot to help children within the context of community trauma. It encourages teachers to allow children to have their sad and angry feelings and to give children the opportunity to talk about what happened without forcing them to participate in the discussions. It cautions against going back to "the ordinary" too quickly (NIMH, 2001). The NIMH encourages schools to offer art and play therapy in the wake of community trauma, as well as groups for parents. The research shows that children under 5 are especially affected by their parents' reaction to the traumatic experience and are not likely to adjust if their parents are acutely traumatized. It alerts teachers to watch for the symptom of emotional numbing in children or lack of feeling about the event as a risk factor for the development of PTSD (NIMH, 2001). In addition, H. S. Koplewicz of the New York University Child Study Center notes that children who watch TV coverage of the events in the wake of the original trauma are twice as likely to develop PTSD symptoms as children whose parents do not allow them to watch (Koplewicz, 2005). Young children who are exposed to repeated media portrayals of a disaster often experience the disaster as though it were happening over and over and do not understand that the pictures they are seeing are depicting the original event.

In the 2005–2006 schoolyear, the staff at the Center for Emotionally Responsive Practice at Bank Street College heard an unusual number of teachers reporting high levels of anxiety and disorganization in their prekindergarten children. In addition, teachers in preschools located in downtown Manhattan reported a resurgence of building and destroying play buildings between 2003 and 2005. On a trip to explore their downtown neighborhood, a group of children who had turned 4 in 2005 stopped to interview one of the doormen about the building he was attending. To the teacher's surprise, several questions were asked about what would happen if the building were to fall down or another building were to fall on top of it. The doorman responded by reassuring the children that the building was strong and wouldn't fall down. Children responded by informing the doorman that the building "might" fall down if somebody knocked it down, or "another building might fall on top of it and then it would fall down" (Beausoleil, 2006).

The work of Dr. Lenore Terr (1988) suggests that the children who were babies and toddlers during the attacks of September 11 and were directly exposed to the violence may have been traumatized by the event and that the need to represent and express traumatic affects may develop as they children develop. Those babies and toddlers who were not directly exposed were likely impacted by the anxiety that their parents experienced, and outcomes for young children are often directly related to the emotional well-being of their parents (NIMH, 2001).

There have been studies noting a higher prevalence of early and premature births during the fall of 2001 (U.S. Government Accountability Office, 2004). This was thought to be the result of the high level of maternal anxiety during that time. The children in preschools during the schoolyears 2003–2005 were born in 2001–2002, into a world on high alert. Studies of the effect of community trauma on these children may yield important information about the effect of community trauma on infants and on children in utero and in infancy.

COUNTERTRANSFERENCE ISSUES FOR TEACHERS
OF TRAUMATIZED CHILDREN

The behaviors of traumatized children and the awareness of their traumatic experiences can provoke a range of feelings in the adults who take care of them. This phenomenon of countertransference refers to the conscious or unconscious emotional reactions in the therapist or teacher that are evoked by the child's affects, behaviors, and issues. Countertransferential reactions can be powerful and sometimes confusing to the early childhood professional. Since all teachers and therapists were once children, being with children is likely to bring back childhood experiences for the adult. Countertransference may be heightened with traumatized children because they may bring high levels of emotional distress into the classroom and behave in disturbing ways. Understandably, some teachers might be tempted to diminish the intensity of countertransference by maintaining a pretense that the world children inhabit is a perpetually cheerful and sunny place. Many early childhood classrooms model and represent only positive affects with children. Children are encouraged to be "happy" and "nice." Difficult behaviors are addressed so that "not nice" interactions can be eliminated without trying to connect behavior to the child's psychological state and life experience. Sadly, the overly cheerful classroom environment that denies the traumatized child's emotional experiences can leave him alone with his feelings and worries and may be paradoxically as isolating as a harsh, strict, repressive environment.

It is important for teachers to understand their own countertransference issues. Indeed, if a teacher is to become a healing partner in development for a young traumatized child, her own affects, language, and interactions must be genuine. This requires her to take in the whole child, including the part that has been traumatized and may be exhibiting inappropriate or disturbing behavior. The teacher's own history as a young child who went to school and was taken care of by parents and teachers is present in the classroom as children's intense emotions surround her. Fellow staff members can become important resources to teachers overwhelmed by their own countertransference in schools that heal. Administrative support for teachers who work with large numbers of children with traumatic histories is essential for the teacher's ability to create and sustain an empathic, healing environment. The challenges of teaching traumatized children must be acknowledged and given a time and place to be expressed within the school community or the greater community. If countertransference is dealt with positively, it can become a useful tool for teachers seeking to gain insight into themselves and into what the children in their classrooms are experiencing. If a teacher is feeling afraid and inundated by a child's frightening emotional energy, it is likely the child is also awash in fear.

Community trauma can present especially intense countertransferential challenges for a teacher or clinician who has also been affected by the traumatic event. The teachers in New York who were watching children knock their buildings down with toy planes struggled to tolerate the play and reassure children that they were safe when they themselves felt endangered. A teacher in Baton Rouge who watched in horror as young children and their parents were stranded on rooftops for days before the government mobilized an adequate response to Hurricane Katrina found herself in tears when a group of those children transferred into her classroom a few weeks later. Early childhood programs that heal provide support for staff during trying times so that they are able to be truly present for children in crisis. Without support, teachers may need to minimize their empathy for the children's pain in order to feel strong enough to teach through the crisis.

TEACHER–CHILD RELATIONSHIP: THE IMPORTANCE OF ATTACHMENT AND CONTINUITY

How should teachers in healing preschools help those children whose development has been hampered by their traumatic experiences? To begin, the therapeutic teacher can provide traumatized children with an opportunity to develop a trusting and secure relationship with an adult and with the world around them. Many traumatized children have had to contend with disorganized and unpredictable home environments, inconsistent care, and frightening occurrences in their lives. The therapeutic teacher can offer these children another emotional experience by creating a classroom environment that is safe and predictable and by providing care that is nurturing, secure, and reliable.

Preschools that heal create a consistent and containing classroom structure and daily routine. The routines should be easy for children to master and recognize. Within the routines there must be opportunities for self-expression and symbolic representation of affects and events. The teacher must assume that traumatized children need help negotiating change and should assist them in anticipating transitions or variations in the routine. Giving the children time to prepare and helping them to master changes by anticipating them is essential. If the class plans to take a walk to the river, for example, the teacher can have the children try to imagine what they might see there and ask them to draw a picture about it beforehand.

Addressing Specific Vulnerabilities of Traumatized Children

Traumatized children often have a great deal of difficulty tolerating separations without becoming frightened about being hurt or abandoned. The teacher should anticipate the children's anxiety, provide reassurance about routine separations, and help them predict reunion. This helps children feel more secure when adults come and go from the classroom.

Traumatized children frequently perceive their environments as potentially dangerous. These children need help to know that school is a protective place, that a loud noise or a sudden movement does not necessarily indicate danger, and that at school the grown-ups will make sure that everybody stays safe. Therapeutic teachers must verbalize these reassurances several times a day.

Traumatized children often fear for their very survival and can panic when they suspect that their needs will not be met. Eating, toileting, and naptimes can therefore become anxious and difficult. At snacktimes and mealtimes, children might grab and hoard food, avoid or later have difficulty leaving the table, or panic when something is denied them. It helps to provide children with consistent and adequate amounts of nurture and food at snacktimes and mealtimes. Children need to know that at school grown-ups will make sure that all the children get enough.

The teacher should anticipate that naptime might be a particularly anxious time for traumatized children. This is often frustrating for teachers since the children who cannot seem to tolerate rest time are often the same children who are exhausted and really need to rest. Traumatized children often prefer to be active as a way of distancing themselves from traumatic memories and traumatic affects. They may resist rest time because it leaves them vulnerable to being flooded by disturbing memories and feelings. Children may be tired and need to rest but might have frightening associations with the dark, have scary dreams, or fear losing track of the adult. It helps to allow children to hold a transitional object, such as a soft toy or blanket. They may need to rest close to where the teacher is sitting or have a night-light plugged in near their resting spot to remind them that the teacher is present and to keep them oriented. Children who cannot sleep need the option of looking at a book quietly or listening to soft music. The teacher can reassure children that she will be there to keep them safe and talk about what will happen when they wake up so that naptime does not seem never ending.

The therapeutic teacher should also be mindful that toileting might be anxiety provoking for traumatized children. Some children might experience separation anxiety or feel vulnerable to intrusion in the bathroom. Some children might avoid going to the bathroom, while others will want to go every 5 minutes. Some traumatized children might want the adult very close and engage her in constant chatter, while others will want the adult to station herself at a distance. Some children may imagine monsters or become hypersensitive to noises while in the bathroom. It helps to be aware of these difficulties and to empathize with the child's fears. The teacher should reassure the child that she will neither abandon him nor intrude upon him in the bathroom, that she would be sure that he is safe there.

The needs of traumatized children will often require a clinical as well as educational approach. Teachers who can partner with mental health professionals in their programs or develop relationships with clinical consultants who are available to offer guidance and support will have the additional resources needed to manage the care of traumatized children in the classroom. Many traumatized children will require individual therapy, family intervention, and sometimes psychiatric attention in order to ensure their well-being. Educational/clinical partnerships are often the traumatized child's best hope for a better future. The teacher and the clinician may each breath a sigh of relief to know that they are not alone in the experience of caring for this fragile and difficult young child.

Using Therapeutic Language with the Traumatized Child

Teachers frequently feel at a loss for words when confronted with the responses, reactions, and behaviors of traumatized children. Teachers who want to create healing environments can learn to use language that helps to reassure, reorient, contain, and support the traumatized child without negating the traumatic material. For example, when a firefighter came to inspect the sprinkler system at an urban preschool, the teacher asked if any of the kids had questions to ask him. A little boy raised his hand. "Why does the whole world have so many fires? And the firemans took so long to come that it made my sister dead in heaven."

The classroom teacher in a situation like this may feel anxious about responding. She may be unsure how to proceed or whether to intrude in a conversation like that between the child and the firefighter. The firefighter's response was to ignore the personal part of the question and to tell the little boy that firetrucks go as fast as they can and use their sirens and their horns to get to the fire right away. The teacher may be tempted to move on and let the other children have a chance to talk. She may be tempted to pick up on the reference to heaven as a way of comforting both this bereaved child and the other children that heard the story.

In preschools that heal the teacher resists the temptation to move on and uses language to affirm the boy's loss and to reframe his conclusions. She says, "Most of the time the firefighters get to a fire fast enough to save people if they are in the burning building, but the fire in Christopher's building burned very quickly, and his little sister couldn't get out in time to be saved. She died and that is so sad for Christopher and his family." Another child raises her hand. "My stove got a fire and it burned up the rice." The teacher assures the children that at school they are very careful about fires, and that's why sometimes they practice going out of the building in case there was ever a fire, so that everyone would be safe. It is common to hear teachers refer to keeping children safe in preschools that heal. Traumatized children may need to hear that they cannot do dangerous things in school because those things aren't safe and in school the teachers work hard to keep the children safe. Children may also need to hear that teachers will make sure that each child has enough of what they need. They may need the teacher to let them know where she is going when she steps out of the classroom and when she will be back.

When children are panicking, having flashbacks, or in a preoccupied or dissociated state, it may be useful for the teacher to help the children differentiate her past experiences from the circumstances of the here-and-now. The child who is shrieking in the bathroom, or cramming his mouth full of crackers, or hiding under the table shaking when a loud truck roars by the building may need to hear the teacher say "Maybe you remember": "Maybe you remember a time when the bathroom was a scary place for you. Now you're here in preschool and I will make sure you stay safe in the bathroom." "Maybe you remember a time when you didn't have enough food to eat. In our classroom we always make sure that the kids get enough crackers at snacktime." "Maybe you remember a time when a loud noise meant something dangerous. The noise we just heard was a big truck passing by, but it can't come into our school building."

When children affected by community trauma play about the traumatic experience or make drawings about it, teachers can ask the children if they are thinking about what happened and if they want to tell the story of their drawing or play for the teacher to write down. School is a safe place for children to talk and play and draw about scary things that happen. The teacher should acknowledge that she, too, remembers when the traumatic event happened and that it was a scary time for everyone.

Of course, language will not be the teacher's only tool for helping traumatized children in the classroom. The teacher's classroom routines and curriculums should also be infused with her knowledge about the life experiences that her children have had (see Chapters 8 and 9). A curriculum that uses teddy bears as transitional objects during times of crisis was developed after September 11 and can be adapted for different kinds of community trauma (Koplow, 2002).

CONCLUSION

Children with traumatic histories make their presence in the classroom felt in intense, sometimes disturbing, and often compelling ways. The early childhood professional who develops her repertoire of responses will be less anxious and more confident when caring for traumatized children. The traumatized child who is fortunate enough to come into a preschool setting where his experiences are validated and where his emotional needs are recognized will be able to begin the process of healing. Little by little, the early childhood professional can help to facilitate a dialogue between the child's past and present experiences and thus help her to integrate the traumatic material in the safety of the everyday classroom environment. This dialogue can decrease the traumatized child's feelings of isolation and increase receptivity to learning over time.

REFERENCES

American Psychiatric Association (APA). (2000). *Diagnostic and statistical manual of mental disorders* (4th ed., rev.). Washington, DC: Author.

Beausoleil, L. (2006). The youngest witnesses. In Teachers College Press with M. Grolnick (Eds.), *Forever after*, New York: Teachers College Press.

Center for the Advancement of Health. (2001). One year later: Post traumatic stress takes toll on children. *Facts of Life* [Online newsletter], 7(9). Retrieved July 14, 2006, from http://www.cfah.org/factsoflife/vol7no.9.cfm*<http://www.cfah.org/factsoflife/vol7no.9.cfm>

Crowel, R. (2005, November). *In harm's way: Aiding children exposed to trauma* (Grant-makers in Health Issue Brief No. 23). Retrieved February 9, 2007, from http://www.gih.org

DeBellis, M. D., Baum, A. S., Birmaher, B., Keshavan, M. S., Eccard, C. H., Boring, A. M., Jenkins, F. J., & Ryan, N. (1999). Developmental traumatology, Part 1: Biological stress systems. *Biological Psychiatry, 45*(10), 1259–1270.

Gunnar, M. R., & Donzella, B. (2002). Social regulation of the cortisol levels in early human development. *Psychoneuroendocrinology, 27*, 199–220.

Kelley, M. L. (2002). *Children's adjustment in the aftermath of Hurricane Katrina.* Retrieved August 8, 2006, from http://www.lsu.edu/psychology/faculty/documentKelley.htm

Koplewicz, H. (2005, September 10). *TV viewing of Katrina affects children psychologically.* Retrieved August 8, 2006, from http://www.doctorslounge.com/Psychiatry/articles/ptsd_Katrina/index.htm

Koplow, L. (2002). *Creating schools that heal: Real life solutions.* New York: Teachers College Press.

Lupien, S. J., de Leon, M. J., Santi, S. D., Convit, A., Tarshish, C., Nair, N. P. V., Thakur, M., McEwen, B., Hauger, R. L., & Meaney, M. J. (1998). Cortisol levels during human aging predict hippocampal atrophy and memory deficits. *Nature Neuroscience, 1*(1), 69–73.

McEwen, B. S., & Sapolsky, R. M. (1995). Stress and cognitive function. *Current Opinion in Neurobiology, 5*(2), 205–216.

National Institute of Mental Health NIMH). (2001). *Helping children and adolescents cope with violence and disasters* (U.S. Department of Health and Human Services Publication No. 1). Bethesda, MD: National Institute of Mental Health. Available online at http://www.nimh.nih.gov/publicat/index.cfm

Terr, L. (1988). What happens to early memories of trauma? A study of twenty children under the age of five at the time of documented traumatic events. *Journal of American Academy of Child and Adolescent Psychiatry, 27*(1), 96–104.

Terr, L. (1990). *Too scared to cry: Psychic trauma in childhood.* New York: Harper & Row.

U.S. Government Accountability Office. (2004, September 8). *September 11th: Health effects in the aftermath of the World Trade Center attack* (GAO-04-1068-T). Statement of Janet Heinrich before the Subcommittee on National Security, Emerging Threats, and International Relations of the House Committee on Government Reform. 108th Cong., 2nd sess.

Helping Children with Autistic Spectrum Disorders

Lesley Koplow, Suzanne Abrams, Judith Ferber, and Beverley Dennis

CHILDREN WITH AUTISTIC SPECTRUM DISORDERS often have developmental patterns that are perplexing to their parents and teachers. Unlike children with overall delays in general development, children on the spectrum show an uneven developmental pattern, sometimes appearing to be simultaneously "enabled" and "disabled." While these children may be unable to answer a question, join another child in play, or make a routine transition unassisted, they may be able to recite the alphabet flawlessly and identify colors and print number symbols before their peers can. While they may be motivated to assemble a complex puzzle that would be daunting for most other preschool children, they may seem unmotivated and unable to engage in pretend play with other children. It is therefore crucial for the early childhood professional to become well acquainted with the abilities and difficulties demonstrated by the child with a pervasive developmental disorder so that intervention can facilitate the integration of strengths and weaknesses.

Autistic spectrum disorders (ASD), or *pervasive developmental disorders* (PPD), have been seen differently by professionals from various disciplines. ASD is sometimes described as a psychiatric disorder, a communication disorder, and a disorder of sensory integration by professionals of different disciplines. While outcomes for children diagnosed with ASD were historically considered to be poor, recent long-term studies of children who received early, intensive, high-quality intervention for many years showed more positive adjustment (Greenspan, 1997, 2006; Pruitt & Madigan, 1991). The continuum of autistic spectrum disorders is wide. It includes severe autism as well as less debilitating disorders. A complete list of criteria for the diagnosis of severe autism can be found in the *Diagnostic and Statistical Manual of Mental Disorders* (American Psychiatric Association, 2000), but it may be summarized as a profound lack of responsiveness to others, a failure to develop communicative language, and a restriction of activities to those that involve repetitive manipulations of the body or the environment. Severely autistic children are often diagnosed by the time they are toddlers, as their difficulties are global and apparent. However, when children on the autistic spectrum come into the preschool setting without having had early intervention, it may be difficult to assess just where they are on the spectrum until appropriate intervention is put into place.

Also on the continuum of autistic spectrum disorders are *pervasive developmental disorders not otherwise specified* (PDD NOS). While children with PDD NOS do not show the profound lack of responsiveness that characterizes the autistic child, they show some features of autism. There are qualitative differences in their social and emotional interactions that are not indicative of normal developmental processes. They may develop some language and be able to make needs and wants known, but their language is idiosyncratic and lacking in symbolic value. It may seem difficult for such children to enter into a dialogue that involves shared meaning with the other. Yet because PDD NOS children may show evidence of average or even superior cognitive potential and be somewhat responsive to parents and teachers, it may be more difficult for those involved with them to see the need for early intervention. Instead, concerned adults may support what they believe to be the child's strengths while minimizing the observed areas of weakness. Paradoxically, this strategy may reinforce the PDD NOS child's own tendency to compensate for fragility by rigidly adhering to areas of "expertise," which often become ritualistic and can narrow social opportunity. This chapter will describe the child with PDD NOS, analyze his core issues and the meaning of his atypical behavior, suggest intervention strategies, and demonstrate their implementation using a case study format.

CORE ISSUES

While children with general delays in development may benefit from more time to achieve essential milestones, children with PDD NOS are misserved by a "wait-and-see" approach. Adults who care about these children must work hard to understand and address their core issues of relatedness, symbolic functioning, and language development while they are young.

The development of children on the PDD NOS continuum is characterized by qualitative differences and by an atypical sequence of development that seems to circumvent the birth of symbolic capacities. Their play patterns often seem empty, as do their connections to peers. These patterns indicate a clear need for early intervention. Children who are left alone to fill in their own developmental gaps may evolve compensatory strategies and defenses that become increasingly rigid as they grow up, leaving them less and less receptive to participating in healthy relationships.

Relatedness

The young child with PDD has an atypical way of relating to others. Those who have observed PDD children will note a seeming obliviousness to those around them, or a physical merging with others, or a tendency to relate to people as though they existed only to perform certain expected tasks. In order to understand the PDD child, we must explore the issue of relatedness and discover the ways in which relatedness impacts the development of symbolic capacities in young children.

Relatedness may be defined as a state of remaining connected to one's self as well as to others. Relatedness in young children is manifested differently at various developmental stages. For example, relatedness in infancy may be seen in the child's heightened level of receptivity to adult affects, facial expressions, and mood, while relatedness in toddlerhood may be manifested by a need to oppose the adult and to lay a personal claim to the world. Relatedness in the preschool child is expressed in the child's motivation to convey his experiences to the adult, which bridges physical distance and demonstrates his capacity to remain connected even when physically separate. In addition, relatedness in play with other preschool children involves the creation of mutually meaningful play symbols that hold emotional or actual experiences. In each of these domains, relatedness presupposes the existence of an attachment relationship between the child and a primary adult. The opportunity for attachment is a precursor for the development of a related state.

Many psychosocial histories of children with PDD indicate that they certainly had the opportunity for attachment relationships to develop. Many such children received nurturing, attentive, loving care, with a typical range of social opportunity, within the family unit. Indeed, some parents of children with PDD recall that their children showed attachment behaviors and adequate relatedness during infancy. However, many parents describe their children developing difficulties maintaining a related state once they entered toddlerhood. While milestones for walking were sometimes early, often typical, and occasionally delayed, there seemed to be a pattern of decreasing relatedness once locomotion heralded physical separation. Once able to walk away from the adult, children with PDD often seem self-absorbed and act as though they are in a world of their own, failing to return to the adult for frequent "refueling," as the typical toddler does (Mahler, Bergman, & Pine, 1975/2000).

Sometimes, relatedness difficulties in PDD children take a different form. Children who have difficulty maintaining a related state when separate from important adults may avoid experiencing separation by merging with the adult. Such children may strive to achieve a symbiotic union with their parent, acting as though the parent is ever-present and will anticipate and meet all of their needs. If any-one interferes with the child's merged position, she often becomes enraged and panicky, trying desperately to restore the symbiotic union. Such children may have intense separation reactions, such as screaming, crying, and vomiting, when sepa-ration is necessary, or they may remain blissful, as though denying that separa-tion has occurred. Some children may try to compensate for their own lack of individuation by taking on other identities. They may seem to merge with fantasy characters, reciting familiar fantasy scripts from videos or storybooks, as though they were inhabited by the characters or in the company of the characters at all times.

While the child who merges may appear more related and more affectionate than his isolation-seeking counterpart, he is usually unable to relate to others as separate individuals with distinctive identities and personalities. Instead, he in-teracts in a way that does not acknowledge the personhood of the other. For ex-ample, the child who resolves his relatedness issues by merging may insist on sitting on the adult's lap with his face buried in the adult's chest instead of looking at her face or sitting against her to look outward and follow the activities of others. He might approach strangers and significant others alike as if there was no differ-ence between familiar and unfamiliar people.

Symbolic Functioning

Children with PDD are often brought for help because their parents notice a lack of appropriate language development. Yet there are many precursors to the de-velopment of language that may also have failed to develop in children with PDD. A child must connect to her experiences before being able to put them into words or play symbols in order to communicate them. There must be a level of related-ness that motivates the child to share her experiences with another person. In order to develop meaningful language, a child must differentiate herself from the adult, tolerate periods of separation, and then be motivated to use language and play symbols to bridge the physical and psychological distance that separation implies. A child must be able to differentiate herself from items in her intimate environment and discover that these items exist apart from his sensory perception of them.

It is significant that pointing rarely occurs spontaneously in the PDD child, indicating early difficulties in differentiating himself from the world around him. He often neglects to involve adults in discovering and labeling his world through mutual pointing play, bringing the adult into the picture only when he needs some-thing he cannot reach. Explorations and manipulations of the environment may be limited or may take place in an isolated way. It is also significant that many children with PDD do not use a typical transitional object to self-comfort. Use of transitional objects is a precursor to more advanced symbolic capacities, because it requires the child to endow it with representational quality. The blanket must "stand for" Mommy or Daddy in order to be effective. It must serve a symbolic purpose, which seems a difficult achievement for the PDD child.

A child's first words generally symbolize people and experiences in his or her intimate environment. "Mama," "dada," "bath," and "shoes" are examples of typical first words for the well-developing child. Children with PDD may not develop these kinds of first words or may not develop first words at the usual age. If intimate words do develop, they sometimes are used inconsistently or disappear all together as the child proceeds through toddlerhood. More typical of the child with PDD NOS is the tendency for first words to appear that are not typical and do not refer to features of the intimate environment. Later language may be sparse or may be complex, with a pseudo-sophisticated quality, but often includes mainly "borrowed" verbal routines. Likewise, children with PDD often seem to have no interest in symbolic play materials that are compelling to other children their age. They may become rigidly attached to "borrowed" play symbols, such as toys that allow them to reenact television or video routines, but avoid toys that require a personal interpretation or true symbolic value. They may also become very adept at use of manipulative toys or electronic toys that require some precocious abilities but do not require symbolic functioning.

This failure to develop symbolic play capacities frequently coexists with the PDD child's inability to connect to feeling states and recognize and respond to the affective states of other people. This state of emotional disconnection and social disinterest limits interactions between the PDD child and the significant people in her world and may underlie her deficits in representational play, learning, and communication. Greenspan (1997) notes that autistic spectrum children whose communication issues are treated solely with behavioral and cognitive approaches may develop language capacities that are somewhat functional but rote; additionally, they do not generally show marked improvements in play and relatedness. However, children whose relatedness and emotional issues are treated intensively have also been able to develop symbolic play and self-generated, flexible language. Brain research in recent years supports Greenspan's conclusion that the biologically based emotional and social deficits in autistic spectrum children essentially prevent their symbolic capacities from unfolding. There is now evidence that the physiology of emotional intelligence enables the neurological infrastructure of higher-level thinking and communication (National Scientific Council on the Developing Child, 2004a, 2004b)

While preschoolers with PDD often enter programs without the tools of symbolic language and symbolic play necessary for children to make sense of their experiences, they do not lack for experiences themselves. A PDD child may observe a fire on the way to school, have a frightening medical procedure, or endure the birth of a sibling. Without the use of symbols to interpret these experiences, the PDD child may become increasingly overwhelmed, taking refuge in an autistic withdrawal or in a fantasy world in order to avoid feelings of helplessness. He may become dependent on the sameness of external structures and routines to compensate for the lack of internal images that help him feel secure and organized.

Language Development

How does a PDD child's lack of relatedness and failure to develop symbolic capacities affect the actual quality of her language as she grows?

Symptoms of PDD often become most apparent during toddlerhood, when the child enters a stage that requires him to separate from his caregiver. At this time, the child needs to leave the safety of the other and to set out on his own to explore his environment. In order to do this, the child must have a developing sense of his identity separate from his parents. He must be able to take an image of a nurturing adult on his "journeys" and to know that the adult will be there when he returns. This period of separating and reuniting is crucial for communication development. It is during this period that the child develops a stronger interest in his environment and the ways that he impacts it. It is the sharing of these exciting experiential interactions that establishes the foundation for first words and the subsequent growth of more complex early communication.

The PDD child is often less motivated to share newly acquired knowledge. She often shows little interest in the things that others may consider to be salient features of the environment. As a result, a child with PDD acquires language in an idiosyncratic way that departs from the expected developmental course. For example, instead of learning first words for the purpose of encoding meaningful objects and using them to make requests of or comment to others, the PDD child may learn words for objects that hold a heightened significance for her only. The words may seem less personal than is typical for a toddler. For instance, instead of naming a favorite toy or significant person in the household, a child with PDD may develop first words such as "radiator" or "fire extinguisher," or may use words that refer to television or video characters. These words hold little promise for intimate interactions with others because their appropriate context is quite limited.

Children with PDD often interact verbally by repeating all or part of what has just been said to them. In other words, they echo the language that they hear. While echolalia is a developmentally salient language-learning modality for children between the ages of 12 and 24 months, developmentally appropriate echolalia and the echolalia of the PDD child are qualitatively different. Well-functioning toddlers will repeat a salient word or phrase within the sentence they have just heard, as if the repetition has facilitated their focus or understanding. The toddler who is asked "See the taxi, Annie?" may answer "Taxi" or "See taxi." The PDD child is likely to echo the sentence in a way that indicates difficulty comprehending its meaning. She may say "Annie" or "The taxi, Annie" (Fay & Schuler, 1980).

Another feature that often characterizes the PDD child's language is delayed echolalia, or the frequent repetition of previously heard words and phrases. A child may repeatedly recite all the words to his favorite cookie commercial every time cookies are served for snacktime. Another child may repeat the instructions uttered by the subway public address system after having ridden the subway to school.

Production of delayed echolalic utterances may reflect the child's difficulty formulating utterances of his own. His cognitive strengths may allow him to draw an association between his present situation and a past situation, and he then "replays" the words that were used in the initial context. The complexity of these utterances may be deceiving, creating the illusion that a child can generate elaborate utterances when he is actually "borrowing" language that he has heard in the past. Because the child with PDD often has poor self–other boundaries and overidentifies with other people or fantasy characters, the use of "borrowed" language may be a symptom of his lack of age-appropriate ego structure and self-concept.

Language acquisition is highly systematic and is based on a system of rules that is shared with others. "Borrowed" language may indicate that the child with PDD is neither spontaneously acquiring rules of syntax nor adequately acquiring rules that govern semantics. The child cannot organize language in accordance with these rules and therefore may not be able to string words together into meaningful sentences. Therefore, when the child is not relying on "borrowed" language or echolalia, she may generate language that consists of a large vocabulary of nouns. Again, the sophisticated nature of these words and the readiness with which the child learns complex names may be confusing to the adults, who assume that more diverse functions of language will come in time. The child with PDD may be dependent on intervention in order for more diverse language constructions to develop.

Several characteristics of the PDD child's language interfere with her participation in meaningful discourse. The reversal of pronouns is a typical feature that tends to cause breakdowns in communication. A little girl may look at her teacher and ask "You want snack?" sounding as though she wishes to offer a snack to the teacher but actually using the construction to request a snack for herself. The teacher may then attempt to model the appropriate construction, but this becomes extremely confusing. The interchanging of pronouns may be related to the PDD child's difficulty clearly delineating self and other. The symptom perpetuates her interpersonal difficulties because it prevents the other from responding in an effective, self-directed manner.

Verbal perseveration, or the repetitive and noncommunicative production of words and phrases, is another language characteristic common to children with PDD. The child may lock into a verbalization and be unable to break his preoccupation with it. For instance, a child may wander around the room repeating the phrase "Give up already!" all afternoon. He may be unresponsive to the adult's attempts to respond to him or to alter the language pattern. Other children may attempt to question him as to the meaning of the phrase and, when there is no answer forthcoming, may shrug and engage with someone else. This repetitive behavior may be understood as the child's attempt to soothe himself by creating safety through sameness, because he lacks the ability to utilize play and language symbols to process unpredictable experiences.

Since the child with PDD often has difficulty organizing the language that she hears and finding meaning within it, her own language may reflect this confusion and have the quality of jargon, which is the wordless production of consonants and vowel sounds strung together in a way that resembles language in rhythm and intonation. While clearly spoken words may emerge from streams of jargon, the child seems unaware that the whole communication lacks integrity or meaning to others. It is difficult for another child or an adult to offer a response, thus perpetuating the child's isolation and unrelatedness.

While language difficulties are almost always present in the child with a pervasive developmental disorder and are frequently the feature cited by parents for bringing a child into treatment, the language issues exist within the context of the child's overall social and emotional difficulties. Recent brain research confirms the role of emotional development as an organizer of intellectual processing (Greenspan, 1997, 2006; Seigel, 1999; Shonkoff & Phillips, 2000). Children on the autistic spectrum constantly struggle to cope with social and emotional experience. It is essential that the early childhood intervention professionals devote energy to helping them with this struggle. The core areas of relationship and symbol development must be addressed if the child with PDD is to develop ego strengths that are truly his own.

There has been a recent increase in the diagnosis of children with Asperger's syndrome in early childhood. Children with Asperger's syndrome do not have the language issues that characterize other children on the autistic spectrum. Rather, they are able to formulate meaningful language but are not motivated to use their language to connect socially. The child with Asperger's may be overlooked or mistakenly identified as a brilliant child who is bored by the interests of the less sophisticated children surrounding her. Without intervention, this child may be at risk for extreme emotional isolation and more complex psychiatric difficulties as she grows.

PDD NOS IN PRESCHOOL: IDENTIFICATION AND INTERVENTION

The observant teacher or clinician will notice many distinctive patterns of functioning in the preschool child with pervasive developmental disorder. Recognition of the ways that the PDD child's core issues manifest themselves in the preschool setting is essential when designing effective interventions for children with PDD. Typical manifestations of PDD in preschool children include the following:

1. The child shows a lack of relatedness to teachers and clinicians and seems to avoid contact, or the child clings to and merges with teachers and clinicians and is unable to tolerate separation, or the child relates to adults in a diffuse and undifferentiated fashion.

2. The child seems oblivious to peers, or the child overidentifies with peers, or the child relates to peers in a diffuse "friendly" but undifferentiated way.

3. The child's language is atypical, possibly including echolalic language, delayed echolalia, idiosyncratic language, self-language, jargon, television and video scripts, and pseudomature language that is out of the mouths of adults. There is often confused use of pronouns.

4. The child's symbolic play skills are lacking and he avoids representational materials, such as dolls and puppets. However, the child may be at age level or above in the acquisition of "readiness skills" such as identification of numbers, letters, colors, and shapes, and may excel at assembling puzzles, pegboards, and working mechanical toys. The child's decoding of written words may be precocious while comprehension seems limited.

5. The child shows a preoccupation with fantasy characters and fantasy movies, books, or scripts, which coexists with a lack of personal and self-generated fantasy play. The child may be compelled to enact certain scenes from fantasy again and again. The child's identification with fantasy characters seems to diminish responsiveness to others in the present reality.

6. The child shows a high need for sameness, is dependent on routines and the enactment of rituals, lacks flexibility, and disintegrates when routines are disrupted.

7. The child seems focused on details and often misses what is salient to others. For example, the child may focus on the brand name on a doctor bag but fail to explore its contents.

8. The child lacks a full range of affect. She may have a rosy and blissful demeanor that does not seem to vary unless she is in distress, when her emotional reactions become extreme. She may have a bland or unusually tense facial expression.

9. The child may have atypical postures, which are often extremely rigid or extremely floppy. There may be unusual patterns of movement and some degree of self-stimulation. Fine and gross motor abilities may range from excellent to very poor.

These maladaptive patterns of functioning may interfere with the PDD child's participation in the usual preschool routines and activities in ways that are confusing to classroom staff. Figures 11.1–11.6 illustrate behaviors often demonstrated by children with PDD during the preschool day and provide staff with guidance concerning effective intervention strategies. In the case of Melinda that follows, the reader may recognize many of the behaviors and the responsive interventions woven into the narrative.

THE CASE OF MELINDA

Children with PDD have atypical behaviors, but they can be helped to achieve meaningful dialogue with those around them. In the case presentation of Melinda,

FIGURE 11.1 Helping the PDD Child in the Preschool Setting: Outdoor Play—Play in Gym

Behavior	Issue	Intervention
Child becomes overly excited, acts wild and without direction, often pushing others.	Poor self–other boundaries create confusion for child when in outdoor spaces or large gym areas where there tends to be a lot of commotion.	Provide structure by organizing games such as red light, green light, red rover, ball, etc., to help child use physical energy in goal-directed ways; help child to stay connected to himself by emphasizing activities that demand internal controls (such as above) and have child check in with adults frequently; child should be closely supervised as may have poor concept of the cause and effect of his own actions.
Child is very agile and able to climb, ride bike, etc., but shows poor judgment and seems oblivious to injury.	Child disconnects from painful experience; reality testing is not at age level.	Provide close supervision, verbalize safe and unsafe practices; stop child from unsafe activity by physically removing him; attend to injury whether child is able to do so or not, modeling appropriate affects and providing comfort.
Child avoids all physical play equipment and refuses to participate in gross motor activity.	Body integrity issues and fears of injury inhibit the development of gross motor skills; sensory integration difficulties may make certain kinds of physical play a disorienting experience.	Gradually encourage exploration of play equipment, allowing child to watch others before trying; use peers to motivate activity; encourage parents to involve child in swimming, roller skating, and other activities that require child to focus on maintaining her own equilibrium in the context of a relationship with a supportive adult; have child evaluated by an O.T. if interventions don't promote growth.

Note: Things to avoid:
- Avoid traumatizing child by involving him in physical activity without warning.
- Avoid denying sad affects around injury unless the child's affects are borrowed or not genuine.
- Avoid being punitive about out-of-control behavior for PDD children who lack self–other boundaries.

FIGURE 11.2 Helping the PDD Child in the Preschool Setting: Arrival and Dismissal

Behavior	Issue	Intervention
Child is oblivious to separation from parent or caregiver .	Child cannot remain connected when separating.	Help parent to say good bye. Model same for child. Make photograph books for child including caregivers at home. Help child look at, think about, and talk about people who are out of sight.
Child panics and cannot separate from caregivers or parents.	Child cannot remain connected when separating and experiences panic about the disconnected state.	Develop a consistent arrival and departure routine, adult to "receive" child, representations of person child is leaving, transitional object, etc. Teacher-made books or available children's books about separation can be helpful. Helping children predict reunions is important.
Child enters room and immediately plops into the lap of a new volunteer who has never been met before.	Child has not achieved a level of differentiated relatedness with others.	Help child to differentiate between familiar and unfamiliar people. Do not encourage new volunteers or staff to engage PDD children if they will be transient or peripheral members of the classroom whom the child will not have an opportunity to get to know. Try to have staff members who have connections with the children welcome and dismiss them.
Child hides and resists entry into the room, yet wears blissful, detached affect.	Child's affects do not reflect his emotional status; he is probably scared or worried about entering.	Articulate the discrepancy between affects and actions. Implement affect curriculum to help child develop the ability to use affects communicatively.

Note: Things to avoid:
- Avoid assuming that the PDD child's atypical social behavior at arrival or dismissal is due to "bad manners," "manipulative" behavior, or the like.

FIGURE 11.3 Helping the PDD Child in the Preschool Setting: Morning Meeting

Behavior	Issue	Intervention
Child initially resists attending meeting.	Child needs to experience the routine of meeting, in order to feel secure within it.	Help child to come to the meeting by escorting her and holding her on a lap. Meeting should be predictable in sequence so that after a few weeks, routine may provide the needed structure.
Child sings all the words of all the songs at meeting, although he never says the words unless he is singing.	Child remembers words in the context of song lyrics, although he does not yet understand the meaning of what he is singing.	Sing songs about the children and their experiences. Use motions and gestures that may provide clues to meaning.
Child enjoys the meeting time because he reads all of the words on any of the materials that the teacher is using. For example, the teacher bought a photograph album for pictures taken on trips. She forgot to take off sticker saying name and address of store and price of item; PDD child reads this many times.	Child is hyperlexic, and is able to decode any written word: however, he is not able to process the meaning of the words he reads.	Read stories and provide books with simple, relevant themes. Avoid presenting material with extraneous words or letters or number symbols. Meeting activities should include songs, stories, and play routines focused on personal and social issues.

Note: Things to avoid:
- Avoid "pre-academic" rituals that have no meaning to age group, e.g., reciting date, weather, etc.
- Avoid complex language or complex stories.
- Avoid presentation of concepts without experiential component following presentation.

FIGURE 11.4 Helping the PDD Child in the Preschool Setting: Snack Time / Lunch Time

Behavior	Issue	Intervention
Child eats few foods exclusively for a period of time and then rejects them for another few; never tries new foods.	Eating often becomes ritualized and new foods regarded as intrusions.	Have predictable food routines with set times for snack and lunch. Have some foods consistently available and some foods that vary. For example, have crackers, juice, and fruit, but vary the type of juice and fruit. Articulate likes and dislikes of all the children. Include what foods used to be liked and no longer are, and foods that were disliked and are now accepted. Involve PDD children in cooking curriculums.
Child becomes upset if foods are served in ways that differ from what he is used to; for instance, he may love pudding but refuse to eat it if it comes from a box instead of a cup.	Child cannot differentiate essential features from incidental features of foods, therefore reacts as though the food item has been transformed and become unrecognizable.	Child may need to use familiar cups, bottles, packages, etc., to help him adjust to eating at school. Eventually, staff and parent can transition child to less specific forms of foods that he likes. Teachers can make a book about pudding and all the different ways to buy and eat it, cook different kinds of pudding at cooking time, etc.
Child becomes regressed when given food and crushes, smashes, or combines food items.	Child experiences eating on a primary process level.	Teachers can set clear limits at snack and lunch time that define food as for eating only. Children never *have* to eat, but must sit with others and throw away food if they don't wish to eat it. Sensory play such as sand, playdough, and water can be provided at play time.

Note: Things to avoid:
- Avoid making meal times mechanical; be relaxed and social.
- Avoid emphasis on politeness; instead, emphasize experience.
- Never force feed!
- Never withhold food for language!

FIGURE 11.5 Helping the PDD Child in the Preschool Setting: Free Play Time

Behavior	Issue	Intervention
Child spends all free play time rolling cars back and forth on the rug in an isolated fashion.	Child's play is on a sensory level; she loses herself in the motion of the wheels.	Offer alternative sensory play options that may have more social potential, such as water play, sand, etc. Do not allow child access to wheel toy unless an adult is free to engage the child by modeling more meaningful and symbolic uses, e.g., children getting in school bus as child does each day.
Child spends all free play time using single-purpose materials like pegboards, puzzles, and shape boxes; he excels in these.	Child's play patterns are indicative of developing an "expertise" in the visual motor area; however, this co-exists with indifference to other kids and a lack of ability to make believe.	Help child move away from exclusive use of single-purpose activities. Engage him in play with playdough or other materials that have multiple, representational purposes. Talk about your actions and his as you play.
Child uses free play time to dress up as dinosaur in "Land Before Time." He cries when it's time to move on to the next activity, which demands that he resume his own identity.	Child becomes overidentified with fantasy figures and cannot maintain his own ego definition.	Encourage well-functioning peers to interact with child within fantasy arena, which will involve them adding their own personal interpretations to the demands of the play. Limit child's access to fantasy props to which he seems "addicted" (e.g., only during half of play time, etc.). Help parents limit access to fantasy videos. Model playing out of actual experiences to diminish need for borrowed fantasy.
Child becomes anxious and wild during free play, runs around the room and does not focus or elaborate in play.	Due to lack of internal structure, child feels uncontained by open-ended activity.	Help child develop a play routine at free play time. If possible, have adult shadow him, offer lap to provide structure and support for focused, more elaborate play. Adult may need to model more appropriate play, using drawing, symbolic toys, sensory materials, and reciprocal play materials such as nerf balls, etc. Help child put away one material before finding another.

Note: Things to avoid:
- Avoid letting PDD children get lost in their own private rituals.
- Avoid "avoiding" free play! Don't conclude that free play is meaningless to the children and therefore is not needed! Only practice will allow children to develop the symbolic play skills necessary for productive, organized social play.

FIGURE 11.6 Helping the PDD Child in the Preschool Setting: Transitions: In-House and on Trips

Behavior	Issue	Intervention
Child screams if routines are changed; after a long period, child calms down, but becomes obsessed with solitary activity.	Child is disoriented by change; he is dependent on external order, as he lacks age-typical internal organization.	Make experiences predictable initially. Give 5-minute warnings of routine transitions. Take photographs of child engaged in each aspect of the daily routine. Verbalize the reason for his distress and reassure him regarding the next step by using the photograph, etc.
Child panics when class goes on trips.	Child is disoriented by change; he is dependent on external order, as he lacks age-typical internal organization.	Plan short, local trips. Use pictures to help child forecast events. Bring something familiar that the child finds comforting. Assign one adult to be with child. Have adult narrate child's experiences as they happen.
Once engaged in activity, child has difficulty achieving closure; he accelerates his actions and sobs and fights when adult cleans up.	Child merges with activity to the extent that he loses himself and thus experiences panic when he must separate from it.	Use "clean up" marker such as song or timer to create a structure for the activity's conclusion. Articulate the fact that the toy is going to be put away but the child is still OK. Show him his mirror image to assure him that he's still intact. Hold him if he feels uncontained. Talk about where the toy is when you put it away and when he can get it again.
Child gets upset when new people enter the room; he may yell "Go away".	New people are threatening the same way that new experiences are threatening, because they disturb the child's sense of order and well being.	Give warnings about visitors when possible. Explain child's need for order and familiarity motivate his unwelcoming attitude and should not be taken personally. Draw picture with child later in the day, symbolizing his initial distress and the actual experience of having the visitor, which may ultimately have been pleasurable.

Note: Things to avoid:
- Avoid taking children with PDD on field trips that are too long, overstimulating, overcrowded, or not meaningful to the child's own experiences.

readers will follow the process of intervention that allowed her to connect to her teachers and to herself. Relatedness, symbolic functioning, and use of appropriate language were the areas of focus in Melinda's intervention.

Melinda stands in the doorway with a faraway look in her eyes. "Hi, honey, I'm home!" she stiffly intones, making eye contact with no one as she says this. She plops herself down in the lap of an adult she has never seen before, peering at her face intently and touching her cheek. After a few minutes, Melinda gets up and begins to wander around the classroom. Mainly, she hovers at the peripheries of the room, gingerly fingering a few random items she happens to come across on the shelf tops—a paintbrush, the box of tissues, a toy car—then putting them down. Often, she calls out the teacher's name without turning around—"Hey, Judy! Hey, Judy!"— but wanders away again once she has her attention. She plays briefly with the animals, naming a cow, an elephant, and a hippopotamus, but does not develop a theme. She is joined by another little girl who pretends a baby duck is quacking for its mommy. Melinda imitates her, "Quack! Quack!" The little girl looks at her strangely, then says to the teacher, "Why does she always copy me?" At cleanup time, Melinda walks around reciting under her breath what sounds like dialogue from *Cinderella*—"It's time to go to the ball!"—and every so often does a little twirl or pirouette.

This was a typical playtime for Melinda when she enrolled, at age 3½, in a therapeutic preschool. The story of Melinda illustrates how, when relationship-oriented interventions are applied at an early age, a child who has PDD can be helped enormously to develop in a more integrated fashion.

Melinda was the second child of an intact, working-class family. Her mother, Rachel, was very involved in her care and responsive to her needs. Although she wanted very much to provide Melinda with rich childhood experiences, Rachel's own feelings of guilt about Melinda's developmental difficulties caused her to over-compensate, thus overwhelming Melinda with input she could not process or integrate —too much language, too many videos, too many toys, even too much food.

The combination of this and Melinda's inherent difficulties integrating experience had caused her development to proceed in an uneven, atypical fashion consistent with the diagnosis of PDD. Melinda demonstrated many areas of cognitive strength, including mastery of certain isolated concepts (e.g., numbers, letters, color recognition), a good memory for details, the ability to recognize and label objects, and a receptivity to visual information. However, while drawn to the details of things, Melinda had difficulty taking in the gestalt. She could not process any but the most basic language and interpersonal messages and could not use symbols as most young children do to help her organize and share basic experience. Thus both her ability to enter into relationship and her sense of self, which is rooted in relationship, were largely inhibited.

Melinda's affect was bland, rarely varied, and seemingly disconnected from her inner state. What affects she did wear seemed borrowed—for instance, a heightened pseudocheerfulness—and did not match the reality at hand. When Melinda fell on the playground, for example, she showed no response to the pain. Although Melinda was drawn to others, she related in an undifferentiated fashion. While interested in other children, she could rarely do more than imitate their behavior and language.

Melinda rarely initiated and never seemed fully invested in play activities. She used materials in only the most basic symbolic manner (e.g., making the noises of farm animals) or in an imitative fashion but could not elaborate and became quickly ritualized. She was able to replicate in her drawings the most basic features of a face but did so without connection, as if she had been taught. The only other thing she drew was a TV. Melinda liked to dress up, but she would become too immersed in fantasy and would repeatedly play out verbatim the same scene from *Beauty and the Beast*, *Cinderella*, or the like. The themes were idiosyncratic and therefore inaccessible to other children, so Melinda was usually isolated in her play.

While she quickly learned to follow the routines of structured group activities, she had trouble participating and would become preoccupied by internal thoughts—singing a song borrowed from a video or television show over and over. At storytime, she enjoyed looking at books. She could memorize the words in books verbatim but read them in a rote manner, having no idea what they meant. When she read the book *How Do I Feel?* by Norma Simon (1970), she read with the same intonation each time, completely without affect.

Melinda's language consisted of isolated labels and whole phrases borrowed directly, intonation and all, from television, video, or other people's conversations and peppered with jargon and echolalia. When Melinda wanted to look longer at a page in a storybook, for example, she would shout out, "Hey! Hold it! Stop the camera!" When she needed help one day, instead of asking an adult she lay down on the floor and shouted, "Alert! Alert!" She was imitating the character in a television ad she had seen for a medical alert system. Sometimes Melinda would get stuck on a phrase or a song and repeat it again and again until interrupted. Meanwhile, Melinda rarely used language to express even her most basic needs and wants, for example, to ask for more juice at snack.

An intervention plan was formulated that was designed to help bring Melinda into relationship, become more connected to and organize her experiences, and integrate affect and cognition.

Since Melinda's relatedness had been arrested at an early level, the teachers began using reciprocal-play techniques to help build basic relatedness. In therapy sessions, Melinda took turns with her therapist blowing bubbles, playing peek-a-boo in front of the mirror, playing catch, and other activities that highlighted the relationship between self and other. Teachers helped Melinda strengthen her connection to her mother by bridging it through the use of visits to the parents' room, use of photographs, and many references to Mommy. Teachers helped Melinda differentiate between familiar and unfamiliar people—saying to her, for instance, that she didn't know the new volunteer yet, but perhaps she could ask her what her name was. Since Melinda had difficulty maintaining self–other boundaries with her peers and would become imitative, teachers worked on helping her develop greater awareness of her own personal boundaries. They might say, for instance, "You are Melinda. That is Nathan. Nathan is having a hard time. He is jumping. Melinda is not. She is doing a good job eating her snack."

Teachers and therapists helped Melinda use symbols to connect to and organize her experiences by reflecting and highlighting them through language, photographs, drawing, and play. Melinda, like many children who have PDD, was more receptive to visual input than to verbal information. Therefore, staff drew pictures that reflected her experiences. Drawings included pictures of her playing with bubbles, pictures of her riding on the school bus, pictures of her eating snack. In these pictures, staff tried to represent her as accurately as possible so that she would be helped to recognize herself. Teachers also made photograph books that depicted her engaged in a variety of activities and emphasized relationship by depicting the significant people in her life. Staff modeled basic symbolic play themes that reflected her own activities (e.g., cooking, riding on the school bus, bathing). If Melinda introduced a theme, staff helped her to stay with it and elaborate. The curriculum was facilitative for Melinda because it represented and invited representation of basic developmental issues such as going away and coming back, big and little, and affect.

In particular, staff highlighted Melinda's emotional experience, eliciting through modeling and empathic reflection genuine expressions of joy, sadness, fear, and anger, as well as her wants, needs, likes, and dislikes. When another child hit Melinda, the teacher would ask, "Melinda, did you like that?" Often, she would appear confused and say, "Yes." The teacher would respond, "Ouch, hitting hurts. You can say, 'That hurts. I don't like that.'" Other examples include, "Mmm, Melinda likes spaghetti." "Melinda doesn't like eggs. She says, 'Yuk!'" "You want more juice. You can say, 'I want juice.'" "Melinda is sad. She misses her mommy."

Teachers and therapists took advantage of Melinda's interest in pictures and writing and drew many pictures of Melinda in which affect would be salient. Simple captions were written to accompany the pictures, such as "Melinda is angry. She says, 'No cleanup!'" To help Melinda develop a greater understanding of emotional cause and effect, staff made a book in which a series of photographs and captions depicted her becoming sad when she had to wait her turn for the tricycle, getting her turn, and feeling better.

Adults at school offered Melinda clear, reduced, reality-based language messages that she could process more easily, often sticking to two- or three-word phrases. Instead of focusing on the polite trimmings of language, such as *please* and *thank you*, staff emphasized language that was meaningful to Melinda, such as "I want crackers." Teachers helped Melinda differentiate between language that was meaningful and language that was tangential, echolalic, or perseverative. If Melinda was singing a song from a cartoon perseveratively during a group painting activity, a staff member might say, "That's TV, Melinda. No TV now. Now it is time for painting. Do you want red paint?"

Therapists and teachers worked with Melinda's mother, Rachel, to help her understand that for Melinda, less input was actually more helpful. Staff encouraged Rachel to minimize video and television inputs and provide Melinda with active experiences like cooking, rollerskating, and trips to various places, as well as activities that reflected her experiences, such as drawing and looking at photographs. Rachel needed to be encouraged to not overwhelm Melinda with stimulation but rather to give her enough room to initiate both language and activity.

Melinda slowly began to progress. Over the course of several months, Melinda went through developmental processes that ordinarily would have occurred at a much earlier age as the stages of the separation/individuation process. These processes had to do with establishing differentiated relationships and developing her sense of self in the context of these relationships.

During this interim period, Melinda became increasingly connected to the significant adults in her life and went through a stage of separation anxiety, having difficulty separating from her mother and crying for her when she was not there. She elected to spend time with her primary teachers rather than the less familiar volunteers.

Simultaneously, Melinda's sense of self began to emerge. With it came a newly found sense of her autonomy. "No" and "Mine" became her favorite words for a while (e.g., "*No*! I said no meeting!" "Hey, gimme that. That's mine!"). Like a toddler, Melinda was for the first time becoming aware of herself as a separate and autonomous person, able to oppose others and able to possess her own things. Allowing Melinda to go through this process was difficult for her mother, who had a tendency to say things like: "Melinda, stop that. Now be nice." "Listen to your teachers." "Share your things." Staff worked with Rachel to help her understand that these behaviors actually reflected a positive developmental gain for Melinda. Eventually, Rachel came to understand that "better late than never" was the operative concept in Melinda's case.

For the first time, Melinda began to become connected to her affects. She might cry for Mommy, cry when she had to wait her turn for the tricycle, or get angry at meeting time when she did not want to come. Initially she was overwhelmed by her feelings, becoming flooded with them much as a toddler would. At the same time, she was amazed that she was capable of such powerful emotions. She would stand in front of the mirror, tears streaming down her face, saying, "Look! I'm sad. I'm so sad. I'm crying." Over time, Melinda developed more of a middle ground with this and would use the teachers to help her organize her emotional experience through the use of symbols, telling a teacher, for example, "Draw mad. Melinda is mad." With these achievements in ego development came the normative use of pronouns.

Melinda's symbolic development went through stages, too. Her play for a long time was at an early level. At first it involved a lot of sensorimotor activity, such as water and sand play. Later, her play included a lot of looking in the mirror, dressing up, and playing peek-a-boo and hide-and-seek as she practiced both self and object constancy. One day, she put on a Ninja Turtle mask. "Who's that?" she asked the teacher. "Mm, a Ninja Turtle," the teacher said. Melinda removed the mask and said, "No, that's Melinda, silly!"

Melinda's play and drawing demonstrated improved integration of cognition and affect. She became able to use play and drawing symbols in a self-generated, not borrowed, manner, representing developmentally salient themes. She would play about cooking, eating, sleeping, doctors and injury, Mommy going to work, and taking care of the baby. On one occasion, she acted out the experience of being overfed. She took on the role of her mother and repeatedly tried to force the Max doll to eat, despite his protests (as voiced by the teacher): "Eat this food. You need to eat this." When he kept refusing, Melinda pretended to get mad, roughly put away the food and said, "Okay, then you're not going to Grandma's." Since Melinda's play themes were universally accessible to other children, she began to be able to play dramatically with her peers—dressing up with them to go on a trip, playing baby and doctor, and other activities.

As Melinda became progressively more connected to her internal state, she began to be able to generate language to express her needs and wants, feeling states, and likes and dislikes: "I want crackers." "I'm hot." "I want the bike." "I want pink." "Mm, I like chocolate milk." Whereas her language meanings used to be primarily idiosyncratic, she began to use language to establish shared meaning with others and would ask repeatedly "What's this?" in reference to various objects.

As Melinda's core self became increasingly developed and integrated, her symbolic processes evolved. She became able to use symbols in a meaningful fashion and to represent and integrate her experiences in more and more elaborate ways. Her language became more meaningful and communicative, and her use of jargon and echolalia diminished. As she neared age 5, Melinda used phrases such as "Melinda and Pablo play cooking," "Mommy brought her lunch to school," and "Mommy took me to the store—she buy me a toy" to describe her experiences, both present and past. She developed the ability to differentiate between meaningful language and language that was overwhelming and thus had become rote to her.

She was eventually able to use symbols to organize her emotional experience as well. This provided her with an emotional middle ground: Instead of becoming overwrought with emotion as before, she became progressively able to express her feelings symbolically. When upset, she would bring the teacher a paper and marker and tell her, "Draw mad, Judy. Melinda is mad." As the end of the year drew near, she would say with real affect, "It's sad to say goodbye."

One final anecdote reflects the developmental point Melinda had reached as she was about to graduate from the preschool program. As part of a curriculum about self-concept, the group made body tracings of each child on large brown paper, which the children colored in. Melinda carried hers around with her all day long. As she showed it to her mother, she said, "That's me. That's Melinda." She made her mother hang it on the wall as soon as she got home. While Melinda's quest for psychological integration will certainly be ongoing, Melinda had begun to find herself.

REFERENCES

American Psychiatric Association. (2000). *Diagnostic and statistical manual of mental disorders* (4th ed., rev.). Washington, DC: Author.

Fay, W., & Schuler, A. (1980). *Emerging language in autistic children.* Baltimore: University Park Press.

Greenspan, S. (1997). *Growth of the mind and the endangered origins of intelligence.* New York: Perseus.

Greenspan, S., & Wieder, S. (2006). *Engaging autism.* Cambridge, MA: Da Capo.

Mahler, M., Bergman, A., & Pine, F. (2000). *The psychological birth of the human infant.* New York: Basic Books. (Original work published 1975)

National Scientific Council on the Developing Child. (2004a). *Children's emotional development is built into the architecture of their brain* (Working Paper No. 2). Retrieved July 2006 from http://www.developingchild.net/reports.shtml

National Scientific Council on the Developing Child. (2004b). *Young children develop in an environment of relationships* (Working Paper No. 1). Retrieved July 2006 from http://www.developingchild.net/reports.shtml

Pruitt, K., & Madigan, J. (1991, December). *Therapeutic action in one to one therapy with young children diagnosed with pervasive developmental disorder not-otherwise-specified.* Paper presented at the seventh biennial National Training Institute of the National Center for Clinical Infant Programs, Arlington, VA.

Shonkoff, J. P., & Phillips, D. A. (2000). From neurons to neighborhoods: *The science of early childhood development.* Washington, DC: National Academy Press.

Siegel, D. J. (1999). *The developing mind: How relationships and the brain interact to shape who we are.* New York: Guilford.

Simon, N. (1970). *How do I feel?* Chicago: Whitman.

CHAPTER 12

Why Homeless Children Can't Sit Still

Lesley Koplow

Jonathan Kozol's *Rachel and Her Children* (1988) brought attention to the plight of homeless children and their families, offering a sociopolitical analysis of homelessness and its effect on family life. There have been studies attempting to determine whether homeless families differ substantially from low-income housed families (Hart-Shegos, 1999; Molnar, 1988; "Protecting the Mental Health," 2000), and there have been clinical stories focusing on the homeless child and parent as they struggle to remain connected to one another in spite of the lack of shelter for their relationship (Koplow, 1992). While researchers have found that homeless children share many characteristics of at-risk, low-income, multistressed children who are not homeless, early childhood educators have felt a specific need for guidance when working with a homeless population. Curriculums to help teachers work effectively with homeless or formerly homeless populations are available, indicating that early childhood educators perceive homeless children as having distinctive needs (Ennes, 1991).

What do homeless children need in preschool? What are behavioral indicators of unmet need in homeless children? How does homelessness itself impact on the development of a young child? Finally, how can insight into the dynamics of homelessness for young children inform the work of the professionals in the lives of homeless children? This chapter will explore these important questions.

PHYSICAL CONDITIONS: EMOTIONAL CONSEQUENCES

A study of 81 preschools for homeless children showed that close to half of the children were seriously delayed in at least one major area of development (Bassuk, Rubin, & Lauriat, 1986; "Protecting the Mental Health," 2000). Teachers who seek consultations regarding homeless children in early childhood programs frequently have remarkably similar concerns. They describe children who are hypervigilant, possess a low frustration tolerance, "don't listen," can't follow through on their activities, and "can't sit still." These symptoms often coexist with hunger, fatigue, depressed affects, driven behavior, aggression, language delays, precocious self-care abilities, and a lack of joy in mastery of age-appropriate challenges. Research finds that over one-fifth of homeless children ages 3 to 6 have mental health problems serious enough to require clinical intervention ("Protecting the Mental Health," 2000). When young homeless children are brought to the attention of mental health professionals, they are frequently diagnosed with attention-deficit hyperactivity disorder (ADHD) to account for their hyperactive behavior, without sufficient clinical consideration of their pychosocial history, which may indicate that the hyperactivity is secondary to posttraumatic stress disorder (PTSD) or anxiety (Sanchez, 2000).

It is not surprising that children who live in shelters or hotels frequently arrive for preschool feeling hungry or tired. Families may be dependent on shelter-provided meals, which may not include items that appeal to a young child and which are often served in crowded, chaotic dining areas that are not conducive for feeding children. Families in hotels may be forbidden to cook in their rooms and may exist on fast-food items that are affordable on their limited food budgets. Sleeping quarters may be insufficient to accommodate all family members, lack privacy, and be noisy and disruptive.

These conditions clearly do not meet a young child's basic care needs. Neither is it simple to compensate for these inadequacies. The provision of balanced meals and rest mats at preschool cannot fully address the most debilitating aspects of the child's food and sleep deprivation. In essence, in addition to stressing the child physically, homelessness deprives the child of experiencing his or her parent as provider and protector. The homeless parent cannot provide an intimate environment in which to nurture and structure her child. She cannot act on her attunement to her own needs or to her child's needs if they are both hungry at the end of a stressful day and must wait in a long line to obtain food. What are the consequences of this kind of caregiving experience for both parents and children?

HOMELESSNESS AND THE PARENTING OF INFANTS

Parents who feel ill equipped to respond to their children's needs for nurture may defend against feelings of helplessness and inadequacy by distancing themselves from their children's dependency needs. Parents who were well attuned and responsive to dependency needs before the experience of homelessness may be able to compensate for the lack of environmental support at times, but at other times they may feel so overwhelmed by unmet needs that diminishing attunement becomes a necessary form of self-protection. Since nurture is a primary developmental task of parenting an infant and remains a salient part of the parental role throughout childhood, homeless parents who feel they must partially surrender the nurturing role will probably suffer a loss of self-esteem and accompanying depression.

Parents who were not well attuned prior to the experience of homelessness may become even less available to their infants. This group may include women whose homelessness is related to mental illness; drug abuse; or a significant history of early trauma, loss, abuse, foster placement, domestic violence, and other factors. In cases where parental behavior exacerbated difficulties in maintaining housing or actually precipitated the event of homelessness, parents may be unable to tolerate their guilty feelings. They may maintain as much distance as possible from the infant, who may be the perceived source of the unwanted guilt. Because shelter living and hotel living both drastically decrease one's living space, making it impossible to physically gain distance from family members, the need for distance may result in a detached form of caregiving that is unsatisfying for both parent and child. Infants who remain extremely demanding and express their needs and distress through constant crying that pierces the mother's defenses may be at risk for abuse. Statistics show homeless children to be twice as likely as housed children to suffer child abuse ("Protecting the Mental Health," 2000).

Consequences for the Parenting of Toddlers

The parental role becomes more complex as children move into toddlerhood. The walking toddler is eager to explore his environment. He wants to make a claim on the world and to discover his impact on all that he encounters. To do this, he requires a measure of autonomy, yet he feels increasingly ambivalent about moving away from his parents. The parent of a toddler is called on to function as a steady anchor during this tumultuous period. The parent must allow the toddler to explore but remain available to him for emotional "refueling" (Mahler, Bergman, & Pine, 1975/2000). The shifting affects and volatile emotional status of the toddler need to be balanced by a relatively consistent affect state and generally supportive attitude in the adult.

The parental role demands that the parent go beyond providing encouragement to the toddler: It takes on an authoritative dimension as well. Galinsky (1987) refers to authority as the primary parental task of toddlerhood. In order for a young child to feel safe, a parent must be able to set consistent and reasonable limits. This can be an overwhelming challenge for homeless parents, who may feel little authority over their own lives, let alone over their children's lives. Feeling disempowered may result in the parents giving up any measure of authority that might have been attained within the parent–child relationship, thus leaving children feeling uncontained and unprotected. On the other hand, feelings of disempowerment may lead parents to attempt to compensate for feeling generally out of control by becoming controlling and authoritative with their children. This may be likely to occur when the toddler's own autonomy needs are expressed through oppositional responses or behaviors, thus confronting parents with the reality that they themselves have failed to achieve an autonomous position.

The physical constraints of hotel and shelter spaces may impose unreasonable limits for the toddler. While children generally internalize parental expectations and limits within the parental domain of the intimate environment, the homeless family is living in a deeply impersonal environment that lacks the markers of the parents' personalities. It may be harder for the growing toddler to internalize limits in this impersonal environment, causing a heightened need for parental limit setting.

Consequences for the Parenting of the Preschool Child

Well-developing preschool children are fascinated by cause-and-effect relationships. The 3-year-old's first "why?" question announces his discovery of cause and effect, and the persistent "whys" that follow draw the adult into the discovery process. Indeed, the task of parenthood for the parent of a preschool and young school-age child involves interpreting the world to the child and, conversely, presenting the child to the world outside of the household (Galinsky, 1987). This is almost an impossible task for the homeless parent, who may have a tenuous hold on the cause and effect of her own situation. "Whys" may become a threatening question for the parent, who may hear blame in the child's inquiry and may be trying hard to ward off feelings of self-blame. If a parent is single and has many children, most of whom are still nonverbal, there may be a pull toward giving verbal preschool and school-age children a parental role both in the managing of younger siblings and in negotiating with shelter staff. This constitutes a role reversal, where young children are put in the position for interpreting events for their parents and interpreting parental behaviors to the outside world.

Preschool children and their school-age siblings are fully mobile and generally have a high need for activity. Many shelters and hotels recognize this and attempt to provide some on-site children's programming to meet children's educational and recreational needs. Parental adjustment to the temporary housing situation may determine whether these services are facilitative for the children; parents must allow their children to make consistent use of the services in order for them to be effective. It may seem paradoxical that overwhelmed parents wouldn't jump at the chance to gain some respite from their children, therefore ensuring their full participation in any children's programming available. However, parents may have difficulty making consistent use of the children's programs for a variety of reasons. These might include the inability to be organized enough to bring the children on time; fear of feeling lonely and vulnerable if separated from the children; fear that program staff will be unhappy with the quality of the child's physical or emotional care and refer the family for protective services; and fear that the program will not provide adequate supervision.

Since homeless parents must frequently spend hours obtaining public assistance, food allowances, health care, and housing referrals, children who are not in preschool or day care must accompany them on these errands. Needless to say, this creates an untenable situation for both children, who are not having their needs met, and their parents, who are attempting to manage them.

HOMELESSNESS AND THE DEVELOPMENTAL PROCESS: INFANCY

The homeless infant endures a variety of circumstances that may adversely effect his developmental process. The most threatening of these is the lack of emotional availability of his mother during a highly stressful time. Not only may the homeless infant experience a physical surrounding that does not meet his needs for a protected, predictable, responsive, and appropriately stimulating environment, but he may also be in the position of trying to cope with the assaultive elements without the participation of parent as psychological partner. An infant requires an emotionally present parent in order to do the work of infancy even in the most supportive external environment. The homeless infant whose parent is preoccupied may be constantly overwhelmed and need to close down, sleeping often and becoming less responsive overall to the environment. Conversely, he may exhibit difficulties with regulation of state, become hyperalert, and be difficult to soothe.

Erikson (1968) calls the establishing of "basic trust" the primary developmental task of infancy. Ainsworth, Bleher, Waters, and Wall (1978) refer to the provision of nurture and care as the cornerstone of the attachment relationship between parent and infant, and thus it is the nucleus of trust. Homelessness often interferes with responsive nurturing and offers minimal privacy for quiet, shared moments between parent and infant. Homelessness forces parent and child into an impersonal environment instead of an intimate one, making it potentially difficult for homeless infants to achieve a sense of basic trust. This difficulty may be especially likely if the infant experiences disruptive and dangerous intrusions that the parent is unable to prevent in the shelter or hotel setting.

The literature has emphasized the social learning that takes place in infancy through the mutual expression of affect between parent and child. Many readers will be familiar with the visual cliff study, where 6-month-olds read the expressions on their mother's face before deciding whether to proceed to crawl across a plane that appeared to drop off suddenly (Sorce, Emde, Campos, & Klinnert, 1985). While some researchers have theorized that the existence of affect is innate (Siegel, 1999), attunement to affects and the development of affect communication is partially dependent on social opportunity and emotional connectedness (Beebe 2004; Stern, 1985/2000).

Affect development may be complicated for the homeless infant. The need to shut down in order to avoid being overwhelmed by adverse stimuli may have a secondary effect of diminishing receptivity to input in general. If the parent has also shut down as a means of self-protection and becomes depressed, the infant may attempt to maintain an emotional synchrony with her by mirroring the depressed affects (Beebe, 2004; Emde, 1989).

In cases where homelessness is related to mental illness or substance abuse, unstable and abruptly shifting parental affects may in effect alert the child to changes in adult tolerance and level of receptivity. Infants of parents with abruptly shifting affects may become hypervigilant to adult affects as a way of monitoring the availability of the parent, but they may also have difficulty developing their own expression of a normal range of affects reflective of their emotional states.

HOMELESSNESS AND THE DEVELOPMENTAL PROCESS: TODDLERHOOD

The developmental agenda of the toddler is difficult to accomplish during times of family crisis. The toddler requires a stable, secure environment in order to do the developmental work of practicing her newly acquired mobility skills. Not only must the physical environment be safe enough to support her explorations, but the emotional environment must be safe enough to support her desire to venture from her parent without risking her loss.

Neither of these conditions is likely to exist for the homeless toddler. Often, the physical surround is either unpredictable, potentially hazardous, or extremely limited in scope. Parents who find themselves without a home often experience feelings of anxiety, depression, and disorientation, and they may be ill equipped to function as psychological home base for someone else. Toddlers have serious developmental dilemmas if they cannot risk moving away from their mothers for fear of loss or danger or if they move away and are then left to their own devices without the availability of an adult for emotional refueling or participation in mutual discoveries about the world. They are unlikely to develop an adequate orientation to the environment because they lack a parental home base from which to begin their journeys, a psychological "port" from which to build bridges to and from destinations of interests. Their ventures into the world may appear random and aimless.

While many children are able to use transitional objects to help them maintain the maternal image during brief separations, thus bridging intimate and unknown environments, homeless children may be less likely to have access to an object with personal meaning and history. Given the transient nature of the homeless infant's living situation, there may be less opportunity to safeguard her connections to material objects that then must be moved from place to place. The homeless toddler who has been homeless since infancy may have few or no possessions that represent significant relationships or foster a sense of self-continuity.

As toddlers discover their intimate environments, they engage the adult in the process of naming the items that they encounter. Adults are generally eager to participate in this pointing–naming game as a way to be included in the child's venturing forth and as a method of facilitating his use of language. Indeed, the child's first words most often refer to items within his intimate environment and to the primary relationships that he has there.

Homeless children lack an intimate environment as a foundation for verbal language. They may not have opportunities to discover and reexplore a consistent repertoire of objects. Adults may be less available for the personal dialogues that result in the invented baby words that precede standard speech. If a general lack of responsiveness has characterized the parent–child relationship, the child will have had less success in the role of preverbal communication partner and may be delayed in verbal language as well.

HOMELESSNESS AND THE DEVELOPMENTAL PROCESS: THE PRESCHOOL CHILD

The preschooler who suddenly becomes homeless will be highly stressed and probably show signs of regressions. As the loss of home is a significant loss for a young child, she will probably be disoriented, anxious, frightened, clingy, tearful, or perhaps regressed in areas such as toileting or language use.

If a preschool child is homeless and has a history of homelessness beginning in infancy or toddlerhood, his entire developmental status may appear distinctive from that of his peers. It is likely that many salient developmental tasks will be incomplete and many important developmental issues will be unresolved. For instance, consider the preschool-age child who did not have the opportunity to establish a psychological home base as a toddler and has not been able to internalize an image of a nurturing and protective adult to comfort her during adverse situations. When this child enters preschool, she may experience extreme difficulties with separation. Since she lacks experience in using the adult as a source of guidance and as a beacon of orientation to the environment, she may dart about the room randomly, apparently without direction, or she may be unable to take initiative to explore at all. If she feels a great deal of anxiety, she is likely to express it with motoric activity, resulting in the exasperated teacher's comment, "She can't sit still!"

Homeless children may he preoccupied with the whereabouts and well-being of family members when separated from them, as separation may evoke feelings of loss and anxiety about future losses. This will certainly be true if the child or family has had frightening experiences or violent encounters in the shelter or hotel setting. Children who are preoccupied and maintain a hypervigilant state are generally less attentive and less receptive to input. While they may appear cognitively compromised due to their inattention and lack of responsiveness, normal capacity may reveal itself when their concerns are addressed and they feel well supported by the environment.

SYMPTOMS CONNECTED WITH HOMELESSNESS IN CHILDREN

It is not surprising that some of the homeless child's symptoms are similar to those exhibited by children with posttraumatic stress disorder and reactive attachment disorders of childhood. While homelessness may not in itself constitute a trauma for a young child who has never known a home, homelessness deprives children of appropriate care and protection, thus leaving them vulnerable as potential victims of traumatic experience. While homelessness may be a part of the child's psychosocial history and a fact known to the staff, symptoms of traumatic stress may indicate that the preschool child has been exposed to or is a victim of traumatic events not recorded as part of his written history.

In their study *Home Is Where the Heart Is* (Molnar, 1988), Bank Street College observers noted that many homeless preschool children exhibited inappropriate social interactions with adults. Observers noted what could be described as an undifferentiated relatedness with strange adults and a lack of expected attachment behaviors with their own mothers. These symptoms of reactive attachment disorders may be the outcome of the disrupted attachment processes mentioned earlier in our discussion of infancy and toddlerhood. In addition, there is specific mention of children engaging in very physical behaviors such as touching without inhibition, kissing, and hugging. This author has observed the same behaviors often coexisting with difficulties maintaining personal boundaries, sexual play and behavior, and a tendency for affectionate behavior with other children to become abruptly aggressive.

Given the cramped sleeping quarters that are a part of hotel and shelter life, children often have inappropriate access to adult sexuality. Although there are usually house rules designed to minimize illicit sexual activity, these rules are not always sufficient to protect children from exposure. Even if children are sufficiently protected from sexual behavior between adults, logistics may encourage or force children to share beds with their parents, often causing children to feel overstimulated and experience confusing feelings. These feelings may be acted out in the school environment and may require intervention on the part of the teacher or program social worker.

Teachers may be confounded by the homeless child's seemingly precocious abilities to perform self-care tasks and other practical feats that are generally done by adults. These precocious abilities often coexist with a defeated response to age-level challenges and little tolerance for frustration in attempts to master them. Sadly, when children have to devote their energies to maintaining their own survival, there is often little energy left for age-level pursuits. The effort of transcending himself into an adult mode leaves the child exhausted and unfulfilled. The level of skill he achieves may be sufficient to perform the task yet is obviously inferior to an adult attempt, causing feelings of inadequacy.

IMPLICATIONS FOR THE EARLY CHILDHOOD EDUCATOR

The early childhood program can be instrumental in improving the developmental outcome of the homeless child. However, the program must look at the homeless child and his family through the lens of homeless experience in order to be helpful. Once staff is able to understand the homeless child's developmental dilemmas, they can use their energies to address these and facilitate growth.

While the following measures may be useful for all highly stressed children and their families, they may be especially helpful for homeless children and their parents.

The preschool environment should be well cared for, with consistent arrangement of furniture and toys. Storage spaces that are within children's reach should be well organized by category. Broken toys should be discarded. Since homeless children may lack experience with consistent environments, it is important that the preschool environment offer an opportunity to explore items over time. If the environment is chaotic, the child may be unable to experience the ongoingness of items in a well-differentiated fashion, may lack knowledge about the function of items, and may also lack recognition of their cause-and-effect relationships.

It is important that homeless children and families experience themselves as worthy of care in order for their positive self-concepts to develop. Staff who attend to the environment and make sure that it is clean and well cared for are communicating a respectful attitude toward children and families.

Teachers or clinical staff should visit the shelter or hotel whenever possible. Homelessness often leaves both children and adults feeling fragmented and isolated. Programs that can make at least one home visit may be able to help children and families bridge the psychological distance between home and school and may increase the family's feeling of connection. Staff should evaluate the appropriate timing for this visit, which might depend on a degree of parental trust and understanding of the visit's purpose.

The preschool can conceive of itself as a psychological home base for homeless students and their families. The preschool should examine school policies and routines as they relate to this important function. While most preschool settings have features that create a "home-away-from-home" feeling for children and their parents (such as cubbies, parents' room, and so forth), homeless families may derive special benefits from these features. If a center serves some homeless families, staff should be aware of the heightened need for the program to function as perhaps the only intimate environment to which the parents and children have access. Therefore, routines involving arrival and departure, eating, sleeping, and toileting should be made comfortable and personal, and a climate of emotional responsiveness should prevail for both parents and children.

Teachers of homeless children should be aware of the importance of relationship as an organizing influence in the classroom. When teachers of homeless children are aware of the importance of their relationship role with their students, they can take measures to increase personal contact with them at intervals throughout the day. For example, a teacher might realize that a homeless child becomes frantic and disorganized during free time; she may exert an organizing influence over the child by encouraging him to check in with the teacher at the conclusion of each activity. During group time or other "sit-down" times, she may hold the child on her lap or assign another classroom adult to do the holding. She may encourage the child to hold a classroom stuffed animal during rest time each day and help that child to seek the animal out during times of distress.

Classrooms that include homeless children need to offer children reflections of and potential symbols for their experiences. Homeless children may initially lack the foundation for abstract language and symbolic play and therefore seem uninterested in representational activity. In order to develop age-appropriate representational capacities, they may need exposure to symbols of themselves. They may benefit from curriculums that include photographs of themselves and their family members, teacher-drawn books representing classroom activities and affects, and activities designed to highlight social and emotional cause and effect. As all children do, homeless children need dolls and pretend people that look similar to themselves in order to encourage identification with the play symbols. Dramatic-play areas should include props for experiences that teachers know to be salient in the lives of homeless children, for instance, bags and suitcases if the child has moved from place to place, fire hats and boots if the loss of housing was due to fire, and other relevant items.

Teachers of homeless children must offer children a high level of protection in the school environment. Limit setting can be done by stressing the protective function of the limits being set. Homeless children may not be accustomed to appropriate levels of supervision. This may leave them feeling anxious and uncontained. Paradoxically, they may reject the teacher's attempts to limit dangerous behaviors and test the teacher's resolve to offer protection by repeatedly engaging in hazardous physical activity. Supportive holding, verbalizing limits and their rationale, and enforcing safety rules are well worth the struggles with homeless children, who will ultimately benefit from a safe and containing environment.

CONCLUSION

Most teachers and clinicians who work in the public sector in urban areas will encounter homeless children in the preschool and day-care population. Understanding the ways that homelessness impacts on development will allow staff members to attend to those areas that have been neglected for the homeless child. This understanding will inform the creation of a growth-promoting school environment with the potential to meet the educational and psychological needs of the homeless child.

REFERENCES

Ainsworth, M., Bleher, E., Waters, E., & Wall, S. (1978). *Patterns of attachment.* Hillsdale, NJ: Erlbaum.

Bassuk, E., Rubin, L., & Lauriat, A. S. (1986). Characteristics of sheltered homeless families. *American Journal of Public Health, 76*(9), 1097–1101.

Beebe, B. (2004). Faces in relation: A case study. *Psychoanalytic Dialogues, 14*(1), 1–51.

Emde, R. (1989). The infant's relationship experience: Developmental and affective aspects. In A. Sameroff & R. Emde (Eds.), *Relationship disturbance in early childhood* (pp. 33–51). New York: Basic Books.

Ennes, J. (1991). *Connecting: Meeting the needs of formerly homeless pre-school children—A curriculum for child care.* New York: Child Care.

Erikson, E. (1968). *Childhood and society* (2nd ed.). New York: Norton.

Galinsky, E. (1987). *The six stages of parenthood.* Reading, PA: Addison-Wesley.

Hart-Shegos, E. (1999). *Homelessness and its effects on children.* Minneapolis, MN: Family Housing Fund.

Koplow, L. (1992). *The way home: A child therapist looks at the inner lives of city children.* New York: Dutton.

Kozol, J. (1988). *Rachel and her children.* New York: Crown.

Mahler, M., Bergman, A., & Pine, F. (2000). *The psychological birth of the human infant.* New York: Basic Books. (Original work published 1975)

Molnar, J. (1988). *Home is where the heart is: The crisis of homeless children and families in New York City.* New York: Bank Street College of Education.

Protecting the mental health of homeless children and youth [Special issue]. (2000, February). *Healing Hands,* February 2000 [Online newsletter of HCH Clinicians' Network, National Health Care for the Homeless Council].

Sanchez, R. (2000, February). Why homeless children misbehave. *Healing Hands,* February 2000 [Online newsletter of HCH Clinicians' Network, National Health Care for the Homeless Council].

Siegel, D. J. (1999). *The developing mind: How relationships and the brain interact to shape who we are.* New York: Guilford.

Stern, D. (2000). *The interpersonal world of the infant.* New York: Basic Books. (Original work published 1985)

Preschool as Home Base

CHAPTER 13

Caring for Families and Staff

LESLEY KOPLOW

THE PRECEDING CHAPTERS have focused on the many ways that young, emotionally fragile children can be helped to use preschool as a psychological home base, a safe place from which to grow and explore. Preschool experience often becomes a kind of extended family experience for children, who may spend several hours each day at the early childhood center. Ellen Galinsky (1977) referred to this phenomenon in her *The New Extended Family*.

PRESCHOOL AS EXTENDED FAMILY

Since the time of Galinsky's publication, increasing numbers of preschools have expanded their hours of operation to meet the needs of working parents. The increased numbers include parents affected by welfare reforms that have mandatory work requirements for families receiving public assistance. Not only does this mean that many more children are having their care needs met by preschool staff, but parents have to have sufficient trust in the center in order to support the attachment relationships that underlie high-quality care. They have to feel at home in the center when they drop their child off and when they pick their child up, and they have to communicate their comfort level to their children. Parents are dependent on school staff to give them the nuances of their child's affects and activities during the schoolday so they do not feel cut off from their young children's experiences or too guilty about leaving their children in the center to go to work.

Preschool staff who provide hours of care and psychoeducational experience to young children every day must also have trust in the preschool environment that employs them. They have to feel that the ground that they walk on at the center is secure before they can give children a feeling of security in the classroom. Preschools that heal have to nurture and enable parents and staff members as well as children in order to thrive. Preschool teachers and assistant teachers make relatively little money. If they are not well supported and valued as important members of the school community, they may have no motivation to stay in the preschool setting. Staff turnover is debilitating to fragile children, who need ongoing, nurturing relationships with their teachers and caregivers.

FAMILIES ON SITE

Competent preschools know what to do with young children when they enter the classroom setting. The program's mission to provide a developmentally appropriate and emotionally supportive learning environment is clear, and staff members know what activities to undertake in service of that mission. Teachers know what constitutes acceptable behavior and what language to use with children who need guidance.

When parents come to school, program staff must know what to do with them as well. The urban preschool with an open-door policy to parents must be clear about the nature of the invitation they are extending. Staff must define their mission first to themselves and then to parents and families. Bringing a young child into group life is a meaningful transition for parents, and the preschool must be prepared to make room for families who are struggling with that transition as well as families who are ready to enter and feel comfortable bringing their child into the school environment.

Most preschools advocate a partnership between school and families on behalf of children. However, it is sometimes difficult to operationalize this concept with stressed populations of parents who may not always appear to act in their children's best interest (Christenson, 2004). Therefore, the welcome mat may be extended with considerable ambivalence. It may say, "Welcome if you are 'good,' culturally familiar parents who are seeking help and speak the language of childhood. Otherwise, please stay home."

Certainly, each program formally or informally communicates expectations for parent activity and behavior while parents are on site. Just as the classroom teacher sets a tone that will influence the behavior of the students toward one another and affect their inclination to express themselves freely, the attitude of the program director, teachers, and clinicians toward families will affect and partially determine the ways that parents make use of the preschool program. Therefore, it is important that staff be self-reflective about their own feelings and attitudes toward the parent population because this will surely influence the outcome of parent intervention.

A DIALOGUE OF DIVERSITY

Urban preschools are likely to serve a diverse population of parents. One class of 18 children may include several families from varied ethnic and cultural backgrounds. Some families are highly educated while others have had minimal formal education. There may be economic diversity as well as cultural diversity, with some centers including both families on public assistance and families with abundant financial resources. Many families may be raising their children in an environment unlike the one in which they themselves were raised. At the end of the schoolday, the hallways may echo with several languages and dialects as parents collect their children and begin bridging the psychological distance between school and home.

In the multicultural urban environment, each family may come to school with its own cultural imperatives for child care and its own culturally rooted response to the program's mission for parents. When the parent population includes parents of developmentally arrested, traumatized, or emotionally fragile children, it is essential for staff to recognize that the meaning of each child's difficulty will be deeply embedded in the parents' own personal and cultural experiences. Therefore, the preschool parent program must strive to recognize and value each parent's personal and cultural experiences and employ structures that enable parents to connect, value, and share their experiences with one another and with program staff.

At the same time, the preschool itself must recognize that *it* is part of a subculture—the subculture of the early childhood community. Indeed, all strong, healing programs have premises about child care and family development that are born of collective experiences with the early childhood population. All programs with clear philosophies evolve a specialized language that allows them to refer specifically to aspects of the work that might remain invisible to the casual observer. Just as the early childhood program has a responsibility to help parents articulate the meaning of their own personal and cultural experiences, it also has a responsibility to clearly communicate *its* "cultural" and philosophical premises. The ensuing dialogue can enrich both parents and staff and widen the sphere of meaning for each.

A PLACE TO FIND COMMON GROUND

Given a diverse parent population, program staff must help parents to find common ground within the school community (Koplow, 1992). The family mission of preschools that heal is threefold. Programs must (1) help parents develop a healthy connection to their own children; (2) help parents find meaning in their own personal and cultural experiences, past and present; and (3) help parents connect with one another. These goals may be intimidating to the preschool administrator who has only modest resources available for parent programs. Therefore, the following interventions include a range of possibilities for programs with and without well-supported parent programs.

Parents' Room

Parents' rooms should be comfortable spaces where parents are welcome to relax during the hours that their children attend preschool. The parents' room decor need not be elaborate but should be warm and include a rug and soft furniture, a coffee/tea corner, and some infant/toddler toys for parents who bring their younger children along.

Parents' rooms are important because they convey a welcoming attitude to the parent, make parents feel provided for, and allow separation-anxious parents and children to be reassured by reuniting with each other in a predictable location.

While many parents may have no interest in making use of a parents' room during the schoolday, others will feel tremendous relief in knowing that there is a safe place available for them where they may converse with other parents, rest, and care for younger children. Some parents' rooms have arts and craft supplies on hand. Others provide parents with materials and invite them to work on projects that are helpful to the classroom teachers, such as sewing doll clothes.

Parents' rooms may be essential for parents who need the preschool program to function as a psychological home base for themselves as well as for their children. Psychosocial histories may reveal that many parents lacked continuity in their own childhoods and therefore had no opportunity to organize themselves by building stable relationships with important adults in a nurturing environment. When parents have the opportunity to be present in the therapeutic milieu of the preschool for a period of months or even years, the experience may be a powerful one. Parents may feel a greater capacity for organization and achieve a more planful outlook for themselves and their children.

Parent Group

The reader may have absorbed the previous paragraphs with skepticism, wondering how the provision of a space can in itself accomplish so much psychological work. Indeed, while parents' rooms are an essential component of preschools that heal, the potential benefits increase when the parents' room also houses a weekly parent group.

Many preschool programs have a parent-group component. These groups vary in method and purpose. Some are led by teachers, others by directors, and still others by social workers or psychologists. Some are educative groups, assuming that parents grow when given instruction regarding parenting practices. These groups often focus on imparting information that might assist parents in managing their children. Other groups are essentially support groups, encouraging parents to talk about difficulties so that other parents can be empathic and everyone can feel less isolated. Other groups are therapeutic, making use of the techniques used in educative and support models but also emphasizing spontaneous contributions that emerge during an open-ended group process. The therapeutic-group model will be elaborated on here as a possible component of preschools that heal.

While educative groups are leader-facilitated and topic-oriented, therapeutic groups are leader-facilitated but open-ended. Participants raise topics and group leaders respond by listening, reflecting, clarifying content, inviting further comment by other members, or offering interpretations that may help parents make connections to the content. The open-ended nature of the therapeutic parent group may be compared to the open-ended nature of the children's free-play period (see Chapter 8). Certainly, difficult issues and themes will arise that would not have surfaced in a more tightly structured format, and these might frighten both other group members and leaders at times. On the other hand, as in the expertly led free-play period, group facilitators may often act to direct and contain material that comes up. The structure of the therapeutic group does not come from the leader's prescheduled agenda, but this does not imply that the therapeutic parent group lacks structure. Rather, the structuring elements emerge from the alliance between group members and facilitator as well as from the facilitator's commitment to conveying and maintaining the threefold goals of parent intervention.

The therapeutic parent group may have one or two leaders, depending on the size, fragility, and explosive potential of the group population as well as on the program's resources for parent intervention. The group leaders should initially define the parameters of the group so that members are well oriented to the group experience and rules of interaction are clearly stated. For example, the leader may introduce the group by saying,

> We want the group to be a place where people can feel connected to their present experiences as parents and their past experience as children. Since the group is so diverse, we'll have to find a common language to talk about these feelings of connection. We think that language will come from being together over time and talking and listening to one another. In the group, everyone needs to respect everyone else's right to their feelings and opinions, and no one is allowed to intentionally hurt anyone else physically or emotionally.

The leader of the therapeutic group composed of a culturally diverse parent body assumes that each group member can make a valuable contribution to the group. She is aware that the initial areas of commonality for group members are their status as parents of young children and the fact that all members were once young children themselves. Using Selma Fraiberg's (1980) premise that parents who are in touch with their own childhood experiences and affects have a greater capacity to connect with and empathize with their own children, the group leader invites the parents to remember their own childhood experiences and feelings within the group whenever possible. This invitation can be extended only if the group leader conveys her ability to contain the material. Ultimately, the leader's consistent reappearance week after week will show her ability to survive whatever topics arise and make members feel that the group is a safe place for remembering.

Hello/Goodbye: A Group Dialogue

The following portions of group process illustrate the ways that therapeutic group intervention can address essential issues and promote growth among diverse groups of parents. Ten parents of needy preschoolers are in attendance.

EARLY SESSION

It is the second month of school, and several children are still having difficulty separating from their parents to come into the classroom.

MIGUELINA [A kinship foster mother who has had many losses, including an adult child]: Misty is drivin' me crazy. She don't let me out of her sight since school started. If I leave her with my sister to go out for a quart of milk, forget it! You can hear her around the block.

HANNAH [a former school psychologist who stopped working when her son was born]: Do you tell her where you're going and that you'll be right back? It helps if I tell Sammy.

MIGUELINA: I ain't makin' any promises I can't keep. What if I get run over by a car on my way home? (*silence; some smiles and some uncomfortable shifting of positions of group members*)

LEADER: It must be hard to reassure Misty if you don't feel secure about always being there for her.

THEA [an older woman, also a kinship foster parent who was in last year's group as well]: You feel like that 'cause Misty's your foster child. You don't have no legal claim on her. I know what that's like. One day the judge will say, all right now, Jimmy and Keisha are going to live with their mother and that will be that.

LEANA [a highly educated woman who has been reading child development literature avidly since enrolling her two children in the program]: I know, but don't you think Miguelina should reassure Misty anyway? I mean, so at least she feels reassured for *now*? (*Miguelina looks up at the leader, wary of her reply.*)

LEADER: I wonder if anyone remembers being in Misty's position as a child? Being very young and worrying about your parents not coming back for you?

MIGUELINA: I can't go back that far.

CHRISTA [a banking executive who suffered abuse as a child]: Oh, dear. You are asking a lot!

WINTER SESSION

A teacher who has been at the school for years recently went on maternity leave. All parents participated in a special event for Karen, the departing teacher.

MIGUELINA: Now Misty thinks that I have a baby in my tummy like Karen.

LEANA: Does that make her happy or sad? [Leana is considering becoming pregnant again.]

MIGUELINA: I don't know, but she probably thinks I'll leave her if I get a baby, like Karen did.

THEA: That's right. What's Keisha gonna think? Her birth mother's pregnant again.

LEADER: I don't know. Does anyone with younger siblings remember how you felt waiting for the baby to come?

MONIQUE [a victim of domestic violence who had been in a shelter when she entered the program 3 years ago]: There go that question again! She keep on askin' every time even though nobody do remember. (*Monique looks at the leader with a provocative, playful smile.*)

HANNAH: I remember my older sister telling me that she hated me for coming, and I think she still does! (*Leana looks disturbed at this.*)

JEFFERY [an engineering student and father of an aphasic child]: I remember being really upset after my mother had my sister, not because I was jealous of my sister, but because my mother didn't look the same anymore. I guess I was so young when she got pregnant, about 1 year old, I didn't remember her being so thin—I got used to her being sort of . . . round, you know? I felt like I didn't know her.

CHRISTA: I had that same reaction! Not after my sister was born, but after they sent me from my grandparents in Hungary back to my mother in Germany. I was about 3, I guess, and I looked at her and I thought "Who *is* this lady?" She didn't look a thing like I remembered her.

LEADER: Were you scared?

CHRISTA (*looks blank*): I don't know. Isn't that strange? I can't remember that part.

JEFFERY: I was. I remember crying for my mother and she would come and I still kept crying.

LEADER: Hmm. That sounds really scary, and so does Christa's story. Kids need to have an image of their parents in their heads to comfort themselves with when they're separated. It sounds like your images didn't work anymore for a while. It's an important story because so many of the kids here have trouble keeping the image of important people in their minds. That's why separation is so difficult—that's why we use photographs so often in the classroom. Also, think about the book we made when Karen got pregnant that explained about the baby and showed pictures of what Karen used to look like and what she looks like now.

MIGUELINA: You people are photography crazy. You got more pictures of Misty than I do. It makes me nervous—like every time I turn around, there she is. Why do you think I gave her the nickname Misty?

LEANA: Isn't Misty her real name?

MIGUELINA: No. Her given name is Juana Marie. I call her Misty because
for me she's like the mist. It looks like she's settled in with me, but
one day, I could look around and she'll be gone.

HANNAH: Don't say that! That gives me the chills!

THEA: No. She's yours now and you gotta fight to keep it that way.

END-OF-YEAR SESSION (6 WEEKS BEFORE ENDING)

The group leader has announced several staff changes for the fall, including one teacher leaving, one former staff member returning, the reintegra-
tion of the staff member on maternity leave in a new capacity, and the
leader's own plans to work part-time in the fall. She makes it clear that she
will continue to lead the group and will maintain any treatment cases
currently in progress.

LEADER: That's a lot to take in. A lot of change.

MONIQUE: That's fine by me! Now we got Karen and Marcy back. That's
all I care about.

LEANA: You're not upset about [leader] not being here every day? [Leana
knows that Monique is one of the parents who makes use of the
parent room on a daily basis and frequently checks in with group
leader.]

MONIQUE (shrugs, smiles, and denies having a reaction to this): It ain't
like she leavin'. She still be here for us.

(The group suddenly becomes aware that Hannah is crying.)

JEFFERY: Hey! Don't cry! Sammy's teachers are both staying.

HANNAH: I'm sorry . . . (gets up to leave)

LEADER: You don't have to leave the room to cry. You can cry here.
(Hannah does leave, but returns instantly.)

CHRISTA: Don't you cry! Then I'll start.

LEADER: Maybe you can tell us what's making you feel so sad.

HANNAH: I know you'll still be here for the group and for Sammy and
I, but what about in the future? After Sammy graduates? If you
work part-time now, it makes me think that eventually you'll be
gone.

THEA: So? By that time you'll be in another school and you'll already be
workin' with other people helpin' Sammy out. It won't matter by that
time!

HANNAH: But what if we want to come back for a consultation? I just
want to think that she'll be here—that the program will still be here—
that it won't change.

MIGUELINA: What about Misty? Her teacher is leaving! Poor child.

CHRISTA: I'm not going to tell Donna. Why should she have to know? She's graduating this year. Let her think about this place the way she remembers it.

LEADER: This is really important. Everyone is really reacting not only to the actual fact of losing people that are important, but to the idea of losing the image of this place which has become a source of security. (*to Christa*) Can you say more about why you feel strongly about not telling Donna too much about the changes?

CHRISTA (*with tears in her eyes*): When I look at Hannah crying, I think I can remember the way it felt when I was a kid and I was sent back and forth all those times—really without a home—I don't want Donna to feel that way.

MONIQUE: I'll take pictures of you all on the last day, so that way Bri can remember the way it is now.

MIGUELINA: Maybe I'll bring a video camera for Misty.

These important dialogues allowed parents to address complex child development issues, such as the relationship of separation anxiety to object constancy, and enabled parents to remember and connect with some of their own early childhood experiences and affects. The connections fostered a greater empathic response to their own children's situations. The opportunity to listen to one another gave parents a way to consider difficult material while maintaining their own defenses if necessary. Some parents elected to remain silent for months before voicing thoughts or feelings. However, their contributions indicated that their receptivity to psychological issues had been greatly influenced by the group dialogue.

Parent Guidance

If program resources allow for individual parent sessions as part of the parent intervention program, individual parents' reactions to the group dialogue can be explored and elaborated. This individual time may be especially important for extremely fragile group members whose leaders worry about the continued affects and reactions of provocative material on them.

Apart from using individual parent sessions as a follow-up to group dialogue, there are many possibilities for this parent component, which has traditionally been described as "parent guidance." While parents can find common ground in a group milieu, there are many personal, familial, and cultural issues that are not easily explored in a group but have a profound impact on parent and child dynamics. Parents, like their children, may need to establish a strong, therapeutic relationship with a clinician in order to feel safe enough to address personal material. School-based clinicians, on the other hand, may feel a need to give direction to parents who seem unable to meet their young children's needs. Historically, these two clinical objectives have been considered contradictory. Only directive parent guidance was provided on the school site, while parents were referred for treatment to discuss their own personal issues.

Selma Fraiberg's (1980) work with emotionally fragile, potentially abusive parents revolutionized the early intervention process by applying a psychoanalytic model to parent guidance work. She hypothesized that parents interacted with their children in counterproductive ways not because they lacked information about "correct" ways to parent but because they were unconsciously reenacting their own traumatic early childhood experiences, which they could no longer feel or remember. Therefore, according to Fraiberg, parent intervention work had to be personal and therapeutic in nature so that parents could connect to their own early experiences and affects before educative approaches could be effective.

It may be especially important to implement these premises when doing individual parent work. Indeed, if one uses solely educative approaches with fragile populations of parents, parents may learn what they "should" be doing but remain unable to do it. This may feel worse than "not knowing" what to do, as it may create guilt that some parents are ill equipped to tolerate. Alicia Lieberman's recent work with parents who have had difficult histories also shows clinical value in helping parents remember and connect to the positive influences in their early lives that may have gotten overshadowed by trauma and fragmentation (Lieberman, Padron, Van Horn, & Harris, 2005).

When resources exist for individual parent counseling, preschools that heal may use an approach similar to the one demonstrated by the group process mentioned previously. This approach would encourage open-ended dialogue with an ongoing invitation to remember early experiences within the containing relationship with the therapist. The therapist may provide a developmental framework from which to organize and interpret the early experiences and may make connections between the parent's issues and the child's. The therapist may feel it is productive to include dyadic sessions or whole-family sessions in the work with parents and children so that interactive issues can be addressed as they occur. This family or dyadic modality may be more comfortable for those parents who easily feel spotlighted or judged if they are the focus of clinical attention.

The following material from one parent's sessions may demonstrate the benefits of psychodynamically informed parent work.

Wendy was the 33-year-old mother of Georgie, a 4-year-old boy with atypical ego development. Wendy grew up in a major urban area and felt she could identify with many urban subcultures because her father and mother were immigrants from the Caribbean. Most people assumed Wendy was African American because she was Black and spoke English with no accent, although she was equally fluent in French.

Wendy was clearly an attentive, devoted mother who cared deeply for Georgie. Yet she worried the staff by acting in ways that were preventing Georgie from making progress. Specifically, Wendy stuffed Georgie with food continually, as if food was the answer to any distress Georgie might express. Consequently, Georgie was considerably overweight. In addition, Wendy was overprotective of

Georgie to the extent that she limited his opportunity for physical activity for fear that he would fall and get hurt.

Staff patiently tried to intervene with Wendy and Georgie. Teachers modeled alternate responses to Georgie's distress that did not involve food but worked to comfort him. Staff encouraged Wendy to consult her pediatrician concerning what constitutes a normal diet for a 4-year-old boy and what physical pursuits were healthy for an active preschooler. Wendy voiced interest in these suggestions but seemed to be made anxious by them. Her behavior with Georgie did not change. Wendy used her individual sessions to explore these issues:

WENDY: Marcy and Karen think Georgie is overweight. I don't think he's that bad. What do you think? (*Therapist opens her mouth to respond, but Wendy keeps talking.*) Well, I did do what you said and I checked with the doctor. She agrees that Georgie has a little weight problem. She referred me to a nutritionist.

THERAPIST: What did the nutritionist say?

WENDY: She said I have to put Georgie on a diet!

THERAPIST: How do you think that will be for you?

WENDY: I don't know. It will be okay, I guess. Well, hard, really hard. I know it's the right thing to do. My grandmother told me the same thing. You think she'd be happy with Georgie being kind of pudgy— you know grandparents like children to look well fed . . .

THERAPIST: Why do you think it's so hard to let Georgie eat less?

WENDY: Well, he likes candy and he likes sweets, and now he's used to me putting food in his mouth every time he turns around. If I say no, he'll probably cry . . .

THERAPIST: Is it hard to hear him cry and not give in?

WENDY: I'll tell you, that child has me wrapped around his little finger!

THERAPIST: How was it for you and your mother when you were small? In the food department, I mean.

WENDY: I was a little-bitty thing, believe it or not, and my mother didn't worry about it either. Now, if I go over there for the weekend, it's ridiculous! My father says, "Wendy, have a little bit more of this! Is that all you're going to eat?" I say, "Papa, please!"

THERAPIST: So it's your dad who thinks there's not enough of you. (*Wendy laughs.*) Well, you're telling me that you know giving too much is bad for him but it's hard not to do it. I wonder if there was a time you felt like you weren't giving Georgie enough?

(*Wendy disengages from the therapist by breaking eye contact—she looks guilty and anxious.*)

THERAPIST: Is this too hard to think about?

WENDY: Well, you know from the papers . . . but I still feel ashamed to talk about it . . . you know . . . when I was pregnant with Georgie . . .

THERAPIST: You were drinking.

WENDY (*tearful*): I didn't take good care of him then.

THERAPIST: I know you feel a lot of guilt about that, and I wonder if the overfeeding is a way to compensate for the guilty feelings—to make up for the past by being extra motherly in the present?

WENDY: Yeah and it's not working either, because it's making the whole thing worse.

THERAPIST: I think what will make it better is if we keep talking about the guilt.

The therapist and Wendy kept talking about the guilt over time, and soon Wendy was able to let go of the maladaptive feeding behavior.

Parent–Child Day

Monthly parent–child days are an indispensable feature of preschools that heal. Parent–child days can be integrated into the program year, even if the preschool lacks resources specifically earmarked for parent intervention. On parent–child days, at least one parent or significant adult must attend school with the child for part of the morning. The morning begins with a parent–child group where the entire school community, including all staff members, sing together. Songs can include familiar children's songs that are part of the usual classroom music times or songs featured in the therapeutic curriculum, as well as songs that may be part of a family's repertoire and have personal and cultural meaning to group participants. After the group sing-along, an activity is planned that fosters reciprocity between parents and their children, and focuses the whole group on an important issue or a special occasion.

For example, many young children need help to make sense out of the way that Halloween is celebrated. Age-appropriate difficulty differentiating between reality and fantasy makes the donning of masks and costumes frightening and sometimes terrifying to young fragile children. Watching family members assume monstrous qualities is especially horrifying. Therefore, Halloween provides an inspiration for a parent–child group theme because it offers an opportunity to reassure children in their parents' presence and constitutes an educative and pleasurable activity for parents. At the parent–child group for October, each child in turn is given a choice of some nonthreatening Halloween accessories to put on himself and his parent. (For example, bunny ears and cat whiskers might be provided.) Other children and parents watch the process, while the leader calls everyone's attention to the fact that the parent and child are still the same people they have always been, with or without the costume. Parents and children may share a special Halloween snack made by the children in cooking time the day before. A goodbye song is sung to signify the end of the parent–child group, and children then return to their classrooms while parents are free to socialize with one another. However, teachers can make plans involving parents in classroom activities later in the morning as well, such as inviting parents to accompany children on a neighborhood walk, having parents join their children for lunch, and so forth.

Parent–child day activities can be varied, creative, and connected with a therapeutic curriculum, or they can be simple and involve no complex metaphors, as long as they are designed to be pleasurable for both children and parents. Having parents and children work on a leaf collage together can be an occasion for feelings of parent–child connection. Having children listen to a tape recording of each of their parents singing or telling a story can be an occasion for promoting personal and cultural identification.

Parent–child days are a powerful form of intervention for several reasons. Parents of emotionally fragile or developmentally arrested children rarely experience themselves and their children as valuable members of community life. Parents often report feeling helpless and embarrassed when their children cry or act out in stores or on the street. Some parents painfully recall incidents of feeling rejected at church or synagogue because of their children's difficult behavior. Parent–child groups give parents a place to be with their children where they can feel that their children are both accepted and contained.

Parent–child activities also give parents an opportunity to be part of the process of facilitating mastery for their children and a chance to feel pride in their children's accomplishments. Many parents are surprised when they find that their child knows the words or motions to a familiar song or can risk participation in a group activity. In addition, it gives them a firsthand feeling for aspects of the therapeutic curriculum, which helps to create a stronger alliance between parents and school staff.

Parent–child day activities are always photographed, and the photographs are assembled in albums for parents and children to review at their leisure. The photograph albums help to foster a strong family feeling in the program because special parent–child moments are captured and children's physical and psychological changes are recorded and treasured.

In order for preschools to be viable as a psychological home base for parents and children, they must function as strong and stable places from which a family can move forward. Programs must meet the challenge of a diverse group of parents with an evolved philosophy; an attentive, empathic ear; and a readiness for dialogue. Parents may alternately reject and embrace various aspects of the program, but it is the reconciliation of these two positions that may ultimately empower parents to provide their children with a model for integrating new experiences.

THE COMMUNITY OF STAFF

Building a psychological home base in the early childhood center may be a clear mandate for administrators in centers where parents and children depend on high-quality, emotionally responsive care each day in order to thrive. Administrators of preschools that heal must also invest heavily in administrative practices that promote staff cohesion and unity so that staff feel well supported and valuable in the work-place, where they spend many hours each day. The business of healing young children demands constant energy, creativity, intelligence, and compassion. If administrators neglect to attend to the emotional life of staff, it is likely that staff members will feel overburdened and overwhelmed. These are feelings that lead to burnout and high rates of staff turnover. Since few people other than educators and caregivers under-stand what it is like to care for emotionally needy children for many hours a day, it is critical that directors, supervisors, and teachers themselves be able to acknowledge this and realize the need for support and refueling.

PHILOSOPHY: ADMINISTRATOR AS SPOKESPERSON

The importance of program philosophy as an organizing force promoting staff integrity and cohesion cannot be overstated. Indeed, every early childhood pro-gram has a statement of its overall mission and intervention philosophy stored neatly in a loose-leaf notebook outlining the program's policies and procedures. Some programs include references to program philosophy in brochures advertis-ing their services to prospective clients and referral sources. Others avoid defin-ing philosophy in specific terms in their public statements, describing themselves as "open" to "doing what works." The literature pertaining to staff effectiveness in programs serving multiproblem families and their children emphasizes the need for administrators to clearly define and articulate program philosophy and to en-sure that practice is actually in accordance with the stated philosophy. This alerts staff members with incompatible beliefs to seek employment in a program that is more in tune with their particular orientation.

The infant mental health literature lends a much-needed human perspective to the existing literature on early childhood administration. Fenichel (1992) ana-lyzed the administrative practices of supervision and mentorship and spoke of the need to create a parallel process between a program's philosophy and practice in the education and treatment of children and families and its philosophy and prac-tice regarding staff issues, advising administrators to "do unto others as you would have them do unto others" (p. 16).

A graduate study of staff dynamics in a psychodynamically oriented preschool program with little staff turnover found commonly held philosophy to be a key factor in the staff's feeling of effectiveness. Briccetti (1993) found that the staff had developed a common language to communicate their philosophy that all be-havior was meaningful and that this philosophy characterized staff interactions with one another as well:

> The philosophy of the pre-school was to construct a psychological home, a "safe space," a holding environment for children and families. The staff had constructed a common frame of reference and language regarding this philosophy and practice.

They were committed to helping children heal and develop by enabling them to represent and share experiences. This process was mirrored in the interaction between staff which became the glue that held the program together and a vital link to the children's treatment. (p. 22)

Preschools that heal have embraced a particular philosophy that acknowledges the primary role of emotional life as an organizer of developmental processes. Therefore, these preschools must support the children's relationships as a foundation for emotional growth, and curriculum must reflect and affirm actual emotional experience. If the administrative goal is to implement a parallel process for staff in order to facilitate their professional development and learning, the director must find ways to translate these premises into the working milieu. Staff must be encouraged to connect to their work and to build supportive relationships with one another.

THE WORKING MILIEU

Staff members may feel overwhelmed at the prospect of broadening their intervention models to include a focus on emotional life, and they may wonder whether they will have sufficient resources to face the challenges described in this book. Practitioners who already address emotional life in preschool know that the work requires a high level of commitment and that, while it can be compelling, it can also be exhausting. Certainly, intense connections with young children will evoke complex emotional responses in teachers and therapists as well as in parents and other caregivers.

Work involving fragile children and multiproblem families can feel all-consuming. Few professionals can tolerate the necessary level of deep involvement if they feel isolated in their efforts. Early intervention specialist R. S. Shanok (1992) expresses this beautifully in her article addressing key issues for staff in early intervention programs:

Making relationships across classes and cultures, or with people who have been wounded and cannot join us reciprocally, who cannot give us the feedback that would let us know that we are doing all right, requires the insight, courage and resilience born of collaboration. (p. 39)

Collaboration is essential to healthy early intervention practice. Yet it is difficult to find programs where staff feel camaraderie in spite of differences in educational background or training expertise. Interviews with staff in a special education preschool yielded several accounts similar to this one:

At [Pre-school X] we were supposedly working as a team. In actuality, everyone just stuck with other people in their own area. The teachers thought that the therapists weren't working hard enough. The therapists made the teachers feel like they didn't know what they were doing, and case conferences were a joke. All they did was read evaluation reports that we could have read ourselves. Everyone was afraid to say what they really thought.

The tendency for staff members to become divisive "along party lines" may be attributed to what Bertacchi and Coplin (1992) call "the continuum of identification from baby to parent" (p. 89). This refers to the ways that one's career choice may relate to one's own identification with infants, toddlers, young children, or parents; an early childhood teacher may have a strong identification with young children, while a parent guidance professional may have a stronger identification with parents. Issues that arise during a young child's education and treatment may polarize staff if their own identifications are unexamined.

Another challenge for the early childhood setting in the 21st century is to develop a strong enough core to actively collaborate with other service providers and to accommodate the flow of outside therapists who are often assigned to come into the program to meet the special needs of individual children. Many school systems support special-needs preschoolers within the mainstream early childhood community by having additional service providers come into the center from outside agencies. This model presents many learning opportunities as well as many challenges to the staff of the preschool community. The identity issues explored above often become magnified when staff actually are employed by other agencies outside of the preschool. Not only does the system present logistical dilemmas making opportunities for communication difficult to find, but it can present a crisis of sorts for a preschool that has not yet struggled to define its educational philosophy and for the provider who may not have worked within the context of a preschool setting.

Classroom teachers must have the time to communicate with the service providers so that they know the nature of the educational experiences that children in the group are having when they leave the classroom and can learn about the service provider's way of working and the ideas that underlie her work. Service providers have to make time to communicate with teachers so they understand the program's way of working and core beliefs about children and can develop their individual interventions in sync with the overall learning environment. Not only must teachers and service providers work together if young children are to be able to integrate the interventions given, but they must develop a true collaboration in order for core staff and agency staff to feel empowered and effective in their work. It is demoralizing to feel that your efforts are being undermined by other professionals! Teachers must feel respect for and from the outside providers, and the intervention philosophies need to be in sync for children to benefit. These administrative issues require forethought, planning, energy, and talent on the part of the program director. The issues are real and require real work to address.

In order to provide a milieu that is safe enough for staff members to express and listen to one another's viewpoints and feelings, certain programmatic structures must be put into place. They include (1) supervision, (2) opportunity for anecdotal exchange, and (3) opportunity for professional empowerment. The value of these structures will be explored in the following sections.

Supervision

An effective litmus test of a preschool staff's overall health may be the measure of staff receptivity to supervision. Supervisory sessions can be conceived of as a way to manage or monitor staff activity, instruct staff, mentor beginning staff, or facilitate self-reflection in a professional context. If staff members consider supervision a burden or feel that it is inadequate, it is probable that the program is not meeting the supervisory needs of the staff and possible that the staff has become unreceptive to input. This creates a potentially hazardous situation, because staff must then attempt to meet the needs of fragile children and families while feeling that their own professional needs are unmet.

Programs concerned with facilitating developmental processes by strengthening relationships as the social-emotional foundation for learning will probably be well served by a clinical supervision model. Clinical supervision in schools is a reflective process that helps professionals integrate their work experiences and see themselves grow professionally within the context of a supervisory relationship. The supervisory relationship has been considered an essential element for staff attempting effective early intervention with young children and multistressed families (Bertacchi & Stott, 1991; Brown & Thorp, 1989; Fenichel & Eggbeer, 1989; Shanok, 1992). Given the constant challenges that arise when working with fragile children and families, a consistent supervision hour, which includes experienced staff members as well as novices, should be set up and adhered to.

There are variations in supervisory modalities within the clinical supervision model. Some programs provide individual supervision for each staff member. Others arrange group supervision, supervise staff in teaching or clinical teams, or provide a combination of supervisory experiences. No matter what model of supervision is used, the supervisory experience in preschools that heal include the following component: the provision of a safe relationship context for the expression of feeling related to work experience; the provision of a safe relationship context for reflecting on and analyzing practice issues and experiences; and the opportunity to analyze conceptual issues related to practice.

While a supervision hour that is consistently adhered to and a private, adequate supervision space help to define the supervisory context, the actual relationship between supervisor and supervisee is what allows the hour to become instrumental. Shanok (1992) describes the supervisory relationship as "a holding environment, a place to feel secure enough to expose insecurities, mistakes, questions, and differences" (p. 37). Anyone who has done work with fragile children and their families knows that, at times, it is difficult to "hold" all that they bring to the preschool setting. Supervision ensures that no one will have to hold troubling experience or material alone. This is important, because one's own emotional responses to the work or countertransference issues are likely to be aroused and may diminish professional effectiveness if left unattended (Fields, 1991). In order to create a safe context where these issues can be explored, the supervisor must maintain an empathic stance and be able to validate the supervisee's experiences, even if they are different than the supervisor's. This kind of empathic stance can be seen as parallel to the one that the professional assumes in her work with young children and parents.

The supervisor must go beyond creating a supportive relationship context for the supervisory work and help the supervisee reflect on her practice, analyzing what has occurred and what her responses have been. The supervisor can use the kind of reflective techniques that have been recommended in earlier chapters for heightening children's and parents' awareness of the meaning of their actions and interactions. For instance, a supervisory contact at the end of the day may include a reflective exchange like the following:

TEACHER: They were crazy today! Wild! Especially at lunchtime. I
   thought 12:30 would never come.
SUPERVISOR: It sounds draining. Any idea why things got so wild? Maybe
   your feeling that the end of the day would never come is a clue.
TEACHER: Actually, now that you say that, the buses were really late
   yesterday, and I think it scared some of the kids. They might have
   worried that they were never going to get home! I'll bring that up
   tomorrow and see if they can talk more about it.

Without the opportunity to reflect on practice, staff members may leave at the end of the week feeling overwhelmed and confused about their effectiveness, arriving the following week with diminished motivation for involvement.

Finally, the supervisor should provide the supervisee with a context for developing a conceptual framework for the work. While encouraging staff members to make deep connections with children and families can be highly therapeutic, it is also important for staff members to maintain a theoretical perspective on their work and to continually deepen their understanding of relevant issues in child development, early childhood education, psychology, and parent development. Staff development opportunities offer professionals an avenue for keeping abreast of relevant theory and practice. While some staff members may be motivated to read, research, and study current issues to follow up on staff development workshops, others may not have a realistic opportunity for this kind of learning, given other demands in their lives, or may learn more readily from discussions or presentations. The supervisor should be sensitive to the supervisee's learning modality. She can model relating to practice issues conceptually by engaging the supervisee in discourse that helps her build a conceptual framework for her practice experience. For example, a teacher may spend several minutes of her supervision hour describing her interactions with a child who screams and curses at her continually while embracing and assuming a compliant stance toward the assistant teacher. The teacher may need to vent her frustration and discuss the several attempts she has made to win this little girl's trust. The supervisor's years of additional experience allow her to recognize the child's behavior as a probable splitting defense. The following dialogue might ensue:

SUPERVISOR: It sounds like she's splitting, and her history of abuse would really support the development of that defense. She's making you all bad and Jan [the assistant] is all good.

TEACHER: Oh! Yeah, that makes sense. I had been relating it to what happened during the first week of school when she kept hurting kids and I had to hold her. I was thinking that I had to win her over . . . to give her a new kind of experience with me, but it seems to be making it worse.

SUPERVISOR: Well, she does need a more pleasurable experience with you, but it won't be easy for her to take that in. Your efforts in pursuing her may be resulting in her taking a more entrenched position. If she needs you to be all bad and you keep being nicer and nicer, she'll need to go to greater efforts to keep you all bad.

TEACHER (laughs): So I need to be mean?

SUPERVISOR: More neutral, maybe. Available, but not trying too hard. Is part of it that it feels so bad to have her calling you "fucker" all day long?

TEACHER: It does feel bad, and I think it feels really good to Jan to have her be so loving.

SUPERVISOR: You guys need to work together on this! I'm sorry Jan is out today. We need to come up with a united strategy on this one.

TEACHER: Maybe we should make a rule that whoever starts something with Melissa stays with her. No escaping to someone else's arms! We both say the same thing to her.

SUPERVISOR: Great. Do it.

Clearly, in this example the conceptual framework that the supervisor was able to provide allowed the supervisee the needed perspective to develop effective strategies. Without this framework, the teacher might have continued to pursue a course of action that was counterindicated and to use her discussions with her supervisor only to vent her frustration. Ultimately, this would have been unsatisfying for her as well. A supervisory mandate for her to change her behavior without the conceptual reasoning would have left her feeling inept and professionally inadequate. The conceptual framework underlying the supervisory discussion ultimately left the supervisee feeling competent and empowered.

Opportunities for Anecdotal Exchange

Staff members who work on multidisciplinary preschool staffs need opportunities to share their experiences with one another in a way that is available to all program professionals. Formal and informal opportunities for anecdotal exchange can be a powerful tool for bridging distance among diverse professionals.

One avenue that can be used to promote anecdotal exchange within a formal structure is the case conference format. Many programs have case conferences to focus on the status and issues of individual children and families, but these vary greatly in form and content. Clinically oriented programs may focus on presentation of history and formal assessment material, while community-based preschools may use the time to brainstorm solutions to problems like obtaining additional services for needy families. While both approaches to conferencing are informative and productive, carving out a space within them for anecdotal exchange formats may be worthwhile.

The anecdotal exchange format of case conferencing involves asking each staff member who is directly involved with the child and his family to tell a story about interaction with that child and/or parent that demonstrates salient issues. Rather than using hierarchy to determine speaker order, those with the most frequent and intimate contact with that child should speak first, and those with less contact should follow. Supervisors may be helpful in weaving the anecdotal themes together and delineating significant issues once everyone has had a chance to speak. All staff should then feel free to address those issues and to problem-solve for those intervention questions that remain unresolved.

Anecdotal exchange is powerful because the stories told are often compelling and foster identification among staff members across disciplines. Getting a sense of what happens with a child during his or her play or language therapy not only gives all of the staff insight into the child but also demystifies the clinical process and helps staff see connections between each other's work. When stories include difficult moments, listeners may become increasingly empathic to the other person's position; no doubt, listeners have had many difficult moments with this child as well. Anecdotal exchange can feel satisfying to both the storyteller and the listener, offering relief to the storyteller, who may have been feeling isolated with her experiences prior to the exchange, and offering insight to the listener. The practice, once formally instituted, may be more easily carried out informally among staff members as opportunities arise throughout the day. Informal exchanges not only contribute to each staff member's knowledge about the children in her care but also add to the feeling of cohesion in the work milieu. As one staff member put it:

> Working with these kids is like trying to put a puzzle together with some of the pieces missing. If everyone wants to make sense of what's happening with the child and find the missing pieces, they'll want to talk to each other! They need each other to complete the puzzle!

Opportunities for Professional Empowerment

People who work in preschools that heal need to have opportunities for profes-sional growth and empowerment. The latter may seem difficult to ensure because small programs may have few possibilities for lateral moves within the organiza-tion, and state requirements for each position may be quite specific. However, the working milieu of the preschool demands a collaborative spirit that circumvents bureaucratic boundaries. The creative administrator will find ways to honor the learning that staff members have accomplished by affording them avenues for applying newly acquired skills and abilities. For example, a classroom staff mem-ber who is talented in her own therapeutic capacity may become a therapeutic assistant in the treatment of one of the young children in her group, working closely with a clinician and learning about the individual modality. Clinicians who have done years of individual treatment but have never run groups may want to work with classroom staff to acquire group management skills before beginning a trial therapeutic group for a special population within the program. An experienced teacher or therapist who is feeling frustrated by a lack of new challenges may work with a local university to become a supervisor of student teachers or interns in her field. Staff at every level may enjoy participating in workshops or seminars de-signed to share the program's expertise with other schools or agencies.

These opportunities acknowledge the staff member's need to grow within her profession and within the preschool structure. They are empowering on both psychological and practical levels. The teacher or clinician who develops her rep-ertoire of skills within her own setting and over time has a résumé reflecting sta-bility, commitment, diverse experience, and ingenuity.

CONCLUSION

Preschools that heal meet children, parents, and staff members every day, acknowl-edging the different issues and perspectives that each contingent of the school community brings to the center. Parents bring their experiences as parents as well as their past experiences as children into the preschool program. Staff members journey between professional and personal domains as they interact with children and parents each day. The work can be compelling and at times all-consuming, but early childhood professionals must stay in touch with current practice modes and work hard to keep concepts learned in graduate school alive and in working condition. These diverse demands are not rewarded with salaries commensurate with their efforts, and preschool staffs often work without society's acknowledg-ment of the profound nature of their human contribution. If preschools that heal are to thrive, administrators must build in program structures that enable children, parents, and staff to learn, grow, and process the experiences that happen at the center and outside. Supportive practices such as regularly scheduled supervision for staff at every level, opportunities for anecdotal exchange, and opportunities for professional empowerment help to pull staff together. Ultimately, a well-supported staff united by philosophy and connected to clients will design and implement exciting, enduring programs for young children and their families.

REFERENCES

Bertacchi, J., & Coplin, J. (1992). The professional use of self in prevention. In E. Fenichel (Ed.), *Learning through supervision and mentorship: A source book* (pp. 84–90). Arlington, VA: National Center for Clinical Infant Programs.

Bertacchi, J., & Stott, F. (1991). A seminar for supervisors in infant, family programs: Growing versus paying more for staying the same. *Zero to Three, 12,* 34–39.

Briccetti, A. (1993). *Cycles of burnout and renewal.* Unpublished manuscript, Hunter College School of Social Work, New York.

Brown, C., & Thorp, E. (1989). Individualizing training for early intervention practitioners. *Zero to Three, 10,* 8–12.

Christenson, S. L. (2004). The family-school partnerships: An opportunity to promote learning competence of all students. *School Psychology Review, 33*(1), 83–104.

Fenichel, E. (1992). Learning through supervision and mentorship to support the development of infants, toddlers, and their families. In E. Fenichel (Ed.), *Learning through supervision and mentorship: A source book* (pp. 9–18). Arlington, VA: National Center for Clinical Infant Programs.

Fenichel, E., & Eggbeer, L. (1989). Educating allies: Issues and recommendations in the training of practitioners to work with infants, toddlers, and their families. *Zero to Three, 10,* 1–7.

Fields, B. (1991). Toward tenacity of commitment: Understanding and modifying institutional practices and individual responses that impede work with multi-problem families. *Zero to Three, 12,* 3–33.

Fraiberg, S. (Ed.). (1980). *Clinical studies in infant mental health.* New York: Basic Books.

Galinsky, E. (1977). *The new extended family: Day care that works.* New York: Houghton Mifflin.

Koplow, L. (1992). Finding common ground: Facilitating a therapeutic group for diverse parents of young, disturbed children. *Zero to Three, 12*(3), 22–26.

Lieberman, A. F., Padron, E., Van Horn, P., & Harris, W. (2005). Angels in the nursery: The intergenerational transmission of benevolent parental influences. *Infant Mental Health Journal, 26*(6), 504–520.

Shanok, R. S. (1992). The supervisory relationship: Integrator, resource, and guide. In E. Fenichel (Ed.), *Learning through supervision and mentorship: A source book* (pp. 37–41). Arlington, VA: National Center for Clinical Infant Programs.

About the Editor
and the Contributors

Lesley Koplow, C.S.W., is the Director of the Center for Emotionally Responsive Practice at Bank Street College. The Center does staff development training and consultation on Emotionally Responsive Practice in the school setting. She is also a psychotherapist in private practice, and the author of a number of books on child mental health, including *Where Rag Dolls Hide Their Faces*, *The Way Home*, and *Tanya and the Tobo Man*. She lives in New York City with her young daughter.

Suzanne L. Abrams, M.S., C.C.C., is a certified speech and language pathologist with an M.S. from Teachers College, Columbia University. She acts as a consultant to families and professionals on communication and early childhood development.

Beverly Dennis has an M.S. in psychology and has worked in New York and England in programs for children and families. She is currently working in Bermuda.

Judith Ferber, M.S.Ed., LICSW is a licensed clinical social worker currently in private practice in Northampton, Massachusetts, with a specialty in child and family mental health. She holds an M.S. in social work from the Smith College School for Social Work and an M.S. in special education from Bank Street College of Education. Judy has been working with children and families for nearly 20 years in a variety of roles, including psychotherapist, mental health consultant, and educational trainer, as well as having been a therapeutic teacher at the Karen Horney Therapeutic Nursery from 1988 to 1993.

Virginia Hut received her M.S. in early childhood special education from Bank Street College of Education. For the last 20 years, she has worked in the field of early childhood education as a teacher, an administrator, and a learning specialist in private practice. She is currently a Special Education Itinerant Teacher (SEIT) for the Rivendell School in Brooklyn.

Index

Abrams, D., 66
Abrams, Suzanne, chapter by, 194–214
Abuse, 12–13, 217
Acting out
  and affect-cognition curriculum bridge,
    116, 117
  and boundaries/limitations, 52, 61
  and open-ended play, 102, 110
  and opportunities for at-risk children, 25
  parents' reactions to, 241
  and play therapy, 70, 71
  and preschools as psychological "home
    base," 241
  and self-concept, 40
  and teacher-child relationship, 25
  and therapeutic teachers and classrooms,
    50, 52, 61
  and traumatized children, 178
Administrators, preschool, 242–50
Affect
  adult denial of children's, 18
  affirmation of diverse, 18
  and at-risk children, 17, 18, 23–25, 26
  attunement, 35, 219
  and autism/PDD, 196, 198, 202, 210, 212,
    213
  birth of, 18–21
  and cognition, 114–31
  as core self, 39
  and cues from mother, 19
  and curriculum, 18, 114–31, 149–53
  definition of, 21
  and development, 19, 20, 26
  dialogue concerning, 24–25
  and experiences, 18, 19, 26
  false, 21
  function of, 21–23
  and homeless children, 216, 217, 219–20
  and lesson plan guidelines, 134

  as means of communication, 18–19, 20, 24,
    26, 34, 219
  mirroring of, 23, 25, 31
  negative, 17–18, 20, 22–25, 26, 39, 40, 42
  of others, 21–22
  of parents, 220
  and preschools as psychological "home
    base," 233, 237
  prevention of, 24
  regulation of, 22, 23, 26, 32
  and self-concept, 31, 32, 33, 34, 35, 36, 37,
    39, 40
  sharing, 20–21, 34
  and therapeutic teacher and classroom, 53–
    54
  and therapeutic tools, 82, 83
  and traumatized child, 189
  value of children's, 17–28
  See also Emotions
Age-level challenges
  and affect-cognition curriculum bridge,
    117–18
  and homeless children, 216, 222–23, 224
  and preschools as psychological "home
    base," 240
  See also Developmentally appropriate
    practices
Agency, sense of, 33, 38, 41
Aggression
  and affect-cognition curricular bridge, 117
  and development and experiential reality,
    12, 13, 14
  and homeless children, 216, 222
  and image, 12, 13, 14
  and open-ended play, 102, 105–6, 108–9
  and play therapy, 70–71
  and self-concept, 36, 37
  and therapeutic tools, 87–88
  and traumatized child, 183

Ainsworth, M.D., 5, 219
Alpert, A., 71
Alzine, V., 66
American Psychiatric Association (APA), 10,
    175–76, 178, 195
"Ana's Doughnuts" (play theme), 106–8, 117
Anecdotal exchange, 248, 250
Angry Feelings (lesson plan), 150
"Anita's Doctor" (play theme), 110–11
Artwork
    and affect-cognition curriculum bridge, 118
    and autism/PDD, 210, 211, 212, 213
    and lesson plan guidelines, 134
    self-representation in, 37–38
    spontaneous, 84–85, 92
    and therapeutic teacher and classroom, 54,
        56
    as therapeutic tool, 84–85, 90–92
    and traumatized child, 185, 186, 189, 191–
        92
Asperger's syndrome, 201
Assessment, curriculum, 118, 120, 121–22,
    123–24, 126, 128, 130–31, 134
At-risk children
    and affect, 17, 18, 23–25, 26
    and affect-cognition curriculum bridge, 114
    and Asperger's syndrome, 201
    and development and experiential reality, 12
    dilemmas for, 23–25
    homeless children as, 217
    and image, 12
    and open-ended play, 99
    and play therapy, 66, 70
    and traumatized child, 177
Attachment
    and affect, 24
    anxious-avoidant, 36
    and autism/PDD, 196
    and development and experiential reality,
        5–6, 8, 9–10, 11, 12, 14
    disrupted, 11
    and homeless children, 219, 222
    and image, 9–10, 11, 12, 14
    and open-ended play, 102
    and play therapy, 71
    and preschools as psychological "home
        base," 229
    reactive, 10, 222
    and self-concept, 35, 36, 37, 39
    and teacher-child relationship, 189–92
    and therapeutic teacher and classroom, 57
    and traumatized child, 189–92

Attention-deficit hyperactivity disorder
    (ADHD), 178, 216
Authier, J., 88
Autism/PDD, 194–214
    and affect-cognition curriculum bridge, 117
    case study of, 202, 209–14
    core issues of, 195–201
    helping child with, 203–8
    NOS, 195, 198, 201–2
    and open-ended play, 106–8
    symptoms of, 199
Autonomy
    and autism/PDD, 212
    as curriculum theme, 126–28
    and development and experiential reality, 7,
        11, 13
    and homeless children, 217, 218
    and image, 11, 13
    and play therapy, 77
    pseudo-, 38–39
    and self-concept, 29, 32, 38
    and therapeutic teacher and classroom, 53,
        56, 57, 59, 61
Axline, V., 67, 71

Babies: What Do They Need? What Do They
    Do? (lesson plan), 155
Baby Monsters (lesson plan), 157
"Baby Wendy" (play theme), 102–3, 117
Bank Street College, 187, 222
Bassuk, E., 215
Beausoleil, L., 187
Beebe, B., 19, 22, 25, 30, 31, 34, 35, 219,
    220
Beeghly, M., 39
Behavior
    and affect-cognition curriculum bridge,
        115–17, 118, 119
    and autism/PDD, 194–214
    and curriculum, 115–17
    and lesson plan guidelines, 134
    and therapeutic tools, 79–93
    and traumatized child, 177–78, 188
    See also Play: as therapeutic tool; specific
        topic
Behavior modification, 87–88
Bergman, A., 5, 30, 32, 196, 217
Bertacchi, J., 244, 245
"Bianca's Elevator" (play theme), 103–4, 115
Bibliography, for lesson plans, 135–39
Bibliotherapy materials, 82–84
"Big and Little" (lesson plan), 126–28, 166

Bleher, E., 219
"Boats and Bridges" (lesson plan), 128–31, 171
Body integrity, 116, 117–18
Bogat, G.A., 4
Bonvin, P., 23
Books
    and homeless children, 224
    and lesson plan guidelines, 133, 134
    as therapeutic tools, 82–84
    See also Bibliography; Stories
Boundaries/limitations
    and autism/PDD, 200, 211
    as curriculum theme, 122–24
    and development and experiential reality, 7, 8, 11
    and homeless children, 217, 218, 222, 224
    and image, 11
    and preschools as psychological "home base," 233
    self-, 8
    and self-concept, 29
    and teachers as limit setters, 56, 58, 61–62
    and therapeutic teacher and classroom, 48, 49, 51–53, 55
    and traumatized child, 184
Bowlby, J., 4–5, 35
Brain, 176, 198, 201
Bratton, S.C., 65
Briccetti, A., 242–43
Britner, P., 10
Brody, V., 66, 71
Brooks-Gunn, J., 30, 31, 32
Brown, C., 245
Busch-Rossnagel, N., 30, 31

Campos, J.J., 19, 219
Caregivers
    and affect, 19, 24
    and development and experiential reality, 4–14
    and image, 9–14
    and partnerships with child, 4–5, 9–10
    and play therapy, 68, 71
    and preschools as psychological "home base," 230
    and self-concept, 30, 31–32, 34–35, 36, 37, 39
    surrogate, 8, 9, 13, 56, 57–59
    teachers as, 13, 56, 57–59
    and therapeutic teacher and classroom, 56, 58, 63

and traumatized child, 183–84
    See also Parents; Teachers
Carlson, E., 10
Carlson, V., 39
Cassidy, J., 5
Center for the Advancement of Health, 185
Cho, E., 10
Christenson, S. L., 230
Cicchetti, D., 22, 23, 39
Clinical supervision model, 245
Clinicians
    and parent guidance, 237–38
    and preschools as psychological "home base," 237–38
    and self-concept in preschoolers, 40–42
    teacher's partnership with, 190
    and therapeutic tools, 79
Cognition
    and affect curricular bridge, 22, 114–31
    and autism/PDD, 195, 198, 200, 209, 210, 213
    and homeless children, 222
    and lesson plan guidelines, 134–35
    and play therapy, 67, 70
    and self-concept, 32, 37
    and therapeutic teacher and classroom, 48, 53–54, 55, 56
Cohen, L. J., 4
Cole, P., 23
Communication
    affect as means of, 18–19, 20, 24, 26, 34, 219
    and affect-cognition curriculum bridge, 131
    and autism/PDD, 197, 198, 199, 200, 201, 213
    and homeless children, 219, 221
    and open-ended play, 98, 112
    and preschools as psychological "home base," 229, 242–43, 244
    preverbal, 221
    and self-concept, 34
    symbolic, 63
    and therapeutic teacher and classroom, 63
Community trauma, 184–87, 188, 191, 192
Conferencing, 248
"Continuum of identification from baby to parent," 244
Coplin, J., 244
Corrective object relations therapists, 66
Counseling, parent, 238
Crowel, R., 186
Cummings, E. M., 4

Curriculum, therapeutic
  ABCs of, 118
  and affect, 18, 114–31, 149–53
  and affect-cognition bridge, 114–31
  and age-appropriate strengths and abilities,
    117–18
  assessment of, 118, 120, 121–22, 123–24,
    128, 130–31, 134
  and autism/PDD, 211, 213–14
  and behavior, 115–16
  bibliography for, 135–39
  and cognition, 114–31
  conventional curriculum compared with,
    114
  developing early-level, 118–24
  and development and experiential reality,
    14
  embarking on a, 115–18
  end-of-year, 171
  group, 53, 54
  and homeless children, 215, 224
  and image, 14
  lesson plans/themes for, 53, 54–55, 118–31,
    132–72
  methods for developing preschool-level,
    124–31
  and play, 95–113, 115
  and preschools as psychological "home
    base," 240, 241, 243
  purpose of, 114–15
  and self-concept, 41
  and therapeutic teacher and classroom, 48,
    53–55, 62
  and therapeutic tools, 84
  and traumatized child, 192
  See also specific theme

"Darryl's Wife" (play scene), 99–102, 115,
  117
De Roten, Y., 23
DeBellis, M.D., 176, 179
Dennis, Beverley, chapters by, 132–72, 194–
  214
Dependence. See Autonomy
Deprivation
  and development and experiential reality,
    9–14
  or traumatized child, 176–77
Derman-Sparks, L., 18
Development
  and affect, 19, 20, 26
  and deprivation, 9–14

and experiential reality, 3–16
and homeless children, 219–22, 224–25
and image, 4–14
and parent-child relationship, 4–14
and preschools as psychological "home
  base," 243
regressions in, 8, 57, 59, 60, 185, 221
and therapeutic teacher and classroom, 47–
  64
See also specific topic
Developmentally appropriate practices, 29,
  38, 56, 59, 199, 230
Dionne (case study), 72–77
Disassociated states, 179, 191
Distancing, 190, 197, 216, 217
Diversity, 18, 49, 230–31, 233, 234, 241
Donovan, D., 70
Donzella, B., 176, 179
Dougherty, L., 20
Drawings. See Artwork

Early childhood community, preschool as
  subculture of, 231
Echolalia, 199–200, 202, 212, 213
Eggbeer, L., 245
Ego
  and affect, 25
  and affect-cognition curriculum bridge, 114
  and autism/PDD, 200, 201, 212
  and development and experiential reality, 3,
    4, 14
  and image, 14
  and play therapy, 68, 70
  and self-concept, 32, 33, 35
  and therapeutic teacher and classroom, 53,
    55, 60–61, 63
  and traumatized child, 178, 181
Eisenberg, N., 20, 22, 23
Emde, R., 19, 20, 22, 23, 34, 35, 84, 219, 220
Emotionally fragile children. See specific
  topic
Emotions
  dysphoric, 22
  spontaneous, 116–17
  of staff, 85–86
  and therapeutic teacher and classroom, 48,
    55, 56
  See also Affect; specific emotion
Empathy, 22, 23, 24, 36, 39, 55, 63, 183, 188,
  190, 211, 233, 237, 246
Empty/Full (lesson plan), 167
Ennes, J., 215

Environment
    and affect, 18, 24, 26
    and affect-cognition curriculum bridge,
        115
    and autism/PDD, 195, 197, 198, 199
    cheerful, 188
    and development and experiential reality, 5,
        8, 10, 13
    and homeless children, 216, 218–25
    and image, 10, 13
    and play therapy, 67, 68
    and preschools as psychological "home
        base," 230, 231, 244, 245–46
    and self-concept, 27, 33, 35, 36, 37
    and therapeutic teacher and classroom, 47,
        48–49
    and therapeutic tools, 85–86
    and traumatized child, 188, 189, 190
Erikson, E., 49
Essential discoveries, 6
Essex, M.J., 10
Expectations, 3, 35, 218, 230
Experiences
    and affect, 18, 19, 26
    and affect-cognition curriculum bridge,
        114, 115, 117, 131
    and autism/PDD, 196, 197, 198–99, 201,
        210, 212, 213
    and homeless children, 224
    and open-ended play, 98, 102, 112
    of parents, 249
    and play therapy, 65, 69
    and preschools as psychological "home
        base," 229, 231, 233, 237, 244, 245,
        248
    "saving," 60–61
    and self-concept, 33, 34, 36, 38, 40, 41
    of staff, 248, 249
    and therapeutic teacher and classroom, 48–
        49, 53–54, 55, 56, 58, 60–61
    and therapeutic tools, 84, 88–89
    See also Experiential reality
Experiential reality
    and deprivation, 9–14
    and development, 3–16
    and image, 9–14
    and open-ended play, 98
    and teachers, 9
    and therapeutic tools, 92

Fabes, R., 22, 23
Facilitators, teachers as, 4, 62, 63

Fantasy
    and autism/PDD, 197, 198, 200, 202, 210
    and play therapy, 69, 70
    and preschools as psychological "home
        base," 240
Favez, N., 23
Fay, W., 199
Feedback
    reflective, 37
    and self-concept, 30, 31, 36, 37, 40, 41
    and therapeutic tools, 84
Feeding behavior, maladaptive, 238–40
Fenichel, E., 242, 245
Ferber, Judith, chapters by, 29–43, 47–64,
        114–31, 132–72, 175–93, 194–214
Fields, B., 246
Flashbacks, 180–81, 191
Fraiberg, Selma, 31, 233, 238
Freud, A., 71
Freud, S., 32, 67
Friedman, D., 31
Friedman, J., 22, 23

Galinsky, Ellen, 4, 217, 218, 229
Georgie (parent guidance example), 238–40
Giving and Getting (lesson plan) (Valentine's
        Day), 162
Go Away—Come Back (lesson plan), 119–20,
        140
Greenspan, S., 6, 18, 19, 22, 25, 32, 56, 68,
        69, 71, 87, 89, 97, 194, 198, 201
Group
    child within, 62–63
    curriculum, 53, 54
    dramatic play, 63
    parent, 232–37, 241
    supervision, 245
    and therapeutic teacher and classroom, 53,
        54, 63
    and therapeutic tools, 79
Guidance, parental, 237–40
Gunnar, M. R., 176, 179
Guthrie, I., 22, 23

Happy Feelings (lesson plan), 153
Hart-Shegos, E., 215
Harter, S., 30, 31, 32, 37
Hatching (lesson plan), 163
Head Start, 47, 65, 105
"Hello/Goodbye" (group dialogue), 234–37
Holding, 86–87, 224, 245–46
Holes and Peeks (lesson plan), 144

Home visits, and homeless children, 223
Homeless children, 215–25
    development of, 219–22, 224–25
    emotional consequences for, 215–16
    implications for educator of, 223–24
    parenting of, 215–25
    physical conditions for, 215–16
    psychological home base for, 220, 221, 223–24
    role reversals in, 218
    symptoms connected with, 222–23
Honig, A. S., 5
Huebner, R., 20
Hurricane Katrina, 184, 186, 188
Hurting and Healing (lesson plan), 147
Hut, Virginia, chapters by, 114–31, 132–72
Huth-Bocks, A.C., 4
Hyperactivity, 178, 216
Hyperarousal responses, 180
Hypervigilance, 179, 216, 219, 220, 221

Identification with aggressor, 183
Identity, 29, 32, 41, 199, 244
Image
    and autism/PDD, 199
    and development and experiential reality, 4–14
    distorted, 9–14
    divided, 12–13
    and homeless children, 220, 221
    and open-ended play, 102
    and parents, 4, 9–14, 24, 32, 220
    and teachers, 9
    See also Self-image
Infants
    and affect, 18–19, 22
    autistic/PDD, 196
    and experiential reality, 9
    as homeless children, 216–17, 219–20
    and image, 9
    self of, 33–34
    traumatized, 187
Instructors, teachers as, 56–57
Integration
    and affect, 19, 20
    and affect-cognition curriculum bridge, 117, 118
    and autism/PDD, 209, 210, 213, 214
    and development, 8
    and lesson plan guidelines, 134
    and open-ended play, 98, 102, 112
    and play therapy, 77

and therapeutic teacher and classroom, 55, 56
and therapeutic tools, 84, 92
and traumatized child, 183, 185
Intelligence/IQ, 3, 66, 67, 77
Internalization
    and affect-cognition curriculum bridge, 118
    and development, 8
    and homeless children, 218, 221
    and play therapy, 72
    and therapeutic teacher and classroom, 55, 62
Interpretations, as therapeutic tools, 88–90
Ivey, A., 88
Izard, C., 20

Johnson, C., 90
Jones, L., 65
Jones, S., 22, 23

Kagan, J., 30, 31
Kalin, N. H., 10
Kaplan, N., 5
Katz, L., 87
Kelley, M. L., 186
Klein, M. H., 10, 71
Klinnert, M. D., 19, 219
Knoblauch, S., 30, 35
Kochanska, G., 35
Koga, S. F., 10
Kohut, H., 30
Koplewicz, H. S., 186–87
Koplow, Lesley
    chapters by, 3–16, 17–28, 65–78, 79–93, 97–113, 114–31, 132–72, 175–93, 194–214, 215–25, 229–50
    references to work by, 22, 67, 114, 117, 186, 192, 215, 231
Kozol, Jonathan, 215

Lachmann, F. M., 19, 22, 30, 34
Language
    and affect, 21, 22, 23, 24, 25
    and affect-cognition curriculum bridge, 118
    and autism/PDD, 195, 197, 198, 199–201, 202, 209, 210, 211–12, 213
    "borrowed," 200
    and development and experiential reality, 6, 8, 11, 13, 14
    echolalic, 199–200, 202, 212, 213
    and homeless children, 216, 221, 224
    idiosyncratic, 202, 213

and image, 11, 13, 14
and lesson plan guidelines, 134
and open-ended play, 109–10
perseverative, 200–201, 212
and play therapy, 66, 67, 68–69, 70
and preschools as psychological "home
 base," 230, 231, 233, 242–43
preverbal, 24
self-, 202
and self-concept, 30, 31, 33, 34
symbolic, 22
therapeutic, 79–90, 190–92
and therapeutic teacher and classroom, 54,
 55, 56, 63
and traumatized child, 178, 190–92
verbal, 221
Lauriat, A. S., 215
Learning
and affect-cognition curriculum bridge, 118
and autism/PDD, 198
and homeless children, 219
and lesson plan guidelines, 134
motivation for, 48
and open-ended play, 97, 112
and play therapy, 66, 72
and preschools as psychological "home
 base," 244, 245, 246–47
and therapeutic teacher and classroom, 48,
 56, 59, 63
Lesson plans/themes, 53, 54–55, 118–31, 132–
 72
Levendosky, A. A., 4
Lewis, M., 30, 31, 32
Lieberman, Alicia, 4, 10, 238
Light/Dark, Day/Night (lesson plan), 165
Limit setters, teachers as, 56, 58, 61–62, 184,
 224. See also Boundaries/limitations
Lost and Found (lesson plan), 160
Lupien, S.J., 176

McCormick, S., 22, 23
McEwen, B. S., 176
Macfie, J., 22, 23
Mcginnes, G. C., 20
McIntyre, D., 70
Madigan, J., 194
Mahler, M., 5, 30, 32, 33, 39, 196, 217
Main, M., 5
Mann, D., 66, 95
Marvin, R., 10
Meade, A., 66
Melinda (case study), 202, 209–14

Messy/Clean (lesson plan), 158
Michael, M., 23
"Michael's Monster" (play theme), 105–6
"Mine" (lesson plan), 122–24
Mirroring
affect, 23, 25, 31
and affect-cognition curriculum bridge, 131
and homeless children, 220
and mirrors as therapeutic tools, 84
and therapeutic teacher and classroom, 57
Molnar, J., 215, 222
Mommy and Baby Animals (lesson plan), 156
More/No More (lesson plan), 141
Mother. See Caregivers; Parents
Motor skills, 5–6, 10, 11, 32, 202, 203, 220,
 221
Multiculturalism, 231
"My Special Animal" (lesson plan), 121–22,
 154

Naptime, 189, 190
"Natalie's Rabbit" (play theme), 108–9
Nathanson, D., 19
National Association for the Education of
 Young Children (NAEYC), 3
National Institute for Mental Health (NIMH),
 176, 185, 186, 187
National Scientific Council on the Developing
 Child, 18, 21, 22, 23, 198
New School/Old School (lesson plan), 170
Nir, A., 20, 23, 35, 84

Object constancy
and affect, 24
and development and experiential reality, 7,
 8, 13
and image, 13
and play therapy, 70
and preschools as psychological "home
 base," 237
and self-concept, 32
and therapeutic teacher and classroom, 55,
 58, 59, 60–61
and traumatized child, 180, 183
Object permanence
and development and experiential reality, 6,
 8, 14
and image, 14
and play therapy, 70
and self-concept, 32
and therapeutic teacher and classroom, 49
O'Connor, T., 10

O'Donnell-Teti, L., 23
Olrick, J., 10
Olthof, T., 22
Ontai, L. L., 23
Oppenheim, D., 20, 23, 35, 84
Osofsky, J. D., 37, 39
Other
    and affect, 19, 21–22, 23, 24, 26
    and autism/PDD, 196–97, 198, 200, 210–11
    and development and experiential reality, 6,
        8, 11, 12–13
    and image, 11, 12–13
    internal working models of, 35–36
    self and, 6, 11, 12–13, 19, 22, 23, 24, 27,
        32, 33, 35–36, 37, 38, 40, 41, 61, 63,
        200, 210–11
    and self-concept, 27, 30, 31, 32, 33, 36, 37,
        38, 41
    and therapeutic teacher and classroom, 61, 63
    and traumatized child, 181
    working model of, 40
    See also Peers

Panic attacks, 181–82, 189, 191
Parent group, 232–37, 241
Parent-child day, 240–41
Parents
    and affect, 18–19, 20–23, 24
    and autism/PDD, 196–97
    child's relationship with, 4–14, 18–19, 20–
        23, 24, 31, 32–33, 183–84, 215–25,
        231, 233, 240–41
    and development and experiential reality,
        4–14
    diversity among, 230–31
    as emotional object, 32
    guidance for, 237–40
    of homeless children, 215–25
    and image, 4, 9–14, 24, 32, 220
    and preschools as extended family, 229–30
    and preschools as psychological "home
        base," 229–41, 249
    problems of, 9–14, 19–18, 37, 38, 39, 216–20
    as psychological "home base," 5, 10, 220
    and role reversals, 218
    room for, 231–32
    and self-concept, 31, 32–33, 39
    staff/teacher relationship with, 223, 241
    as therapists, 66, 67
    trauma of, 186
    and traumatized child, 183–84, 186
    See also Caregivers

Partnership
    caregiver-child relationship as, 4–5, 9–10,
        14, 19, 24, 219
    school-family, 230
    staff-parent, 241
    teacher-child, 188
    teacher-clinician, 190
Pavenstedt, E., 67
Peers
    and affect, 21–22, 24, 25, 26
    and autism/PDD, 195, 202, 211, 213
    and development and experiential reality, 8,
        14
    and image, 14
    and open-ended play, 98, 102, 108, 112
    and play therapy, 68
    and self-concept, 36, 40–41
    and traumatized child, 179
    See also Other
Pervasive development disorder. See Autism/
    PDD
"Peter's Crocodile" (play theme), 109–10
"Peter's Job Search" (play theme), 104–5, 115
Phillips, D. A., 18, 22, 201
Piaget, J., 3, 6, 30, 56
Pine, F., 5, 30, 32, 196, 217
Planting and Growing (lesson plan), 168
Play
    and affect, 21, 22, 23, 25
    and affect-cognition curriculum bridge,
        115, 118–19
    and age-appropriate strengths and abilities,
        117–18
    and autism/PDD, 195, 196, 197, 198, 201,
        202, 203, 207, 209, 210, 211, 213
    case study about, 72–77
    cautions about, 98–99
    children who can't, 67–70
    collaborative/cooperative, 8, 98
    and curriculum, 95–113, 115, 118–19
    and development and experiential reality, 5,
        6, 8, 14
    dramatic, 8, 63, 213, 224
    as early intervention therapy, 65–78
    fantasy, 69, 70
    free, 49, 50, 59, 118, 133, 207, 233
    group, 63
    and homeless children, 224
    and image, 14
    importance of, 97–98
    integrative, 185
    isolated, 97

and language, 68–69
and lesson plan guidelines, 133, 134
open-ended, 25, 50, 59, 97–113, 134, 233
outdoor, 25, 92, 118, 203
parallel, 98
and preschools as psychological "home
    base," 233
reciprocal, 57
and routines, 86
and self-concept, 29, 31
space for, 69–70
spontaneous, 53–54, 62–63, 65, 112, 115,
    118–19, 134
symbolic/representational, 8, 14, 22, 23, 25,
    58, 63, 65, 66, 69, 71, 72, 84, 97, 98,
    99, 102, 108, 110, 112, 182, 196, 197,
    198, 201, 202, 211, 224
themes for, 97–112, 115, 185, 213
and therapeutic teacher and classroom, 49,
    50–51, 53–54, 55, 56, 57, 58–59, 60,
    62–63
as therapeutic tool, 65–78, 92, 186
toys and materials for, 69–70
traumatic, 182, 185
and traumatized child, 179, 185, 186, 191–
    92
and trust, 68–69
Pointing-naming game, 221
Posttraumatic stress disorder (PTSD), 175–76,
    178, 184, 185, 186–87, 216, 222
Poulin, R., 22, 23
Praise, and self-concept, 40
Prenatal period, 4, 9, 187
Preoccupied states, 179, 191
Preschoolers. See specific topic
Preschools
    administration of, 241–50
    as extended family, 229–30
    mission/philosophy of, 230, 231, 242, 244,
        250
    philosophical and cultural premises of, 231
    as place to find common ground, 231–41
    policies and procedures of, 242
    as psychological "home base," 223–24,
        229–50
    as subculture of early childhood
        community, 231
    working milieu of, 243–49
Progressive early childhood education, 66,
    114
Project Liberty, 185
"Protecting the Mental Health," 215, 217

Pruitt, K., 194
Psychoanalytic accounts, of self, 31–34
Psychosocial history
    and affect, 24
    and affect-cognition curriculum bridge, 117
    and autism/PDD, 196
    and curriculum, 117
    and development and experiential reality, 4,
        9, 12, 14
    and homeless children, 216, 222
    and image, 9, 12, 14
    and preschools as psychological "home
        base," 232
    and traumatized child, 175
"The Pumpkin" (lesson plan), 124–26, 149
"Purple crayon," 90–92

Qing, Z., 20, 22
Questions, and therapeutic tools, 80

Ray, D., 65
Readiness, 202
Real/Pretend (lesson plan), 148
Reality
    developmental, 3–16
    experiential, 3–16
Reality testing, 69
Reflection
    by staff, 230, 245, 246
    and therapeutic teacher and classroom, 52–
        53, 60–61
    verbal, 52–53
    visual forms of, 52–53
Relatedness
    and autism/PDD, 196–97, 198, 199, 201,
        209, 210, 212
    and homeless children, 224
Representation. See Symbols
Rhine, T., 65
Risser, D., 20
Robertson-Jackson, B., 37, 39
Robinson, J., 22, 23
Rogosch, F.A., 22, 23
Room, parents', 231–32
Roseman, L., 23
Roth-Hanania, R., 30, 31
Routines/daily schedule
    and autism/PDD, 199, 202, 210
    and homeless children, 223–24
    importance of, 48, 49–51, 86
    and therapeutic teachers and classrooms,
        48, 49–51

Routines/daily schedule (*continued*)
  as therapeutic tool, 86
  and traumatized child, 189, 192
  See also Boundaries/limitations
Rubin, L., 215
Rustin, J., 30, 35
Rutter, M., 10

Sad Feelings (lesson plan), 151
Samuels, S., 66
Sanchez, R., 216
Sapolsky, R. M., 176
"Sarah's House" (play theme), 110
Scared Feelings (lesson plan), 152
Schuler, A., 199
Self
  and affect, 19, 21, 22, 23, 24
  and affect-cognition curriculum bridge, 116
  and autism/PDD, 196, 200, 209, 210–11,
      212, 214
  awareness of, 34, 36
  boundaries/limitations, 8
  challenge to toddler's, 6–7
  core, 33, 34, 35, 36, 39
  definitions and themes concerning, 30, 35
  developing, 29–43
  and development and experiential reality,
      6–7, 8, 11–13
  disrupted, 11–12
  emergent, 13, 33, 36
  emotional, 48
  existential, 31
  false, 35, 39, 40, 41–42
  idealization of, 39
  and image, 7, 11–13, 30, 31, 32, 41, 77
  internal working models of, 35–36, 40, 41
  intrapsychic foundation of, 32–33
  and other, 6, 11, 12–13, 19, 22, 23, 24, 27,
      32, 33, 35–36, 37, 38, 40, 41, 61, 63,
      200, 210–11
  process view of, 34
  regulation of, 34, 35
  sharing of inner, 34–39
  subjective, 33–34
  and therapeutic teacher and classroom, 48,
      55, 57, 61, 63
  "true," 34
  visual recognition of, 30–31
  See also Self-care; Self-concept; Self-
      confidence; Self-constancy; Self-
      continuity; Self-discovery; Self-
      esteem; Self-expression; Self-worth

Self-care, 67, 216, 222
Self-concept
  and autism/PDD, 200, 214
  definition of, 30, 31
  and homeless children, 223
  and implications for teachers and clinicians,
      40–42
  in infants, 33–34
  internal working models of, 35–36
  and other, 35–36
  in preschoolers, 29–43
  psychoanalytic accounts of, 31–34
  and sharing of inner self, 34–39
  and teacher-child relationship, 40–42
  unstable, 39
  and validation of self, 34–39
Self-confidence, 37, 40
Self-constancy, 8, 11, 32, 39, 116
Self-continuity, 220
Self-discovery, 93
Self-esteem, 12, 29, 37–38, 40, 53
Self-expression, 84–8. *See also* Artwork
Self-worth, 40
Separation
  and affect, 20, 24
  and affect-cognition curriculum bridge,
      116
  and autism/PDD, 196–97, 199, 201, 204,
      212
  as curriculum theme, 118, 119–20, 128–31,
      132
  and development and experiential reality,
      10, 11, 12, 13, 14
  and homeless children, 218, 220, 221
  and image, 11, 12, 13, 14
  as play theme, 115
  and self-concept, 31–32, 33
  and therapeutic teacher and classroom, 61
  and traumatized child, 189
  See also Attachment; Separation anxiety
Separation anxiety, 60, 70, 92, 114, 190, 212,
      221, 232, 237
September 11, 2001, as traumatizing event,
      184–187, 192
Sexuality, 222
Shankoff, J., 18, 22, 201
Shanok, R.S., 243, 245
Sharing
  affect, 20–21, 34
  and development, 8
  and self-concept, 34–39
Shepard, S., 22, 23

Shore, R., 18, 19
Siegel, Daniel, 6, 18, 19, 20, 25, 31, 68, 84, 97, 201, 219
Simon, Norma, 210
Slade, A., 4, 66, 71
Sloate, P., 19
Smith, M., 22, 23
Smyke, A. T., 10
Social interactions
    and affect, 18, 20–21, 22, 23, 24
    and affect-cognition curriculum bridge, 116, 118
    and autism/PDD, 195, 198
    and development and experiential reality, 10, 12, 13
    and homeless children, 219, 222, 224
    and image, 10, 12, 13
    and play therapy, 71
    and self-concept, 34, 35, 40–41
Socioeconomic status, and play therapy, 66
Solnit, A., 19
Some Things Change, Some Things Stay the Same (lesson plan), 159
Sorce, J. F., 19, 219
Sorter, D., 30, 35
Special education, 47–48, 50, 66, 244
Spitz, R., 9–10
Splitting, 183–84, 247
Sroufe, L. A., 20, 35
Staff
    administrator as spokesperson for, 242–43
    anecdotal exchange with, 248, 250
    collaboration among, 243–44, 249
    conceptual framework for work of, 246–47
    countertransference issues for, 187–88
    divisiveness among, 244
    emotions of, 85–86
    experiences of, 248, 249
    and open-ended play, 98–99
    and other service providers, 244
    parents' relationship with, 223, 241
    and preschools as psychological "home base," 230, 236–37, 241–50
    professional development of, 243, 249, 250
    relationships among, 243–44, 249
    self-reflection of, 230
    supervision of, 245–47, 249–50
    support for, 188, 242, 243, 246, 249–50
    trauma of, 185–86
    turnover of, 230, 236–37
    working milieu of, 243–49
    See also Teachers; Therapists

Stark, M., 19
Stern, D., 6, 30, 33, 34, 35, 56, 68, 219
Sticker books, 88
Stories
    and lesson plans, 134
    as therapeutic technique, 80–90
Stott, F., 245
Stranger anxiety, 20
Strayer, J., 22
Stress
    and homeless children, 216, 221, 222
    and traumatized child, 176, 177, 179
    See also Posttraumatic stress disorder
Structure
    and autism/PDD, 198–99, 210
    and preschools as psychological "home base," 231, 233, 245, 249
    and play therapy, 70
    in therapeutic classroom, 47–55, 58
    and therapeutic tools, 86
    and traumatized child, 189
"Superheroes," 8–9, 41
Supervision, staff, 245–47, 249–50
Symbols
    and affect, 18, 22, 23, 25
    and affect-cognition curriculum bridge, 131
    and autism/PDD, 195, 196, 197–99, 201, 209, 210, 211, 213
    and development and experiential reality, 6, 7, 8, 10, 14
    and homeless children, 224
    and image, 10, 14
    and open-ended play, 102
    and play therapy, 66, 69, 71, 72, 77
    poverty of, 11
    and self-concept, 30, 32, 34
    and therapeutic teacher and classroom, 53, 54, 55, 56, 58, 59, 60, 63
    and therapeutic tools, 84, 92
    and traumatized child, 189
    See also Play: symbolic/representational

Teachers
    and affect, 21–22, 24, 25–26
    child's relationship with, 48, 55–62, 86–87, 184, 189–92, 224, 230
    clinicians and, 190
    countertransference issues for, 187–88
    and development and experiential reality, 4, 9, 13, 14
    as facilitators, 4, 62, 63

Teachers (*continued*)
  and homeless children, 223–24
  and image, 9, 13, 14
  importance of, 26
  influence of, 40–42
  as instructors, 56–57
  as limit setters, 56, 58, 61–62, 184, 224
  as mirrors, 25–26
  and open-ended play, 98, 112
  as partners, 188, 190
  and play therapy, 68
  "purple crayon" of, 90–92
  rewards of, 63
  as role models, 25–26, 54, 61, 84, 134, 200, 211
  roles of, 55–62, 63
  and self-concept, 37–38, 40–42
  as surrogate caregivers, 13, 56, 57–59
  therapeutic, 40–42, 47–64
  and therapeutic tools, 79, 84
  as therapists, 56, 60–61
  trauma of, 185–86, 187–88
  and traumatized child, 189–92
  See also Staff
Temper tantrums, 181
Terr, Lenore, 177–78, 187
Terwogt, M., 22
That's Mine (lesson plan), 142
Therapeutic classroom, 47–64
  characteristics of, 47
  cheerful, 188
  and child within the group, 62–63
  curriculum for, 53–55, 62
  definition of, 47
  organization of environment in, 48–49
  role of teachers in, 55–62, 63
  routine and daily schedule in, 48, 49–51, 61, 189
  rules and limits in, 48, 49, 51–53, 55, 58
  structure in, 47–55, 58, 189
  teacher-child relationship in, 48, 55–62
  teachers as models in, 54, 61
  See also Environment
Therapeutic technique
  and art of interpreting, 88–90
  and behavior modification, 87–88
  containing, 85–87
  reflective, 80–90
  and teacher's "purple crayon," 90–92
  that invites expression, 84–85
  tools of, 79–93

Therapeutic tools, 79–93. *See also specific tool*
Therapists
  child's relationship with, 69, 71–72
  corrective object relations, 66
  countertransference issues for, 187–88
  parents as, 66, 67
  role of, 71
  staff relationship with, 244
  teachers as, 56, 60–61
  and therapeutic tools, 79
  and traumatized child, 187–88
Things I Don't Like (lesson plan), 134–35, 146
Things I Like (lesson plan), 134–35, 145
Thompson, R. A., 23
Thorp, E., 245
Threats, 87
Together/Apart (lesson plan), 164
Toileting, 7, 12, 14, 39, 178, 189, 190, 221, 224
Toth, S. L., 22, 23, 39
Toys/materials
  and affect-cognition curriculum bridge, 118
  and autism/PDD, 198
  and bibliotherapy, 82–84
  and homeless children, 223, 224
  and lesson plan guidelines, 133
  and open-ended play, 98
  and play therapy, 69–70, 72
  and preschools as psychological "home base," 232
  and therapeutic teacher and classroom, 48–49
  as transitional objects, 71
  and traumatized child, 182
Transitional objects
  and autism/PDD, 197–98
  and curriculum, 121–22
  and homeless children, 220
  and play therapy, 71
  and therapeutic teacher and classroom, 53, 56, 58, 59
  and traumatized child, 182, 190, 192
Transitions
  and autism/PDD, 208
  as curriculum theme, 121–22
  and preschools as psychological "home base," 230
  and traumatized child, 189
  See also Transitional objects

Transportation (lesson plan), 169
Trauma
    and children as traumatized, 175–93
    community, 184–87, 188, 191, 192
    and countertransference issues for teachers,
        187–88
    and defenses of traumatized child, 182–84
    definitions of, 175–78
    and deprivation compared, 176–77
    diagnostic indicators of, 178–82
    disguises of, 177–78
    and homeless children, 222
    of parents, 238
    and play, 182
    secondary, 185–86
    of teachers/professionals, 185–86
    and therapeutic language, 190–92
    and vulnerabilities of traumatized children,
        189–90
    See also Curriculum; Play: as therapeutic
        tool; specific topic
Trust
    and development, 8
    and homeless children, 219, 223
    and play therapy, 68–69
    and preschools as psychological "home
        base," 229
    and routines/daily schedule, 49–50
    and self-concept, 41

and therapeutic teacher and classroom, 58,
    59, 62
and traumatized child, 189

U.S. Government Accountability Office, 185,
    187

Visual cliff study, 219
Visual forms of reflection, 52–53
Visual self-recognition, 30–31
Von Eye, A., 4

Wall, S., 219
Warren, S., 20, 23, 35, 84
Waters, E., 4, 219
We Can Share (lesson plan), 143
Weil, A. M., 66
Wendy (parent guidance example), 238–40
Westby, C., 68
Wieder, S., 6, 18, 19, 22, 25, 32, 56, 68, 69,
    71, 87, 89, 95
Will I Have a Friend? (lesson plan), 161
Wilson, M., 22, 23
Winnicott, D. W., 26, 32–33, 34, 56, 66, 68, 99
Wolf, D., 66, 71

Zeenah, C. H., 10
Zelman, A., 66
Zilberstein, K., 10